In Search of Canadian Liberalism

The Canadian Rainbow

"I propose the adoption of the rainbow as our emblem. By the endless variety of its tints the rainbow will give an excellent idea of the diversity of races, religions, sentiments and interests of the different parts of the Confederation. By its slender and elongated form the rainbow would afford a perfect representation of the geographical configuration of the Confederation. By its lack of consistence – an image without substance – the rainbow would represent aptly the solidity of our Confederation. An emblem we must have, for every great empire has one; let us adopt the rainbow."

Henri Joly de Lotbinière, in the debates in the legislative assembly of Canada on the proposed scheme of a British North American Confederation, Quebec, 20 February, 1865.

In Search
of Canadian
Liberalism

Frank H. Underhill

The Macmillan Company of Canada Limited
Toronto 1961

Copyright, Canada, 1960
Reprinted 1961

BY FRANK H. UNDERHILL

PRINTED IN CANADA

Table of Contents

Part II   Political Controversy
in the 1930s and 1940s

Part III   The Calm of the 1950s

For Mike Pearson

Introduction

This volume contains a selection of articles written by me over the last thirty years. They have to do directly or indirectly with the subject of Canadian liberalism, and so I have given the volume its title, *In Search of Canadian Liberalism*. They are not presented as in any way forming a comprehensive study of the subject of liberalism in Canada; they are simply a collection of some of my writing on this theme in the past; and, as in all writing of this kind, the topic tends to shift to and fro between liberalism (with a small l), *i.e.* the ideas and values of liberally minded men and women, and Liberalism (with a capital L), *i.e.* the policies of the political party calling itself Liberal.

I was born a North York Presbyterian Grit. For a large part of my life I took for granted that this fact made it certain that I should grow up into a liberal, an assumption which I now see not to have been fully justified. Something, however, in my heredity or in my environment, whatever it was, did make it certain that I should never belong or want to belong to the Establishment. This seemed to me in my early days to be one of my particular virtues. Other people would say that I was just a natural minoritarian, an individualist who never fitted into institutions very well and who always found his most congenial companions among those who were protesting against something or other. My belief is that they were justly protesting. At any rate I cast my first vote, in 1911, for Reciprocity, and thus began a long career of disagreeing with the majority of my fellow citizens. Since then, as far as I can remember, when I have voted in federal elections it has been for some minority party to the left of the Liberals. As far as I can foresee, I am likely to continue voting in this way for the rest of my life.

What crystallized all my natural tendencies into a more or less definite political philosophy of the left — though not very far to the left of centre — was the experience of my formative years as a student and young man. The Toronto of my student days (1907–11) was pretty well devoid of political ideas; but I had the advantage of working under one classical professor, Milner, who had a genius for stirring up interest in ideas, and under the history department of Wrong and the English department of Alexander. I read Thucydides and Herodotus, Plato and Aristotle, Cicero and Tacitus, Milton, Hobbes, Locke, Burke and Mill. The Oxford to which I went from Toronto seethed with politics. I was there (1911–14) in the exciting days of the House of Lords and Home Rule crises, when everybody seemed to be a politician. My chief tutor in Greats was A. D. Lindsay who was a notorious socialist and whose wife went out addressing women's suffrage demonstrations. I joined the Fabian Society, though only as an associate member, since I wasn't quite sure that I believed in the full socialization of the means of production, distribution and exchange. I was also a member of the Russell and Palmerston Club, it being possible in those days to be both a Liberal and a Socialist. I was swept off my feet by the iconoclastic wit and high spirits of Bernard Shaw's plays, I read H. G. Wells and the Webbs, and became a member of a Balliol Fabian group in which the leading spirit was G. D. H. Cole.

Then came the war of 1914. I did my military service in France as a subaltern officer in an English infantry battalion. I discovered that this Edwardian-Georgian generation of Englishmen made the best regimental officers in the world and the worst staff officers. The stupidity of G.H.Q. and the terrible sacrifice of so many of the best men among my contemporaries sickened me for good of a society, national or international, run by the British governing classes.

I had spent the first year of the war (1914–15) as a professor of history in the young University of Saskatchewan. And I returned in 1919 to a Saskatchewan that was being swept by the great prairie fire of the Progressive movement. It used to puzzle me, remembering what Oxford had been like, that the prairie universities remained so detached from this political upheaval. For in Saskatchewan, so it seemed to me, I experienced for the first time what a democracy is really like when it is thoroughly alive. It thrilled me to attend conferences of the Saskatchewan wheat growers and to watch the executive on the platform keeping a precarious hold over the earnest, excited, opinionated, anti-authoritarian delegates in the body of the hall. I saw the wheat pool being launched in a series of mass-meetings which must have been the greatest revival meetings ever held in Canada. Bliss was it in those days on the prairie to be alive, but to be young was very heaven. I exulted in the refusal of the prairie farmers to be fitted into the old two-party system of eastern Canada, or into the orthodox religious denominationalism of Ontario — the United Church was born on the prairie — or into the dominant banking and financial system of Montreal and Toronto.

In the West I had the great good fortune to meet and to become a friend of the two men who seem to me to have been the two greatest Canadians of my adult years, J. W. Dafoe and J. S. Woodsworth. The Winnipeg of the 1920s which contained these two men was for me the intellectual capital of Canada. I was distressed that after the Winnipeg strike they could no longer work together. The Dafoe *Free Press* became my political bible for a time, though I began to disagree with it in the 1930s and followed Mr. Woodsworth to the left. But I still read the *Winnipeg Free Press*, because every now and then it comes out with a magisterial leading article that reminds me of the Dafoe days, whereas the editorial pages of eastern Canada mostly taste like lukewarm soup made out of dishwater. As for Mr. Woodsworth, I suppose now that I must have liked him for some of his bad qualities, which I shared with him, as well as for his good ones. But it is a great thing when you are young, if you are going to spend the rest of your life studying politics, to get to know one politician who does genuinely believe in principles and is prepared to make sacrifices for them; and I agreed with most of his principles. Mr. Dafoe belonged to the group in Winnipeg who were accustomed to exercise power; Mr. Woodsworth was a natural-born protestant.

In 1927 I moved to the history department of the University of Toronto. Shortly after my arrival I was invited to write book reviews for the *Canadian Forum*, then to join its editorial staff, and then to do the regular column "O Canada". This got me started on current Canadian politics and ruined forever all chances that, as a university professor, I would achieve that austere impersonal objectivity which was exemplified by most of my academic colleagues who lived blameless intellectual lives, cultivated the golden mean, and never stuck their necks out. Still, I cannot honestly confess to any very deep regret for having devoted so much of my energies to the controversies of politics. In fact, I think that this experience gave me some insights into Canadian history which I should otherwise have missed.

I had not foreseen that Toronto, the city, would irritate me so much. But living in it from 1927 to 1955 intensified all those feelings which had taken possession of me during my years in the West. If the C.C.F. had not come along when it did, I should have been indeed homeless.

Just before the C.C.F. was launched in 1932 a group of us academic people in Toronto and McGill (Queen's remained stubbornly Liberal) founded the League for Social Reconstruction. This we intended to be a Canadian version of the Fabian Society — without, alas, a Shaw or a Webb among its membership. I was the first president of the L.S.R. and Frank Scott the second. We chose Mr. Woodsworth to be our honorary president. After the Calgary meeting in 1932 at which he became leader of the C.C.F., he invited us to produce a comprehensive programme for it which could be discussed at its next annual conference in Regina.

I made the first draft of this; and my version, as revised by a small group of L.S.R. friends in Toronto, was sent to him just before the Regina meeting. The men who were responsible for this draft, as well as those who produced the book *Social Planning for Canada* in 1935, were all of them, except one, as far as I can remember, either Canadians by birth who had gone on from their Canadian universities to Oxford, or Englishmen by birth who had been trained at Cambridge or the London School of Economics. We looked on the C.C.F. as an application to Canada of the familiar British form of political evolution which had made the Labour party the party of the left in the 1920s and 1930s. I should have liked to include in this present volume that first draft of what became the Regina Manifesto. My recollection is that it was a better piece of writing than the document which emerged from the Regina discussions. I recall that, none of us having had any farm experience, we were very clear as to what should be done about the Canadian agricultural crisis. And I don't think that our document had in it that final declaration that a C.C.F. government would not rest until it had eradicated capitalism from Canada. But I cannot find a copy of the original draft anywhere, and my friends cannot supply me with one.

I was one of the first in the C.C.F. who began to have doubts about the far-reaching socialism of the Regina Manifesto. I wrote articles and delivered speeches about the need for a new political party in Canada until I was wearied with my own arguments. This was good for me because I discovered thereby that I was not cut out to be a practical politician, since the more I repeated my arguments for my party the more I began to doubt them or to feel that the cause needed revision. I never doubted that socialism must be liberal (with a small l). By the 1940s I was annoying my political friends by writing revisionist articles and book reviews in the *Canadian Forum;* and I welcomed the revised Winnipeg declaration of 1956. By the 1950s I had become considerably less interested in the fortunes of political parties as such and more concerned with the climate of opinion in our time which determines to a great extent what parties accomplish or try to accomplish.

The articles which appear in this volume are printed as they were written at the time, though, to save space, a few deletions have been made. I have not tried to make it seem that I have been fully consistent in my political views throughout my life, though I think there is a fairly strong core of consistency in what appears here. If there had been space to reproduce more of the mass of articles and reviews from the past, my changes of opinion would stand out more than they do in the present collection. Going through these old writings again now, I have been surprised to find how completely, in earlier days, I accepted economic interpretations of history, how fervent an isolationist I was before 1939, how confident I was that new political movements were about to prevail, that the old order was coming to an end, that "planning" would emancipate us from our social and economic confusions and frustrations. For now that I have reached my seventieth birthday I wish that I could be as sure about anything as some people I know are about everything. But perhaps this slowly acquired humility doesn't show in my writing.

The volume is divided into three sections. Part I consists of purely historical articles concerned with the liberal point of view as it was expressed in Upper Canada just before Confederation and in English-speaking Canada in the period from 1867 to 1914. I am surprised on looking back that I do not seem to have written anything specifically on Wilfrid Laurier, the greatest of all Canadian liberals. I have not included anything about Edward Blake since I hope to deal with him in another volume; but I have put a list of my articles on him in the Appendix. An essay on J. S. Ewart had to be left out because of space limitations. About the history of liberalism in French Canada there is nothing here because my historical reading about French-Canadian politics, like that of most English Canadians, has been so deplorably superficial.

Part II contains a selection of articles, mostly controversial, on current political topics in the 1930s and 1940s. I have included only one of those on external policy that gave expression to my strongly isolationist point of view at that time, though I did an appalling amount of writing on this theme in the three or four years before 1939. My arguments now seem to me to have been based on a mistaken analysis of the world situation before World War II. I was not a pacifist, but my inarticulate major premise was the assumption that the power of Britain and France was sufficient to hold Hitler's Germany in. I have put a list of some of the most important of these articles in the Appendix.

Part II also contains a series of discussions of the statesmanship of Mr. Mackenzie King. These articles from the *Canadian Forum* will show how much the man irritated persons of my way of thinking, how over-eager I was to announce the end of the King era, and also how I revised some of my opinions and ended with a certain reluctant admiration of him as a statesman. Politically, of course, Mr. King did not die until 1957.

Part III contains some of my reflections on Canadian culture and politics during the 1950s. By 1950 I was sixty years old. And if I had not become wiser, I hope I had become a little more urbane. But perhaps this also doesn't show in my writing.

I have to thank the editors of the various journals in which my articles were first printed, and the institutions at which some of these articles were first presented as addresses, for permission to reproduce them here. I am indebted to the Social Science Research Council of Canada for a grant of money to make the publication of this volume financially possible.

F. H. U.

Ottawa, July, 1960

PART I
The Liberal Past

1. Some Reflections on the Liberal Tradition in Canada

(This paper was read by me as President of the Canadian Historical Association at its annual meeting in 1946.)

"The reader is about to enter upon the most violent and certainly the most eventful moral struggle that has ever taken place in our North American colonies. . . . That I was sentenced to contend on the soil of America with Democracy, and that if I did not overpower it, it would overpower me, were solemn facts which for some weeks had been perfectly evident to my mind." So wrote Sir Francis Bond Head in his *Narrative*,[1] the famous apologia for the policy of his governorship of Upper Canada. The issue as he saw it, and as his contemporaries in Canada saw it, was not merely whether the British North American colonies were to set up a responsible form of government; it was the much deeper one of whether they were to follow the example of the United States and commit themselves to achieving a democratic form of society. And good Sir Francis appealed with confidence to all right-thinking property-owning Englishmen against what he termed "the insane theory of conciliating democracy" as put into practice by the Colonial Office under the guidance of that "rank republican", Mr. Under-Secretary Stephen. No doubt, if the phrase had been then in use he would have accused Stephen, and Lord Glenelg and Lord Durham, of appeasement. In rebuttal of Durham's criticisms of the Upper Canada Family Compact he wrote:

> It appears from Lord Durham's own showing that this "Family Compact" which his Lordship deems it so advisable that the Queen should destroy, is nothing more nor less than that "social fabric" which characterizes every civilized community in the world. . . . "The bench", "the magistrates", "the clergy", "the law", "the

---

[1] Sir Francis Bond Head, *A Narrative* (London, 1839), 64.

3

landed proprietors", "the bankers", "the native-born inhabitants", and "the supporters of the Established Church" [these were the social groups which Durham had defined as composing the Family Compact] form just as much *"a family compact"* in England as they do in Upper Canada, and just as much in Germany as they do in England. . . . The *"family compact"* of Upper Canada is composed of those members of its society who, either by their abilities and character, have been honoured by the confidence of the executive government, or who by their industry and intelligence, have amassed wealth. The party, I own, is comparatively a small one; but to put the multitude at the top and the few at the bottom is a radical reversion of the pyramid of society which every reflecting man must foresee can end only by its downfall.[2]

Sir Francis' statement is as clear and as trenchant an enunciation of the anti-democratic conservative political philosophy of his day as could be quoted from the American conservatives who were fighting Jacksonian Democracy at this same time or from the English conservatives who were fighting the Reform Bill or Chartism. As we all know, this "moral struggle" over the fundamental principles on which society should be based, which Sir Francis correctly discerned as representing the real meaning of the Canadian party strife of the 1830s, was to be decided against him and his tory friends. The century since his *Narrative* was published has been, in the English-speaking world at least, a period of continuously developing liberal and democratic movements. Liberalism has merged into democracy. Today the people of Canada are recovering from the second world war within a generation in defence of democracy. Presumably, considering the sacrifices we have shown ourselves willing to make for the cause, we Canadians cherish passionately the liberal-democratic tradition which is our inheritance from the nineteenth century. Presumably, the growth of liberal-democratic institutions and ideas in our political, economic, and social life is one of the main themes in our Canadian history, just as it certainly is in the history of Great Britain and the United States, the two communities with which we have most intimately shared our experience.

Yet it is a remarkable fact that in the great debate of our generation, the debate which has been going on all over the western world about the fundamental values of liberalism and democracy, we

---

[2] *Ibid.*, 464

Canadians have taken very little part. We talk at length of the status which our nation has attained in the world. We have shown in two great wars that we can produce soldiers and airmen and sailors second to none. We have organized our productive resources so energetically as to make ourselves one of the main arsenals and granaries of democracy. We have achieved political autonomy and economic maturity. But to the discussion of those deep underlying intellectual, moral and spiritual issues which have made such chaos of the contemporary world we Canadians are making very little contribution.

Our Confederation was achieved at the very time in the nineteenth century when a reaction was beginning to set in against the liberal and democratic principles which, springing from eighteenth-century Enlightenment, had seemed up to that moment to be winning ever fresh victories. The liberal nationalism of the early part of the century was beginning to turn into something sinister, the passionate, exclusive, irrational, totalitarian nationalism that we know today. The optimistic belief in human equality and perfectibility was beginning to be undermined by new knowledge about man provided by the researches of biologists and psychologists. At the same time technological developments in mass production industries were building up a new social pyramid with a few owners and managers at the top and the mass of exploited workers at the bottom; and new techniques of mass propaganda still further emphasized this division of mankind into élite and masses. The freedom which our Victorian ancestors thought was slowly broadening down from precedent to precedent seemed to become more and more unreal under the concentrated pressure of capitalistic big business or of the massive bureaucratic state. In such surroundings, the liberal spirit does not flourish. And the more reflective minds of our day have been acutely aware that the mere winning of military victories under banners labelled "liberty" or "democracy" does not carry us very far in the solving of our deeper problems.

Canada is caught up in this modern crisis of liberalism as are all other national communities. But in this world-debate about the values of our civilization the Canadian voice is hardly heard. Who ever reads a Canadian book? What Canadian books are there on these problems? What have we had to say about them that has attracted the attention of our contemporaries or has impressed itself upon their imagination? In the world of ideas we do not yet play a full part. We are still colonial. Our thinking is still derivative. Like other peoples Canadians have of late expended a good deal of misdirected energy in endeavours to export goods without importing other goods in return. But we continue to import ideas without trying to develop an export trade in this field. We are in fact, as I have said, colonial. For our intellectual capital we are still dependent upon a continuous flow of imports from London, New York, and Paris, not to mention Moscow and Rome. It is to be hoped that we will continue to raise our intellectual standards by continuing to import from these more mature centres, and that we will never try to go in for intellectual autarchy. But international commerce in ideas as well as in goods should be a two-way traffic at least, and preferably it should be multilateral.

Incidentally, it is worth remarking in passing that one sign of this colonialism in our intellectual world is to be seen in the present state of Canadian historiography. The guild of Canadian historians confine their activities very largely to the writing of studies in local national history. South of the border American historians have long been demonstrating their intellectual equality by pouring out books on English and European and world history as well as on local subjects. But how little of this kind of research and writing has been done in Canada! During the past year we have lost one of our most distinguished colleagues, in the person of Professor Charles Norris Cochrane; and his book on *Christianity and Classical Culture* is a notable example of the sort of thing I mean. But one cannot think of many cases like this, in which we have asserted our full partnership in the civilization of our day by Canadian writing upon the great subjects of permanent and universal interest.

Now it seems to me — and this is more or less the main theme of the present rambling discursive paper — that this intellectual weakness of Canada is a quality which shows itself through all our history. In particular it is to be discerned in that process of democratization which is the most important thing that has happened to us, as to other kindred peoples, during the last hundred years. When we compare ourselves with Britain and the United States there is one striking contrast. Those two countries, since the end of the eighteenth century, have abounded in prophets and philosophers who have made articulate the idea of a liberal and equalitarian society. Their political history displays also a succession of practical politicians who have not merely performed the functions of manipulating and manoeuvring masses of men and groups which every politician performs, but whose careers have struck the imagination of both contemporaries and descendants as symbolizing certain great inspiring ideas. We in Canada have produced few such figures. Where are the classics in our political literature which embody our Canadian version of liberalism and democracy? Our party struggles have never been raised to the higher intellectual plane at which they become of universal interest by the presence of a Canadian Jefferson and a Canadian Hamilton in opposing parties. We have had no Canadian Burke or Mill to perform the social function of the political philosopher in action. We have had no Canadian Carlyle or Ruskin or Arnold to ask searching questions about the ultimate values embodied in our political or economic practice. We lack a Canadian Walt Whitman or Mark Twain to give literary expression to the democratic way of life. The student in search of illustrative material on the growth of Canadian political ideas during the great century of liberalism and democracy has to content himself mainly with a collection of extracts from more or less forgotten speeches and pamphlets and newspaper editorials. Whatever urge may have, at any time, possessed any Canadian to philosophize upon politics did not lead to much writing whose intrinsic worth helped to preserve it in our memory.

At least this is true of us English-speaking Canadians. Our French-speaking fellow citizens have shown a much greater fondness and capacity for ideas in politics than we have; but their writings, being in another language, have hardly penetrated into our English-Canadian consciousness.

We early repudiated the philosophy of the Manchester School; but in the long history of our Canadian "National Policy" it is difficult to find any Canadian exposition of the anti-Manchester ideas of a national economy, written by economist, business man, or politician, which has impressed itself upon us as worthy of preservation. Our history is full of agrarian protest movements, but the ordinary Canadian would be stumped if asked to name any representative Canadian philosopher of agrarianism. And the most notable illustration of this poverty of our politics at the intellectual level is to be found in the fact that while we were the pioneers in one of the great liberal achievements of the nineteenth century — the experiment of responsible government, which transformed the British Empire into the Commonwealth, and which has thrown fresh light in our own day on the possibility of reconciling nationalism with a wider international community — even in this field, in which our practical contribution was so great, there has arisen since the days of Joseph Howe no Canadian prophet of the idea of the Commonwealth whose writings seem inspiring or even readable to wider circles than those of professional historians.

This seeming incapacity for ideas, or rather this habit of carrying on our communal affairs at a level at which ideas never quite emerge into an articulate life of their own, has surely impoverished our Canadian politics. Every teacher of Canadian history has this fact brought home to him with each fresh batch of young students whom he meets. How reluctant they are to study the history of their own country! How eagerly they show their preference for English or European or (if they get the chance) for American history! For they instinctively feel that when they get outside of Canada they are studying the great creative seminal ideas that have determined the character of our modern world, whereas inside Canada there seem to be no ideas at issue of permanent or universal significance at all. I can myself still remember the thrill of appreciation with which as a university freshman I heard a famous professor of Greek[3] remark that our Canadian history is as dull as ditchwater, and our politics is full of it. Of course, there is a considerable amount of ditchwater in the politics of all countries; my professor was more conscious of it in Canada because he missed here those ideas which he found in the politics of classical Greece. And as far as I have been able to observe, young students of this present generation are still repelled by Canadian history because they find in it little more than the story of a half-continent of material resources over which a population of some twelve million economic animals have spread themselves in a not too successful search for economic wealth.

It will, of course, be said in answer to these mournful reflections upon the low quality of intellectual activity in Canadian politics that they are exaggerated and extreme. So I should like to buttress my position by referring to observations made at different times by students from the outer world upon the nature and quality of Canadian party politics. The name of Goldwin Smith comes to mind at once. He watched and studied Canadian politics continuously from the early 1870s to the early 1900s, applying to them

---

[3] Maurice Hutton, Principal of University College in the University of Toronto.

the standards of an English Manchester liberal; and his verdict was adverse. He felt that Canadians after 1867 had failed to rise to their intellectual opportunities, that they had failed to grasp in their imagination the potentialities of the new nationality, that their political parties operated only to debase and pervert the discussion of public issues, and that in the absence of great guiding, inspiring ideas Canadian national statesmanship had degenerated into a sordid business of bargaining and manoeuvring amongst narrow selfish particularist interest groups. He took a certain sardonic pleasure in noting the skill with which Macdonald played this low game as contrasted with the clumsiness with which Mackenzie and Blake played it; but he could see in it nothing but a low game after all. The obvious reply to Goldwin Smith is that he was embittered by the disappointment of his own ambitions and that his testimony is therefore to be discounted. But no one who studies the politics of the period 1867 to 1914 can be convinced that this is a wholly satisfactory defence against his criticisms.

At the period of the turn of the century, we were studied by another overseas observer who has given us the most penetrating and illuminating analysis of our politics that has yet been written by anyone, native or foreign. In 1907 André Siegfried published his book, *The Race Question in Canada*, and set forth the somewhat paradoxical conclusion that, while (to quote his opening sentence) "Canadian politics are a tilting ground for impassioned rivalries", they operated so as to suppress the intellectual vitality which would be the natural result of such a situation.

> Originally formed to subserve a political idea, these parties are often to be found quite detached from the principles which gave them birth, and with their own self-preservation as their chief care and aim. Even without a programme, they continue to live and thrive, tending to become mere associations for the securing of power, their doctrines serving merely as weapons, dulled or sharpened, grasped as occasion arises for use in the fight. . . . This fact deprives the periodical appeals to the voting public of the importance which they should have. . . . Whichever side succeeds, the country it is well known will be governed in just the same way; the only difference will be in the *personnel* of the Government. That is how things go save when some great wave of feeling sweeps over the Dominion, submerging all the pigmies of politics in its flood. In the intervals between these crises . . . it is not the party that subserves the idea, it is the idea that subserves the party. Canadian statesmen . . . undoubtedly take longer views. They

seem, however, to stand in fear of great movements of public opinion, and to seek to lull them rather than to encourage them and bring them to fruition. Thus, deliberately and not from short-sightedness, they help to promote the state of things which I have described. The reason for this attitude is easy to comprehend. Canada, with its rival creeds and races, is a land of fears and jealousies and conflicts. . . . Let a question involving religion or nationality be once boldly raised. . . and the elections will be turned into real political fights, passionate and sincere. This is exactly what is dreaded by far-sighted and prudent politicians, whose duty it is to preserve the national equilibrium. . . . They exert themselves, therefore, to prevent the formation of homogeneous parties, divided according to creed or race or class. The purity of political life suffers from this, but perhaps the very existence of the Federation is the price. The existing parties are thus entirely harmless. The Liberals and Conservatives differ very little really in their opinions upon crucial questions, and their views as to administration are almost identical. . . . They have come to regard each other without alarm: they know each other too well and resemble each other too closely.[4]

Mr. J. A. Hobson, the well-known English economist, published a little book about Canada at almost the same moment as M. Siegfried — *Canada Today*, which appeared in 1906. It also gives a rather unfavourable impression of Canadian politics, although the author's main interest was in the economic question of protection and the British preference.

More recently another great student of politics from overseas has given us his observations upon Canada. James Bryce had played an active part in the politics of his own country, had made himself intimately acquainted with the American Commonwealth, and applied to Canada a mind that was deeply learned in comparative politics. In his book, *Modern Democracies*, published in 1921, he devoted some chapters to the working of Canadian democracy.

Since 1867 the questions which have had the most constant interest for the bulk of the nation are . . . those which belong to the sphere of commercial and industrial progress, the development of the material resources of the country . . . — matters scarcely falling within the lines by which party opinion is divided, for the policy of *laissez-faire* has few adherents in a country which finds in govern-

---

[4] André Siegfried, *The Race Question in Canada* (English translation, London, 1907), 141-3.

mental action or financial support to private enterprises the quickest means of carrying out every promising project. . . . The task of each party is to persuade the people that in this instance its plan promises quicker and larger results, and that it is fitter to be trusted with the work. Thus it happens that general political principles . . . count for little in politics, though ancient habit requires them to be invoked. Each party tries to adapt itself from time to time to whatever practical issue may arise. Opportunism is inevitable, and the charge of inconsistency, though incessantly bandied to and fro, is lightly regarded. . . . In Canada ideas are not needed to make parties, for these can live by heredity. . . . The people show an abounding party spirit when an election day arrives. The constant party struggle keeps their interest alive. But party spirit, so far from being a measure of the volume of political thinking, may even be a substitute for thinking. . . . In every country a game played over material interests between ministers, constituencies and their representatives, railway companies and private speculators, is not only demoralizing to all concerned but interferes with the consideration of the great issues of policy on a wise handling of which a nation's welfare depends. Fiscal questions, labour questions, the assumption by the State of such branches of industry as railroads or mines, and the principles it ought to follow in such works as it undertakes — questions like these need wide vision, clear insight, and a firmness that will resist political pressure and adhere to the principles once laid down. These qualities have been wanting, and the people have begun to perceive the want.[5]

This general failure of our Canadian politics to rise above a mere confused struggle of interest groups has been no doubt due to a variety of causes. In the middle of the twentieth century it is rather too late for us to keep harping on the pioneer frontier character of the Canadian community as the all-sufficient answer to criticism. The young American republic which included a Jefferson and a Hamilton and a Franklin, not to mention many of their contemporaries of almost equal intellectual stature, was a smaller and more isolated frontier community than Canada has been for a long time; but it was already by the end of the eighteenth century the peer of Europe in the quality of its political thinking and was recognized as such. We still remain colonial in the middle of the twentieth century.

---

[5] James Bryce, *Modern Democracies* (New York, 1921), I, 471-505. Bryce's analysis was based mainly upon observations made before World War I.

One reason for our backwardness, and the reason which interests me most at the moment, has been the weakness of the Radical and Reform parties of the Left in our Canadian history. A healthy society will consist of a great majority massed a little to the right and a little to the left of centre, with smaller groups of strong conservatives and strong radicals out on the wings. If these minority groups are not present in any significant force to provide a perpetual challenge to the majority, the conservatives and liberals of the centre are likely to be a pretty flabby lot, both intellectually and morally.

For this weakness of the Left in Canada, the ultimate explanation would seem to be that we never had an eighteenth century of our own. The intellectual life of our politics has not been periodically revived by fresh drafts from the invigorating fountain of eighteenth-century Enlightenment. In Catholic French Canada the doctrines of the rights of man and of Liberty Equality Fraternity were rejected from the start, and to this day they have never penetrated, save surreptitiously or spasmodically. The mental climate of English Canada in its early formative years was determined by men who were fleeing from the practical application of the doctrines that all men are born equal and are endowed by their Creator with certain unalienable rights amongst which are life, liberty and the pursuit of happiness. All effective liberal and radical democratic movements in the nineteenth century have had their roots in this fertile eighteenth-century soil. But our ancestors made the great refusal in the eighteenth century. In Canada we have no revolutionary tradition; and our historians, political scientists, and philosophers have assiduously tried to educate us to be proud of this fact. How can such a people expect their democracy to be as dynamic as the democracies of Britain and France and the United States have been?

Then also it has never been sufficiently emphasized that our first great democratic upheaval a hundred years ago was a failure. In the United States, Jacksonian Democracy swept away most of the old aristocratic survivals and made a strong attack upon the new plutocratic forces. The Federalists disappeared; and their successors, the Whigs, suffered a series of defeats at the hands of triumphant Democracy. But the Canadian version of Jacksonian Democracy represented by the movements of Papineau and Mackenzie was discredited by the events of their abortive rebellions. And Canada followed the example of Britain rather than of the United States. Responsible government was a British technique of government which took the place of American elective institutions. Our historians have been so dazzled by its success that they have failed to point out that the real radicals in Canada were pushed aside in the 1840s by the respectable professional and property-owning classes, the "Moderates" as we call them; just as the working-class radicals in Britain, without whose mass-agitation the Reform Bill could not have been passed, were pushed aside after 1832 for a long generation of middle-class Whig rule. The social pyramid in Canada about which Sir Francis Bond Head was so worried in 1839 was *not* upset; and after a decade of excitement it was clear that the Reform government was only a business men's government. When Baldwin and LaFontaine were succeeded by Hincks and Morin this was so clear that new radical movements emerged both in Upper and in Lower Canada, the Grits and les Rouges.

Now in North America the essence of all effective liberal movements — I assume in this paper that liberalism naturally leads towards democracy — must be that they are attacks upon the domination of the community by the business man. This was what the Democratic party of Jackson and Van Buren was. As Mr. Schlesinger has recently been pointing out in his brilliant book, *The Age of Jackson*,[6] the effectiveness of the Jacksonians was due to the fact that their leading ideas about the relations of business and government came primarily not from the frontier farmers of the West but from the democratic labour movements in the big cities and their sympathizers amongst the urban intellectuals. Jefferson had been mainly interested in political democracy; Jackson tackled the problem of economic democracy in a society becoming increasingly industrialized. The social equality of the frontier has never given agrarian democrats a sufficient understanding of the problems of a society divided into the rich and the poor of an urban civilization. Here we seem to come upon an important explanation for the weakness of all Canadian radical movements from the 1830s to the end of the century. They were too purely agrarian. The only force that could ultimately overcome the Hamiltonians must, like them, have its base of operations in the cities.

Mr. Schlesinger has also pointed out that American conservatism

---

[6] A. M. Schlesinger, Jr., *The Age of Jackson* (Boston, 1945).

was immensely strengthened when it transformed itself from Federalism to Whiggism. In the 1830s, as he puts it, it changed from broadcloth to homespun. "The metamorphosis revived it politically but ruined it intellectually. The Federalists had thought about society in an intelligent and hard-boiled way. The Whigs, in scuttling Federalism, replaced it by a social philosophy founded, not on ideas, but on subterfuges and sentimentalities."[7] But the Whigs learned the techniques of demagogy from the Jacksonians and set out to guide the turbulent new American democracy along lines that would suit the purposes of business. Surely we should remark that exactly the same metamorphosis took place just a little later in Canadian conservatism. The clear-cut anti-democratic philosophy of Sir Francis Bond Head and the Family Compact Tories was as obsolete and out-of-place in the bustling Canada of the 1850s as Federalism had been in the United States in the 1820s. The Macdonald-Cartier Liberal-Conservative party was American Whiggism with a British title. (And no doubt the British label on the outside added considerably to the potency of the American liquor inside the bottle.) The Liberal-Conservatives had made the necessary demagogic adjustments to the democratic spirit of the times; they had a policy of economic expansion to be carried out under the leadership of business with the assistance of government which was an almost exact parallel to Clay's Whig "American System". But there was no Jackson and no Jacksonian "kitchen cabinet" in Canada to counter this Liberal-Conservatism.

The Grits and les Rouges did not quite meet the needs of the situation. What Rougeism, with its body of ideas from the revolutionary Paris of 1848, might have accomplished we cannot say; for it soon withered under the onslaught of the Church. Grittism in Upper Canada was originally a movement inspired by American ideas, as its early fondness for elective institutions and its continuing insistence on "Rep by Pop" show. But Brown's accession tended to shift the inspiration in the British direction. Brown himself became more and more sentimentally British as he grew older. Moreover, as publisher of the *Globe*, he was a business man on the make, and Toronto was a growing business centre. As Toronto grew, and as the *Globe* grew, the original frontier agrarianism of the Grits was imperceptibly changed into something subtly

---

[7] *Ibid.*, 279.

different. As early as January 3, 1857 the *Globe* was declaring: "The schemes of those who have announced that Toronto must aspire no higher than to be 'the Capital of an Agricultural District' must be vigorously met and overcome." Brown defeated the radicals from the Peninsula in the great Reform convention of 1859, and by 1867 Grit leaders were more and more becoming urban business and professional men. A party which contained William McMaster of the Bank of Commerce and John Macdonald, the big wholesale merchant, was not likely to be very radical. Oliver Mowat, a shrewd cautious lawyer, was about to take over the direction of its forces in Ontario provincial politics; and its rising hope in the federal sphere was Edward Blake, the leader of the Ontario equity bar. Moreover, as Brown's unhappy experiences with his printers in 1872 were to show, the Reform party under *Globe* inspiration found difficulty in adjusting itself to the new ideas which industrialism was encouraging in the minds of the working class. Blake and Mowat, who dominated Canadian Liberal thinking after Brown, were not American democrats or radicals so much as English Whigs in their temperament, their training, and their political philosophy. For political equality and liberty they were prepared to fight; economic equality did not move them very deeply. And the same might be said about Laurier who succeeded them.

Another point worth noting is the effect of British influences in slowing down all movements throughout the nineteenth century in the direction of the democratization of politics and society. Inevitably, because of geographical proximity and the mutual interpenetration of the lives of the two North American communities, the urge towards greater democracy was likely to appear in Canada as an American influence; and since the survival of Canada as a separate entity depended on her not being submerged under an American flood, such influences were fought as dangerous to our Canadian ethos. Sir Francis Bond Head and the Tories of his time habitually used the words "democratic" and "republican" as interchangeable. Every Canadian movement of the Left in those days and since has had to meet accusations of Americanism, and in proving its sound British patriotism it has been apt to lose a good deal of its Leftism. Canadian Methodism, for example, widely influenced by its American connections, was on the Reform side of politics until the Ryerson arrangement in the 1830s with the British Wesleyans put it on the other side.

When we get down to the Confederation period no one can fail to see how markedly the British influence gives a conservative tone to the whole generation of the Fathers. Later Canadians have had to reflect frequently on the sad fact that the "new nationality" was very imperfectly based upon any deep popular feeling. It has occurred to many of them, with the wisdom of hindsight, that Confederation would have been a much stronger structure had the Quebec Resolutions received the ratification of the electorate in each colony in accordance with American precedents. But the British doctrine of legislative sovereignty operated to override all suggestions that the people should be consulted; and Canadian nationality has always been weak in its moral appeal because "We the People" had no formal part in bringing it into being.

Similarly British example was effective in delaying the arrival of manhood suffrage in Canada till towards the end of the century, though the Americans had adopted it in the early part of the century. The ballot did not become part of Canadian law until sanctioned by British precedent in the 1870s. The Chancery Court which had long been a favourite object of radical attack in Upper Canada remained intact until jurists of the Mother Country had amalgamated the equity and common law jurisdictions there. And that strange constitutional device, the Canadian Senate, with its life appointees, was slipped into our constitution with the plea that appointment by the Crown was the British way of doing things. John A. Macdonald must have had his tongue in his cheek when he presented this Senate as a protector of provincial rights, its members being appointed by the head of the very federal government against which provincial rights were to be protected. In the privacy of the Quebec Conference, when they were constructing the second chamber, he had remarked to his fellow delegates: "The rights of the minority must be protected, and the rich are always fewer in number than the poor." One wonders what George Brown or Oliver Mowat, the Grit representatives, must have said at this point, or whether the secretary, who caught Macdonald's immortal sentence, failed to take down their comments. Generally speaking, the notable fact is that in all this era of constitution making, and of constitution testing in the decades just after 1867, the voice of democratic radicalism was so weak.

On the other hand, when Britain began to grow really democratic towards the end of the nineteenth century, her example seemed to have little effect upon Canadian liberalism. The two most significant features in internal British politics since the 1880s have been

dian politics. Both André Siegfried from France and J. A. Hobson from England remarked upon this phenomenon in the books which they published in 1906. "When the workers of Canada wake up," said Hobson, "they will find that Protection is only one among the several economic fangs fastened in their 'corpus vile' by the little group of railroad men, bankers, lumber men and manufacturing monopolists who own their country."[10]

The Great Barbecue was still in full swing when these observers studied Canada. As I have said already, liberalism in North America, if it is to mean anything concrete, must mean an attack upon the domination of institutions and ideas by the business man. In this sense Canadian liberalism revived after 1918, to produce results with which we are all familiar. Amongst those results, however, we can hardly include any advance in the clarity or the realism of the liberal thinking of the so-called Liberal party, however much we may be compelled to admire its dexterity in the practical arts of maintaining itself in office. In the realm of political ideas its performance may be correctly described as that of going on and on and on, and up and up and up. But I am now touching upon present-day controversies. And, whatever latitude may be allowed to the political scientist, we all know that the historian cannot deal with current events without soiling the purity of his scientific objectivity.

In the meantime Canadian historians must continue to study and to write the history of their country. I have devoted these rambling remarks to the subject of political ideas because I have a feeling that Canadian historiography has come to the end of an epoch. For the past twenty or thirty years, most of the best work in Canadian history has been in the economic field. How different groups of Canadians made their living, how a national economy was built up, how the Canadian economy was integrated into a world economy, these topics have been industriously investigated; and we have been given thereby a new and a deeper understanding of the basis of our national life. The climax in this school of activity was reached with the publication of the Carnegie series on Canadian-American relations and of the various volumes connected with the Rowell-Sirois Report.

---

[10] J. A. Hobson, *Canada Today* (London, 1906), 47.

The best work in the Carnegie collection is for the most part on the economic side. And the volume, published during the past year, which crowns the series — Professor Bartlet Brebner's *North American Triangle* — can hardly be praised too highly for the skill and insight with which the author brings out the pattern of the joint Canadian-American achievement in settling the continent and exploiting its economic resources, and with which he explains the practical working of our peculiar North American techniques and forms of organization. But it is significant that he has little to say about the intellectual history of the two peoples, about education, religion, and such subjects; and especially about the idea of democracy as understood in North America. Materials from research on the intellectual history of Canada were not, as a matter of fact, available to him in any quantity. Volume I of the Rowell-Sirois Report is likewise a brilliant and, within its field, a convincing exercise in the economic interpretation of Canadian history. But it is abstract history without names or real flesh-and-blood individuals, the history of puppets who dance on strings pulled by obscure world forces which they can neither understand nor control; it presents us with a ghostly ballet of bloodless economic categories.

The time seems about due for a new history-writing which will attempt to explain the ideas in the heads of Canadians that caused them to act as they did, their philosophy, why they thought in one way at one period and in a different way at another period. Perhaps when we settle down to this task we shall discover that our ancestors had more ideas in their heads than this paper has been willing to concede them. At any rate, we shall then be able to understand more clearly the place of the Canadian people in the civilization of the liberal-democratic century which lies behind us.

2. The Development of National Political Parties in Canada

(This article was first printed in the *Canadian Historical Review*, December, 1935.)

1

"The most common and durable source of factions," declared James Madison in 1787,[1] "has been the various and unequal distribution of property. Those who hold and those who are without property have ever formed distinct interests in society. Those who are creditors, and those who are debtors, fall under a like discrimination. A landed interest, a manufacturing interest, a mercantile interest, a moneyed interest, with many lesser interests, grow up of necessity in civilized nations, and divide them into different classes, actuated by different sentiments and views. The regulation of these various and interfering interests forms the principal task of modern legislation, and involves the spirit of party and faction in the necessary and ordinary operations of the government."

"In the course of political evolution," declared Mr. W. L. Mackenzie King, addressing the National Federation of Liberal Women in 1928,[2] "we witness a constant struggle of two contending principles, the principle of the future and the principle of the past. ... To the ever-present conflict of these principles we owe the birth and growth of political parties. . . . By whatever names those parties may be designated, they tend more and more to owe their existence to this conflict of principles between the future and the past, a conflict which, when the history of the future is unfolded, will be found to have been continuous from the dawn of civilization to the eve of the millenium."

---

[1] The *Federalist*, no. **X**.
[2] W. L. Mackenzie King, *Liberalism, the principle of the future: An address* (published as a pamphlet, n.d.).

This paper is an attempt to apply to the history of Canadian political parties the materialist analysis of Madison, and to show by implication the irrelevance of commonly offered idealistic explanations, such as that provided by Mr. King. I shall, therefore, not spend time inquiring what Canadian Conservatives have been trying to conserve since the achievement of responsible government or what Canadian Liberals have been trying to liberate. I shall devote myself to studying that struggle of different interests to which Madison drew attention; and I shall discuss how out of "the regulation of these various and interfering interests", involving as it did "the spirit of party and faction in the necessary and ordinary operations of the government", the Canadian party-system was evolved.

Madison and the founders of the American constitution apparently expected a multiplicity of parties in the new republic corresponding to the different forms of propertied interests. Instead, there developed a peculiar North American two-party system, centring mainly about the conflict between the industrial and financial interests on the one side and the agricultural interests on the other. But in the course of the struggle for the control of the presidency each party had to make some appeal to all the sectional groups within the nation; so that the two national parties tended to become loose opportunistic collections of politicians, containing in their membership representatives from competing sectional and class groups all across the continent, maintaining an uneasy unity by appeals to traditional symbols and by an intricate and unprincipled system of bargaining and compromise.

In Canada a similar two-party system grew up and developed with the geographical expansion of the Dominion. The fact that the British names for the parties were preserved and that the parties operated within a British constitutional framework made little difference to their essentially North American quality. The stage properties were imported from Britain, but the plot of the play and the characters on the stage were all native products.

2

The present-day Canadian party system goes back to a starting-point in the old province of Canada, in 1854, in the period immediately following the achievement of responsible government. The so-called Reform party of LaFontaine and Baldwin, which was never quite a party but rather a coalition of groups, was in process of disintegration into its original elements. Out of the confusion there was formed a new coalition, which at the start seemed to contemporaries only one of several possible coalitions. But it gave itself the inspired name of the Liberal-Conservative party, and, under the long leadership of John A. Macdonald, it slowly consolidated itself from a coalition into a party which dominated Canadian politics for forty years. Over against the Liberal-Conservatives, the various groups and individuals who found themselves wandering in the wilderness of opposition gradually in their turn coalesced into a new Reform or Liberal party, claiming to base themselves upon the traditions of Baldwin and LaFontaine, but achieving party cohesion more slowly than the Liberal-Conservatives because, until the day of Laurier, they seldom enjoyed the sweets of national office.

The differences between the two parties were never, before or after Confederation, as clear-cut as the differences between their two outstanding leaders, Macdonald and Brown. In fact, in the early days they never quite became parties at all in the modern sense. There were too many individuals whose allegiance was uncertain — "loose fish", "shaky fellows", "waiters on Providence". There were too many constituencies whose practice it was to elect "independents" of one stripe or another — i.e., representatives who were expected, by a realistic bartering of their votes, to get the utmost possible concessions for their locality or their economic group from the party leaders who sought their support. Members of the legislature, both front benchers and back benchers, passed with remarkable ease from one political camp to another. The reader of Canadian newspapers in the 1850s and 1860s is struck at once by the fact that the papers never agree with one another in reporting the results of general elections. Each claims for its side all the doubtful members, and the controversy is not cleared up until there have been two or three divisions in the newly elected house. Nor is it entirely cleared up then. For, as Macdonald was wont to complain, the trouble with so many of these independents was that, after being bought, they often refused to stay bought. Hence the extreme instability of Canadian governments in the 1850s and 1860s, and the bewildering rapidity with which new experimental combinations of politicians succeeded one another in office. Hence the general low level of political morality. Hence also the ferocity with which the fight was carried on.

Still it was out of this confused turmoil that the lines of party division were gradually laid down. And, since it was this party system of the original province of Canada which established itself over the whole dominion after 1867, it is necessary to begin by inquiring what these lines of division were.

Who, then, were the Liberal-Conservatives? Popular tradition has it that Macdonald brought together all the moderate elements in Canadian politics into his new party, leaving the extremists in the cold of opposition. Yet one reads the books in vain to discover in what sense these moderates were moderate, or what were the two extremes between which they formed the golden Canadian mean. To be sure there were the Clear Grits and the Rouges at what may be called the one extreme; but the representatives of the other extreme, the old Family Compact Tories, were, as a matter of fact, part of Macdonald's "moderate" party. And why, after all, should the railway promoters and manufacturers who supported the Liberal-Conservatives because that party looked after their interests be called moderate, while the frontier farmers who fought for their interests in the Clear Grit party are designated as extreme? Historians who apply such adjectives to competing party groups demonstrate merely that they have prejudged all the issues by accepting in advance the standards and the scale of values of one side in the discussion.

The Liberal-Conservative coalition of 1854 was composed of four main groups. A short examination of each of them in turn will reveal what was their chief bond of union.

The group which was numerically strongest was that of the French-Canadian Roman Catholics of whom George Etienne Cartier was by 1854 rapidly becoming the recognized leader. We have been told that Macdonald sensed the natural conservatism of the French and set out from the start of his career to woo them. This is no doubt true as far as it goes, but it does not take us very far. There still remains a blank period in the political evolution of the French Canadians which has never been properly explored. In the 1820s and 1830s there was going on in Lower Canada a bitter struggle between the Montreal mercantile interests, who were dreaming of a commercial state which should extend across the continent and pour its traffic (and profits) into the St. Lawrence, and the French-Canadian peasants who had no taste to be taxed for such far-reaching purposes but wished only to be left to enjoy their accustomed static agricultural civilization. Lord Durham reported in alarmist language in 1839 that relations between the two races were so embittered that neither would ever again accept the government of the other. Yet fifteen years later they are living together in beautiful amity. In the fifteen years after Durham there somehow or other developed that alliance which has been the permanent dominating factor in Canadian politics ever since — the alliance between the Montreal commercial and industrial interests intent upon consolidating an economic empire and the great mass of the French-Canadian voters who accepted the leadership of the church.

In support of this alliance of French and English interests in Quebec, Macdonald brought from Upper Canada a sufficiently large body of Orange Loyalists to give his party a fairly continuous majority from the 1850s to the 1890s. To regard this Anglo-French *entente* of Macdonald and Cartier as merely a case of mutual racial and religious tolerance, and to neglect the dynamic economic purposes which lay behind it, is to take a very superficial view of Canadian politics.

We have very little light on the processes, between the 1830s and 1850s, by which this new alignment of forces in Lower Canada was brought about, but at any rate it is clear that in the career of Cartier we find its personification. Cartier was the avowed and recognized spokesman of the French-Catholic hierarchy. He was also the solicitor of the Grand Trunk Railway Company and the recognized spokesman for Grand Trunk interests during the fifties and sixties when the affairs of the Grand Trunk were the most important subject of political controversy. Cartier represents in his own person the break with the long previous French-Canadian tradition of opposition to the commercial ambitions and policy of the English elements in Montreal. On the eve of Confederation, looking back over his own career, he took occasion to explain that he had never accepted all of Papineau's policy, — "Mr. Papineau not being a commercial man, and not understanding the importance of these measures. He considered Mr. Papineau was right in the struggle he maintained against the oligarchy of that time in power; but he had never approved of the course which he took with reference to commercial matters and in opposition to measures for the improvement of the country."[3]

---

[3] *Parliamentary debates on the subject of the Confederation of the British North American provinces* (Quebec, 1865), 61.

In the thick volume of 817 pages in which Joseph Tassé collected the speeches of Sir George Cartier, the first speech printed is one in the election campaign of 1844 on responsible government; but the second is on the Montreal and Portland Railway. It was delivered on August 10, 1846, at a great open-air meeting, presided over by LaFontaine, and held for the purpose of working up popular enthusiasm in behalf of this project of equipping Montreal with a winter port. "The prosperity of Montreal," Cartier told his hearers, "depends upon its position as the entrepôt of the commerce of the West. . . . We can only maintain that position if we assure ourselves of the best means of transport from the West to the Atlantic by means of our canals and of this railway."[4] Here in 1846 is the whole gospel of the Montreal mercantile class upon the lips of a French Canadian; and, at the close of the meeting, so M. Tassé informs us, many shares were subscribed in the projected railway, "Messrs. LaFontaine and Cartier giving the example".

When he became a member of the legislature Cartier continued his active interest in railway development. He served as legal adviser to the Grand Trunk promoters, and the first resolution of the board of directors of the Grand Trunk Company in 1853 appointed him as its solicitor for Canada East. In the later 1850s and through the 1860s the Grand Trunk had to come repeatedly to the legislature for financial help of one kind or another, and it was Cartier who took the leading part in seeing that the help was forthcoming. "The Grand Trunk," he boasted, "and the Victoria Bridge have flooded Montreal with an abundance of prosperity. What would Montreal be without the Grand Trunk? It has assured for us the commerce of the West."[5] His biographer, Mr. John Boyd, quotes the admiring comment of William Wainwright, one of the leading Grand Trunk officials: "It was undoubtedly through the Arrangements Act, the passage of which by the Canadian parliament was secured by George Etienne Cartier, that the company was saved at that time [1862]. . . . Cartier in this connection rendered a service that should never be forgotten by Canadians, for through his influence the collapse of a railway enterprise that

---

[4] Joseph Tassé, *Discours de Sir Georges Cartier, Baronnet, accompagnés de notices* (Montréal, 1893), 7.
[5] John Boyd, *Sir George Etienne Cartier, Bart.: His life and times* (Toronto, 1914), 161.

meant so much for the country was undoubtedly prevented. George Etienne Cartier was the biggest French Canadian I have ever known."[6] Exactly. On Montreal standards, the test of bigness in a French Canadian was the degree of his assistance in advancing the cause of the commercial empire of Montreal.

"For fourteen years, from 1852 to 1867, Cartier was chairman of the Railway Committee of the Legislature of United Canada"; and finally, to quote Mr. Boyd's delightful euphemism, "he crowned his career by having passed by parliament the first charter for the construction of the Canadian Pacific Railway."[7] The charter to which Mr. Boyd refers was that which was granted in 1872 to Sir Hugh Allan of Montreal and his associates and which gave rise to the incident famous in Canadian history as the Pacific Scandal.

So much for the French-Canadian place in the Liberal-Conservative party. It should be added, of course, that during the same time that it provided this support to business enterprise, the Catholic vote obtained many things which were of interest to the church — the incorporation of religious communities with the locking up of large landed estates in mortmain, the clerical control of education in Lower Canada, the extension of separate schools in Upper Canada, and so forth.

The second group in the Liberal-Conservative party consisted of Montreal big business and such voting support from the Eastern Townships as it could command. Numerically the Lower-Canadian English did not count for much, but they had an importance out of all proportion to their numbers because of their connection with the commercial and industrial enterprises of Montreal. On the whole, the Eastern Townships tended to follow this Montreal leadership in politics; and it is interesting to observe the arguments by which the majority of their votes were attracted into the Liberal-Conservative camp. If race and religion had been the dominating factors in Canadian politics of the fifties and sixties, as the traditional accounts of the pre-Confederation period would have it, the Lower-Canadian English would surely have been attracted into an alliance with the Upper-Canadian Grits; and it was a frequent complaint of the Toronto *Globe* that they did not vote with their western fellow citizens who shared their language and religion.

---

[6] *Ibid.*, 165.
[7] *Ibid.*, 167.

Alexander Galt[8] was the outstanding representative in politics of the Lower-Canada English section. Note the arguments which Galt addresses to his constituents in his great speech at Sherbrooke on November 23, 1864, when he is presenting the project of Confederation to them and when he has to allay their fears of handing themselves over to a permanent French majority in the Province of Quebec:

> The interests of the British population of Lower Canada were identical with those of the French Canadians; these peculiar interests being that the trade and commerce of the Western country should continue to flow through Lower Canada. . . . He felt that in taking his position in the [Quebec] Conference he was charged, not altogether with the simple duty of a representative of the British portion of the population of Lower Canada, but he felt that he equally represented his French Canadian friends; and his conviction was that, instead of there being any clashing and division of interests, they would be found in the future more closely bound together than ever before. It would be found that the effect of the combination of all the Provinces would be to benefit Lower Canada — not French Lower Canada or British Lower Canada — but the whole of Lower Canada — by giving it the position of being the commercial heart of the country. . . . He thought our material interests would have to govern us in this respect. . . . He thought it was plain that Lower Canada was going to be the great commercial centre for the whole of the Provinces, and even when we extended the boundaries of our Empire to the countries bordering on the Saskatchewan and the Rocky Mountains, the whole wealth of that great country must pour down the St. Lawrence and stimulate the industry of the cities of Lower Canada.[9]

Confederation, in other words, meant the final realization of the dream of a commercial empire with the lower St. Lawrence for its

---

[8] Galt had gone into politics in 1849 in order to advance the interests of the British American Land Company of which he was the Canadian manager. Explaining his action to the directors in London, he wrote: "I consider the interests of the Company and of the country to be identical. . . . I ought perhaps to add that I am not the least likely to become a political partisan; my views are all for objects of material advantage" (see O. D. Skelton, *The life and times of Sir Alexander Tilloch Galt*, Toronto, 1920, 143). Here speaks the perfect "moderate".

[9] A. T. Galt, *Speech on the proposed union of the British North American provinces, delivered at Sherbrooke, C.E., 23rd November, 1864* (Montreal, 1864).

focus; and, in face of such an opportunity, it behoved the two races on the St. Lawrence to rise above their mutual suspicions. Let me repeat that, of course, the Liberal-Conservative party stood for a policy of appeasement between French and English; but the dynamic purpose for which appeasement was sought was the establishment of Montreal's "commercial state".

In the field of journalism the chief exponent of the ideas and ambitions of the Montreal business group was, then as now, the Montreal *Gazette*. Copious quotations could be extracted from the *Gazette* illustrating this same thesis which Galt expounded at Sherbrooke, and it is worth noting that in all these quotations from the *Gazette*, from Galt and from Cartier, there is practically no talk about those vague abstractions which are called political principles. The emphasis is entirely upon interests. "Their politics," said the Toronto *Globe* of the two Montreal papers, the *Gazette* and the *Pilot*, "have been conducted on a mercantile basis. . . . The five loaves and two fishes are their seven cardinal principles."[10]

On the other two groups, both from Upper Canada, who made up the Liberal-Conservative coalition, there is no need to dwell so long. It is clear that the Hincksite Reformers, the third group in the coalition, the so-called "moderates" amongst the Upper-Canadian followers of Robert Baldwin, were primarily urban. Francis Hincks himself was notoriously on very intimate terms with the Grand Trunk promoters — too intimate, so his critics charged. When he retired from active politics in 1854, he bequeathed to Macdonald the Hincksite group and its leader, John Ross. Ross had gone to England to complete the Grand Trunk deal, and he was one of the five cabinet ministers sitting upon the directorate of the railway company to denote the close connection between the Canadian government and the transportation enterprise. In due course he became president of the Grand Trunk Railway Company.

Macdonald's own Upper-Canadian Tory following, the fourth element in the Liberal-Conservative coalition, is important for the voting power which it contributed and for the intensification of anti-American feeling which it gave to the party, but for little else. We need only note here that it was the old high and dry Family Compact Tory hero, Sir Allan MacNab, who contributed the

---

[10] Nov. 2, 1859.

slogan of the new coalition when he declared in a famous phrase that "railways are my politics".

The main element in the coalition which gradually formed itself in opposition to the Liberal-Conservatives was, of course, composed of the Clear Grits of Upper Canada. Grittism had the centre of its strength in the pioneer farming area of the Ontario peninsula, and was a characteristic expression of frontier agrarian democracy. The vigorous and growing young city of Toronto, from which railways were beginning to radiate westward and northward, formed the intellectual as well as the economic capital of these pioneer wheat farmers; and its relation to them was like that of Winnipeg in our own day to the radical pioneer wheat farmers of the prairie. In Toronto the Grit movement found an incomparable leader with an incomparable organ through which the gospel of Grittism might be preached — George Brown and his *Globe*. East of Toronto the strength of the Grits gradually declined; and along the eastern end of Lake Ontario, down the St. Lawrence and up the Ottawa, while there were men calling themselves Reformers, pure Grittism made little appeal. These districts were connected economically with Montreal rather than with Toronto. When the Montreal *Gazette* appealed for the interests of the St. Lawrence route against the "Peninsular interest" of western Grittism, it met with sympathetic response in the eastern parts of Upper Canada.

The appeal of the *Globe* was essentially to the West. The commercial and financial interests of Toronto often joined hands with the *Globe*'s "intelligent yeomanry" of the peninsula in fighting against the schemes of Montreal for tariffs that gave differential advantages to imports *viâ* the St. Lawrence, and against Montreal's monopolistic control of transportation, credit, and wholesale distribution. The *Globe* criticized the protectionist tendencies of Galt's tariffs in 1858 and 1859, but Brown could not get the Reformers nearer Montreal to agree with him in his free-trade views. It was the *Globe* which initiated and led the campaign for the extension of Canada westward to the Red River and the prairies; and on this question the Grit attitude was very much like that of the radical Republicans to the south with their free-homestead policy and their election cry of "Vote yourself a farm". The main purpose of this campaign and of the "Rep by Pop" agitation, as Montreal interests very clearly perceived, was to increase the influence of the western agricultural districts in the provincial legislature so that they could more effectively checkmate policies which had their origin in Montreal head-offices.

The *bête noire* of the *Globe* and the Clear Grits was the Grand Trunk Railway. In spite of popular tradition to the contrary, it is the Grand Trunk Railway rather than the French Catholic Church which occupies the major portion of the *Globe*'s space during the decade before Confederation. To the *Globe* the Grand Trunk stood as a symbol for the whole corrupt system, as it believed it to be, of the domination of the country's government and politics by eastern business interests.

> With the Grand Trunk and the Bank of Montreal at his back, there is no saying how far the reckless financier of the present government may carry his schemes. These institutions are the enemies of the people and of popular rights. They have special interests to advance in Parliament. . . . It is time that Upper Canadians were united together in resisting these monopolies, and the Government which has created and supported them. It is time that we had a Government above being the servant of railway or banking institutions. It is time that we had a Government which would consider the interest of the whole people and not of a few wily money-makers who can bring influence to bear upon Parliament. It is above all a necessity that the people of the West . . . should elect men who will be able to prevent the mischief which Mr. Galt is still anxious to do to the interests of the Western country.

This is from an editorial in the *Globe* of August 10, 1867, an editorial written in the midst of the first general election of the new Dominion of Canada which had just come into existence on July 1. Nothing could show more forcibly the *Globe*'s clear understanding (in those days) of the economic basis of politics, and nothing could show more clearly the class and sectional lines dividing the Liberal-Conservatives of the 1860s from the Grits.

The Rouge group from Lower Canada, who worked in cooperation with the Grits in the legislature, were never able to attain the numerical strength in their French-Canadian community which the Grits attained in Upper Canada. Their anti-clerical tendencies made the church a bitter enemy, and by 1867 they were steadily declining in strength under clerical attack. The democratic and republican ideas which they derived from the revolutionary Paris of 1848 made them unpopular both with the church and with Montreal business, though they did form a short alliance with the Montreal mercantile interests in 1849 for the purpose of advocating annexation to the United States. (This is the only occasion on which Montreal ever lost faith in its mission.) But their voting strength was mostly in the pioneer agricultural districts south of the St. Lawrence. Dorion, their leader, opposed Confederation partly because he thought it was a Grand Trunk "job", which it partly was. They shared with the Grits a general sympathy for the democratic ideas which came from the United States. Some of the more advanced of them had imbibed from France an economic radicalism which went far beyond any native North American doctrines, and were beginning to talk about bourgeoisie and proletariat. But these were a small minority of what was only a minority party. The focus of Rouge interest was mainly local; the party had its hands full in fighting the declining power of French-Canadian feudalism and the growing power of the French-Canadian church.

3

Such were the main lines of party division in the pre-Confederation province of Canada. After 1867 these party divisions of Liberal-Conservatives and Reformers were gradually extended from the central area to the outlying sections of the dominion. Inevitably the politics of Canada dominated the politics of the Maritime Provinces and of the little far-western communities of Manitoba and British Columbia. In 1871 the population of Ontario and Quebec together was 2,812,367 (Ontario, 1,620,851; Quebec, 1,191,516) out of the dominion's total population of 3,689,257; while Nova Scotia had only 387,800; New Brunswick, 285,594; Prince Edward Island, 94,021; Manitoba, 25,228; and British Columbia, 36,247. Confederation had been due primarily to the continental ambitions of the Canadians; it was they who had brought the other partners into the union. And it was Canadian ambitions, reaching their highest intensity in Montreal and Toronto, which continued to supply the driving force for both the economic and the political life of the new dominion.

In the politics of the new federal state after 1867, accordingly, there is to be discerned a double process. Most important and fundamental is the continuing drive of great business interests for the conquest and consolidation of this expanded economic empire which lay open to their exploitation; and it was the primary function of Macdonald's Liberal-Conservative party to make the state a partner in this enterprise, a function which was taken over by Laurier's Liberal party after 1896. But to achieve this end of a united centralized economic empire a great variety of particularist sectional, racial, and religious interests had to be conciliated, manipulated, and kept moving together in some kind of practical concord. It was the second function of the party system to perform this task of conciliation and management of the diverse sectional interests in the new loosely knit nation.

The first generation after Confederation is dominated by Macdonald's Liberal-Conservative party. Clearly it was a constructive nation-building party and it earned its support, as against its Reform rival, by the wider sweep of its national ideas and ambitions and by the greater vigour of its administrative policies. But the nationalism of the Liberal-Conservatives was of a particular quality. The nation which they were helping to build up was a nation under the strong centralized control and leadership of the great capitalist *entrepreneurs* of Montreal and Toronto.

In short, the Liberal-Conservative party under Macdonald was a Hamiltonian federalist party. Macdonald would never have subscribed to Alexander Hamilton's whole-hearted contempt for the common people, but he and Cartier and their lieutenants were agreed in opposing the manifestations of American democracy which expressed themselves in Canada through the Grit and the Rouge parties. "The rights of the minority must be protected," said Macdonald to his fellow delegates at Quebec when they were discussing the proper constitution of the Senate, "and the rich are always fewer in number than the poor."[11] In all essential points Macdonald's fundamental policy was Hamiltonian. A strong central government was needed to carry through the drive for westward economic expansion, to win the confidence and attract the capital of the investing classes whose support was necessary for this expansionist policy. The great interests of finance and industry and transportation must be tied to the national government by putting the national government solidly behind their ambitions for power and profit. So the "National Policy" lays the basis for the development of a many-sided economic life, and at the same time fosters a class of industrialists who depend for special privileges upon the

---

[11] Sir J. Pope (ed.), *Confederation, being a series of hitherto unpublished documents bearing on the British North America Act* (Toronto, 1895), 58.

national government. Similarly the Canadian Pacific Railway makes an economic unity out of the half-continent where hitherto there has been only the framework of a political unity, but again the result is achieved by the creation of a specially privileged group who depend vitally upon the incitement and patronage of government. Most important of all, the development of these interlocking groups of railwaymen, manufacturers, and financiers serves to bring about not merely a closer national unity within the northern half of the continent, but a unity which is set off against the United States, which is based predominantly upon the St. Lawrence and its tributary routes, which is constructed for the purpose of consolidating this area against American penetration, of making it a closed preserve to be triumphantly exploited by Canadian business enterprise.

While, however, the economic process of expansion, consolidation, integration, and concentration went on steadily, the accompanying political process by which the diverse sections of public opinion were managed and manipulated towards the one supreme end was carried on only with great difficulty. It was Macdonald's genius in the arts of bargaining and conciliation that gave him his unquestioned position of leadership. Ontario and Quebec were constantly at odds over racial and religious issues. The outlying sections of the dominion were only slowly incorporated into any real union. "Seven years have elapsed since Confederation was accomplished," said the young idealists of the Canada First movement in 1874, "and to this day neither one nor the other of our old parties has established itself, as a party, in Nova Scotia, New Brunswick, Manitoba or British Columbia. Patronage and vituperation were equally inefficacious to give a lasting foothold to either party."[12] "Their politics were and perhaps still are 'better terms'."[13] A decade later when Goldwin Smith visited British Columbia *via* the new Canadian Pacific Railway, he reported with grim enjoyment that a citizen of the Pacific province, on being asked what his politics were, had replied "Government appropriations".[14] In fact "government appropriations" formed the basic element in the technique by which Macdonald kept the different sections of the

---

[12] *Canada first: A memorial of the late William A. Foster, Q.C.* (Toronto, 1890), 55.
[13] *Ibid.,* 59.
[14] Goldwin Smith, *Canada and the Canadian question* (London, 1891), 220.

dominion marching together in some semblance of order and by which he slowly constructed a united party out of diverse sectional groups.

Let me select but one incident in the long history of the Macdonald system, an incident which throws a vivid light on the inherent sectionalism of Canadian politics, on the kind of difficulties Macdonald had to meet, on his methods, and also on the dominant purpose which his whole system subserved.[15]

In 1884 the Macdonald system had reached its zenith. The old chieftain had lived down the disgrace of the Pacific Scandal, and the crisis of the Regina scaffold was not yet upon him. The National Policy had been established and the C.P.R. was being pushed rapidly across the continent. The country seemed at last about to reap the economic harvest which had been promised by Confederation. But the C.P.R. was in financial difficulties. In the winter of 1883-4, Stephen, Angus, McIntyre, Van Horne, and Abbott came up to Ottawa to interview Macdonald. They could raise no more money in the open market in London or New York, and if the government did not come to their help the company would have to go out of business. They proposed a temporary loan from the government of twenty-two and a half million dollars.

Macdonald saw them at his home, at Earnscliffe, late one evening, and rejected their proposal. He told them that they might as well look for the planet Jupiter. He wouldn't give them the money; if he did agree, the cabinet wouldn't follow him; and if the cabinet did agree it would smash the party. They returned disconsolate to their lodgings where they met J. H. Pope, acting minister of railways during Tupper's absence as high commissioner in England. Pope went back to Earnscliffe, woke Macdonald up out of bed, and persuaded him to reverse his decision. "The day the Canadian Pacific busts," said John Henry Pope, who was famous for his homely language, "the Conservative party busts the day after." Next morning the C.P.R. delegation saw the cabinet, and Pope's arguments were again successful. But there still remained the party majority in the House. Tupper was brought back from England and he rammed the loan through caucus. In due course the resolutions and then the bill for the loan were introduced into Parliament.

---

[15] This account of the proceedings concerning the C.P.R. loan of 1884 is based upon O. D. Skelton, *Life and letters of Sir Wilfrid Laurier* (Toronto, 1921), ch. vi, and the columns of the *Week* for the early part of 1884.

Here difficulties arose. Macdonald was vitally dependent upon the large bloc of Bleu votes from Quebec and the French members saw their opportunity. The province of Quebec, like the C.P.R., was in financial difficulties. It had undertaken the construction of a north-shore line from Ottawa to Montreal to Quebec. At this critical moment the premier of Quebec arrived in Ottawa, and together with the French members of the dominion house he proceeded to hold the government up. They demanded that three million dollars be paid to Quebec by the dominion as a subsidy in assistance of the north-shore line on the ground that it was a work of national importance, and they announced that they would not vote for the C.P.R. loan until Macdonald came to terms. The C.P.R. debate began in the House and the seats of the Quebec members were ominously vacant. Macdonald sat with anxious face as the debate progressed from day to day, while agents negotiated for him with the recalcitrant Quebecers in a committee room down the corridor. The debate went on, finally the last speech was delivered, Mr. Speaker called for a division, and still there were no Quebec members in the House. At the last moment, on the second division bell, they trooped in; the C.P.R. loan was carried, the C.P.R. was saved, the government was saved, and the unity of the Conservative party was saved — but the Quebecers got their black-mail.[16] The members from the other provinces, who had been interested spectators at these manoeuvres, then demanded compensation also. Finally it was agreed that there should be a general levelling up all round of provincial subsidies.

On the whole incident and on its implications as to the nature of Canadian politics the comment of Goldwin Smith in the *Week* is very illuminating:

---

[16] It was not only fastidious persons like Goldwin Smith who referred to this process as blackmail. Next year the C.P.R. came back for a further loan of five million dollars.

Macdonald writes to Tupper on this occasion (March 17, 1885): "The C.P.R. will make its appeal for relief this week. I don't know how Council or Parliament will take it. . . . Our difficulties are immense. The Quebec M.P.s have the line to Quebec up again. The Maritimes are clamorous for the short line, and we have blackmailing all round. How it will end God knows, but I wish I were well out of it" (see E. M. Saunders, *The life and letters of the Rt. Hon. Sir Charles Tupper*, London, 1916, II, 47).

Though the Government majority voted solid at last, a rift was distinctly seen in it, and through the rift a glimpse was caught into a troubled and chaotic future. Sir John Macdonald may be the Prince of Darkness; with some of its imps he is certainly far too familiar. But an angel of light would perhaps have not been so successful in holding together the motley and discordant elements, local, ethnological, religious, social and personal, on a combination of which the Dominion government has been based; or if he had, it would not have been without detriment to his seraphic purity. Not Cavour or Bismarck was more singularly fitted for his special task than Sir John. . . . When this man is gone, who will there be to take his place? What shepherd is there who knows the sheep or whose voice the sheep know? Who else could make Orangemen vote for Papists, or induce half the members for Ontario to help in levying on their own Province the necessary blackmail for Quebec? Yet this is the work which will have to be done if a general break-up is to be averted. Things will not hold together of themselves.[17]

This is the excuse, if not the justification, of Sir John Macdonald. The task of his political life has been to hold together a set of elements, national, religious, sectional and personal, as motley as the component patches of any "crazy quilt", and actuated, each of them, by paramount regard for its own interest. This task he has so far accomplished by his consummate address, by his assiduous study of the weaker points of character, and where corruption was indispensable, by corruption. It is more than doubtful whether anybody could have done better than he has done. . . . By giving the public the full benefit of his tact, knowledge and strategy, he has probably done the work for us as cheaply as it was possible to do it. Let it be written on his tomb, that he held out for the country against the blackmailers till the second bell had rung.[18]

4

A study of the Alexander Mackenzie régime, 1873–8, the only period during which the Reformers were in office before Laurier, throws into relief the same characteristics which we have observed in the Macdonald system.

When Macdonald retired from office over the Pacific Scandal and the new Mackenzie government sought public support in a general

---

[17] The *Week,* Feb. 28, 1884.
[18] *Ibid.,* April 10, 1884.

election, the *Globe* proclaimed: "The poll tomorrow is the Thermopylae of Canadian political virtue" (January 28, 1874), and it announced that the Macdonald system was at an end. "By sectional legislation, by tampering with individual members, by holding out threats and inducements in turn, they [the Conservatives] had utterly destroyed the *morale* of the first Parliament of the Dominion" (January 6, 1874). "The Pacific Scandal shattered at one blow the fabric which Sir John Macdonald kept together by his skill in manipulation of individual interests, and the cohesive power of public plunder" (January 22, 1874). "Appeal will henceforth be made not to warring interests but to a community of hopes, not to rival claims of battling representatives but to a national sentiment co-extensive with our wide domain" (January 10, 1874).

Mackenzie, however, quickly discovered that the Thermopylae of Canadian virtue had not altered any of the essential conditions under which Canadian politics was carried on. The cabinet which he formed was as much a coalition of sectional groups as had been that of Macdonald in 1867. With the outlying sections of the dominion Mackenzie had constant trouble. His government was at odds with British Columbia continuously because he was unwilling to pay enough in railway concessions to win the support of the Pacific coast politicians. With the Maritime Provinces he had similar difficulties. The Alexander Mackenzie letter-books in the Public Archives at Ottawa are full of letters from the prime minister in which he is trying to appease the appetite of his Maritime followers for spoils and to make them see that the new Intercolonial Railway must be run as a railway by technical experts and not as an employment agency for deserving Maritime Reformers. "It seems," he wrote on July 27, 1874, to Lord Dufferin, the governor-general, "that the smaller the province the more trouble it will be. Columbia, Manitoba, and Prince Edward Island give me more trouble than Ontario and Quebec." And about the same time, November 18, 1874, he bursts out to his Nova Scotia lieutenant, A. G. Jones of Halifax: "I am in receipt of your extraordinary letter about railway and other appointments, and I confess nothing has been written to me for months that has astonished me more. It is really too bad. Half my time is taken up with this question of patronage in Nova Scotia and Prince Edward Island. My life has become a torment to me about it."

Mackenzie, in fact, was too scrupulous and stiff-necked in his puritanism to make effective use of the technique by which alone a strong united party could be constructed in a country such as Canada. More important, he was not in sympathy with the intellectual atmosphere of the dominion capital. He was never at his ease with railway-contractors or concession-hunters or with any of that swarming tribe of adventurers who were eager to do their share in building up the new nation by being given a slice of its natural resources to exploit for their own profit. He remained hostile to the whole Hamiltonian tradition of an alliance between government and big business which Macdonald had established at Ottawa. He boggled over the expense of the Pacific railway. He failed to seize the opportunity of winning the manufacturers to the support of his party by giving them the protection which they were demanding with more and more insistence through the 1870s. As Goldwin Smith remarked, if his strong point as prime minister consisted in his having been a stone-mason, his weak point consisted in his being one still. No party equipped with such leadership and inspired by such ideals could compete successfully with the Hamiltonian forces gathered together by John A. Macdonald. Mackenzie's failure provides as clear a demonstration of the fundamental basis of Canadian party politics as does Macdonald's success.

5

It was left to Laurier to take up the work where Macdonald had laid it down. Many observers have remarked on the similarity between the two men and their methods, and it is true that under Laurier Canadian politics continued to consist of an intricate process of sectional bargaining and log-rolling just as under Macdonald, the necessary work of adjustment now being carried out under the auspices of the Liberal rather than of the Conservative party. But what is equally important to observe, and what has not so often been pointed out, is that it was a condition of Laurier's success that he should make of his party an instrument for the same Hamiltonian purposes which had been pursued by the Conservative party under Macdonald. So Laurier had a more difficult and subtle rôle to play, because he led a party in which the radical agrarian Grit tradition in Ontario and the radical anti-clerical Rouge tradition in Quebec were still strong. Under Laurier the old party of Brown and Mackenzie and Dorion had to combine Jeffersonian professions with Hamiltonian practices.

After his struggle with the hierarchy in 1896 Laurier quietly smothered what was left of Rougeism in his party, took over the old Bleu faction, and made his peace with the church. The appointment of Fielding rather than Cartwright to the ministry of finance was a sign that he was about to make his peace with the manufacturers also and accept the National Policy. He succeeded in doing this while at the same time keeping hold of his low-tariff agrarian followers by the most brilliant political coup in Canadian history, the invention of the British preference. This served also to help to wean his agricultural constituents from their dangerous habit — dangerous, that is, to Canadian capitalist interests — of looking southward for markets. Having made these preliminary adjustments, Laurier then proceeded to put his party in charge of the one really first-class boom which the country had enjoyed since 1867. In the rush of prosperity of the early 1900s sectional difficulties for the moment disappeared. At last Canada was a nation, for there was so much prosperity to distribute that every section could be satisfied and every individual could become a capitalist.

Incidentally Laurier built up for his party a railway and banking connection to offset the old alliance of the C.P.R. and the Bank of Montreal with the Conservatives. In his working partnership with the Grand Trunk–Mackenzie and Mann–Canadian Bank of Commerce interests he completed the Hamiltonian alignment of his party. The Laurier of the railway boom had come a long way from the Laurier of the 1877 speech on political liberalism — but he had brought his party all the way with him and had established its place in the essential Canadian tradition. "Consult the annals of Canada for the past fifty years at random," said a twentieth-century observer, "and whatever party may be in power, what do you find? The government is building a railway, buying a railway, selling a railway, or blocking a railway."[19]

At this point we reach the golden age in the evolution of the Canadian two-party system. Both parties were now completely national in the North American sense; that is, both appealed for support to all sections and classes of the nation and both preached the same policy — the continuous fostering of material prosperity through the incitement and patronage of government. The class differences which had been discernible between the original Liberal-

---

[19] Quoted in O. D. Skelton, *Life and letters of Sir Wilfrid Laurier*, I, 244.

Conservatives and the original Reformers in the 1850s had disappeared; class conflicts and sectional conflicts were now reconciled
and settled within each party rather than as between the two parties.
All that remained to distinguish the parties were the two old
English names. Not even in the United States had the functioning
of the North American two-party system achieved a greater degree
of perfection than this.

And then suddenly in 1911 there broke out a storm which showed
that all was not quite so harmonious as appeared on the surface.
The reciprocity election of 1911 bears the same significance in
Canadian political history as the election of 1896 in that of the
United States. It marks the emergence of a movement of protest
against the tightening grip of industrial plutocracy upon the
national economy; and from that time on the murmurs of discontent have grown steadily louder. The old agrarian radicalism of
the Upper Canada Grits was coming to life again in a fresh incarnation among the wheat farmers of the new West.

For the moment, however, the incipient revolt was ruthlessly and
triumphantly crushed. When Laurier made the one serious mistake
of his career and listened to the cry of the western farmers for
American markets he was quickly repudiated by the governing
classes of the country and of his own party. Merely to call the roll
of the famous eighteen Toronto Liberals who deserted Laurier over
reciprocity and brought about his defeat is to provide eloquent
testimony of where the real issue of the election lay. The list begins
with the head of the Canadian Bank of Commerce, includes two
other financiers prominent in the Commerce group, three men high
in the directorates of other banks, the legal adviser of Mackenzie
and Mann, two managers of great insurance companies, several
ex-presidents of the Toronto board of trade, and it concludes with
the head of the largest department store in Canada.[20]

In 1911 Canadian capitalism celebrated its coming of age. The
dream of the Montreal merchants of one hundred years before had
at last come true. The northern commercial state was a reality.
Slowly, in spite of many discouragements and setbacks, it had been
built up, and now its trade flowed in and out by the St. Lawrence,
"the River of Canada". Its three and a half million square miles

---

[20] The names of the eighteen Liberals and the text of their manifesto against
reciprocity may be found in the *Canadian annual review*, 1911, 48.

were well organized under the direction and control of Montreal. Toronto capitalists, who at times had shown some inclination to challenge the position of the senior metropolis, were now working hand in hand with it. And on September 21, 1911, the Canadian people put behind them the temptation to break the economic bonds by which they had been welded into a nation, affirming their determination to remain loyal subjects of St. James and King streets.

Yet perhaps the discerning observer might have felt some reason for uneasiness at the very moment of this triumph. Perhaps the agrarian revolt of 1911 was the first sign that there was developing within the Canadian economy, as in that of the United States, a deeper cleavage of interests, another irrepressible conflict which could not be avoided or adjourned indefinitely by the happy process of geographical expansion. Perhaps the unrest which has shown itself in the Progressive movement of the 1920s, and in the C.C.F. and other movements of political protest in the 1930s has pointed in the same direction. Perhaps the more intense strains and stresses which seem likely to test the social structure in the second generation of the twentieth century will make the old Macdonald-Laurier two-party system no longer adequate. It grew up as a free-and-easy opportunistic adaptation to the sectional divisions of a continental area. It worked well enough in an expanding capitalist economy. But the age of the frontier is passing away, and the sectional divisions of North America tend to be transformed into the European class divisions of the "haves" and the "have-nots". Will the party system also be transformed? Or will Canadians still cling to the orthodox faith, in which idealist academic students and cynical practical politicians find a curious bond of union, and maintain that the North American two-party system has still a long life ahead of it, that age cannot wither it nor custom stale its infinite variety?

3. Some Aspects of Upper Canadian Radical Opinion in the Decade before Confederation

(This paper represented my first appearance in public as a student of Canadian history. It was read at the annual meeting of the Canadian Historical Association in 1927, when most of the programme, on this sixtieth anniversary of Confederation, was devoted to the Confederation period. It was written while I was a professor in Saskatchewan and therefore particularly apt to see the parallels between agrarian movements in Upper Canada in the 1860s and agrarian movements on the prairies in the 1920s. It rather overemphasized the agrarian aspect of Grittism; and I modified this view somewhat by the time of my address in 1946 to the C.H.A. on the Canadian liberal tradition.

The *Canadian Historical Review* for June, 1959, contains another article of mine on "Canada's Relations with the Empire as Seen by the Toronto Globe, 1857-67" which continues this analysis of Upper Canadian opinion in the years just before Confederation. Because it is long, and with many quotations from the *Globe*, I have had to omit it from this volume. It brings out the *Globe*'s faith both in Canadian autonomy and in imperial unity, a faith which has been characteristic of Canadian liberal thinking from the start. What liberals in Canada have sought throughout has not been the breaking of the tie with Great Britain but the changing of its nature to that of a free association of equals.

Professor J. M. S. Careless in *Brown of the Globe, 1818-59: Volume I— The Voice of Upper Canada* gives an illuminating account of the development of Reform movements in Upper Canada during the forties and the fifties, the period just before the decade dealt with in this paper of mine. I think that he rather overemphasizes the British Liberal side of Brown as against his North American radical side.)

Present-day popular knowledge of the Confederation movement seems to be largely confined to biographical details about the leading actors in the drama. The story of the political matchmakings and breaches of promise, of the party marriages and divorces of the time, has been narrated to us ad nauseam; and it is the general familiarity with it which has led, no doubt, to the general acceptance of the dictum that "our Canadian History is as dull as ditch-water and our politics is full of it". What is needed for the Confederation period — as indeed for all periods of our history — is a series of studies of the atmosphere, social, economic and intellectual, in which the political movement took place. If we were more familiar with the ideas which were floating in the air at the time and with the underlying conditions which made these ideas prevalent, the 1927 jubilee celebrations on which we are about to embark would probably display much less rhetorical hero-worship and much more real understanding of ourselves as a people.

This paper is an attempt to discuss some of the ideas which were prevalent amongst one section of the community, the Upper Canada Reformers, during the ten or fifteen years before 1867. It is based largely on the pages of George Brown's *Globe*, which, as everyone knows, stood out in the 1850s and 1860s not merely as the exponent but also as the maker of the radical opinion of its constituency. The long agitation conducted by Brown in the *Globe* and on the floor of the Legislative Assembly eventually produced the political situation in Canada from which Confederation resulted. It is worth while, therefore, to examine what it was for which or against which he was agitating, especially as his *Globe* has by this time become one of those classics that everyone has read about but very few have read.

Today the main thing that is remembered about the *Globe* of those times is its attacks upon the Catholic Church; and in view of its reputation for religious intolerance one is rather surprised to find how small a part religious controversies play in its editorials. Of course, attacks on the supposed superstitions of the Roman faith and on the pretensions of the Vatican or of the local hierarchy to be the repositories of final truth can easily be quoted. But from about 1857 on these become less and less frequent. It was the *political* activities of the hierarchy which roused the *Globe*'s ire; their interference in elections; their refusal to accept the complete separation of Church and State which the Upper Canada Reformers thought the only possible policy in a country of such diverse faiths as Canada; and especially their working alliance with the big business interests of Montreal which regularly delivered some fifty-odd French-Canadian "Moutons" in the Assembly under Cartier's leadership to vote for every job of the Grand Trunk, for tariffs that compelled Upper Canada to buy from Montreal instead of from the United States, or for the mere lack of action that prevented Canada from challenging the monopoly of the Hudson's Bay Company in the North-West. It is true, of course, that Brown was hypersensitive on religious questions; and one suspects that a little skilful baiting by his opponents was not infrequently resorted to in order to lead him to make an exhibition of himself on the subject. Certainly they found his vociferous Protestantism a very useful red herring to drag across the trail whenever he grew particularly hot in the pursuit of some unsavoury job perpetrated by the government or its friends. But I think that an attentive reading of the *Globe* itself will lead one to the conclusion that it was gradually dawning on Brown as the years went by that the real enemy was not the Catholic Church but big business.

For the essential thing about the *Globe* and the movement it led is that it represented the aspirations and the general outlook on life of the pioneer Upper Canadian farmer. The "Clear Grit" party in Upper Canada was an expression of the "frontier" in our Canadian politics just as Jacksonian Democracy or Lincoln Republicanism was in the politics of the United States. It was to "the intelligent yeomanry of Upper Canada"[1] that the *Globe* consciously made its appeal. Though Brown himself sat for one of the Toronto seats from 1857 to 1861, the Grits never succeeded in capturing the main urban centres. Toronto, London, Hamilton and Kingston pretty steadily elected supporters of the Macdonald-Cartier coalition. The *Globe* was never tired of contrasting the higher level of politics in the country districts with the corruption of the cities where campaign money from the Grand Trunk, the breweries and government contractors flowed like water. "It has always been the boast of the Reform party," it remarked on August 1, 1867, "that it was greatly made up of the sturdy yeomanry of the land and of by far the most intelligent, incorrupt, and incorruptible of that."

When the London *Times* in one of its frequent jeremiads on the subject of Canada attributed the low level of Canadian public life to universal suffrage, the *Globe* rejoined[2] "There are undoubtedly many people who believe that the franchise is too low . . . but the fact is beyond dispute that the higher classes, to whom the *Times* alludes in terms of approval, are the authors of the greatest mischief in Canada. They have formed a bureaucracy, and by boundless corruption carried on in alliance with London bankers, have

---

[1] The phrase occurs in an article of April 23, 1867, and similar phrases occur frequently.
[2] Nov. 8, 1861.

retained the control of affairs for many years. . . . Our farmers and mechanics whom the *Times* would consider too low in the social scale to be entrusted with the franchise, are our best politicians." When English papers were predicting as the result of the American Civil War a militarized democracy which would proceed, à la Napoleon, to gobble up the rest of North America, the *Globe* repeatedly reminded them that the basis of North American democracy was not a city mob as in Europe but an intelligent, independent agricultural class.[3] It constantly agitated for reforms in the Crown Lands Department so that the interests of the settler rather than those of the land speculator might be advanced;[4] it made fun of city men in charge of agriculture in the Cabinet, men like "Philip Van Weevil"[5] and D'Arcy McGee, "a poetical lawyer who never raised a cabbage in his life except perhaps in a scrimmage of Young Irelanders".[6] From its office for several years was published a special agricultural journal, "The Canada Farmer".[7] Always its first care was for the "intelligent yeomanry of Upper Canada".

This essential connection between the Clear Grit movement and the western farmer is shown also by the nature of the opposition to it. The Brown Reformers never succeeded in making very deep inroads into the eastern corner of Upper Canada — the St. Lawrence below Kingston and the Ottawa valley. These districts were economically connected with Montreal and the St. Lawrence route and naturally supported a Montreal government. It was in the West, in the Peninsula, that the centre of Grit influence lay; and "the eternal restlessness of the Peninsula" of which the Toronto *Leader* once[8] complained was a temper of mind which Brown found

---

[3] e.g. in an article of Aug. 15, 1861: "It is the rural population, the reading population who rule in the United States and no military dictator could conquer them . . . . The greatest standing army that ever was raised would not keep down twenty million of reading men inhabiting a country thousands of miles in extent."

[4] See articles of June 7, Sept. 7, Oct. 19, Dec. 28, 1859; May 23, 1860; Dec. 3, 1861.

[5] "Van Weevil" was the *Globe*'s nickname for Philip Van Koughnet who was taken into the Cabinet in 1857 and given charge of agriculture. He had announced a campaign for the destruction of weevils.

[6] March 31, 1864.

[7] First issued in January, 1864.

[8] Jan. 22, 1857.

congenial. Eastern Protestants, under the guidance of the Montreal *Gazette*, seldom allowed religious sympathies to draw them towards the dangerous radicals of the West. The *Gazette* steadily preached to them that their community of economic interest with their fellow Easterners, the French Catholics, was of far more importance than any religious difference or than the memory of old feuds in the pre-Responsible Government days. "The ties of race and religion," it declared,[9] "have been ineffectual to bind our merchants, manufacturers and mechanics to the chariot wheels of Western Grittism. . . . But why is it? Simply because the Western Grits always ignored the interests of the merchants, manufacturers and mechanics of Lower Canada; because they showed a disposition to treat us as a mere appendage of the Western Province, to be used against the French Canadians when we consented to be these men's tools, and to be repaid for our aid by having the commerce of the St. Lawrence destroyed, and the manufacturing interests of the country broken down." And again in a review of the Rep. by Pop. struggle,[10] "While the French Canadians have feared a preponderant Western representation as dangerous to their nationality and peculiar institutions, the English-speaking commercial classes have feared, not without reason, that more political power given to the Far West meant a policy calculated to divert trade from the great highway of the St. Lawrence into other foreign channels. They had, therefore, to guard material interests and had clung to the English doctrine that interests in the body politic, not mere numbers required representation."

This calm conviction of the Montreal organ of the 1860s that whatever threatened the dominance of Montreal was *ipso facto* contrary to the true interests of Canada, inevitably reminds a modern reader of more recent Canadian politics. In fact, one is constantly being struck in reading the papers of those days by the many points of similarity between the Clear Grit movement amongst the farmers of Upper Canada and the Progressive movement among the prairie farmers today. Both are protests against much the same factors in Canadian life; and both have been defended or denounced by the contemporary press in much the same terms. The essence of the struggle which produced the political

---

[9] March 29, 1864.
[10] Nov. 16, 1864.

deadlock of the 1860s was not that it was primarily a fight of Protestant against Catholic or of English against French, though both these elements entered into it and embittered it. It was primarily a struggle of West against East; the then West being, like the modern West, in its social structure largely agricultural and in its geographical position a long way from its markets; and the East, then as now, being dominated by the transportation, banking and manufacturing interests which centred in Montreal.

I propose to deal specially with the attitude of the *Globe* towards three questions which bulked very large in the discussion of the pre-Confederation years — the Grand Trunk, the North-West, and Confederation itself.

1. The Grand Trunk

The modern period of our Canadian history is usually taken to begin with the achievement of Responsible Government. But it is the coming of the railways which really makes it modern; and one often wonders in studying the 1850s whether we shouldn't fix the beginning with the introduction of the Grand Trunk rather than with the introduction of Responsible Government. The famous remark of one prominent party leader that his politics were railway politics is the watchword of the new era in which a Baldwin or a LaFontaine was as out of place as Rip Van Winkle; and the problem of how railway development should be carried on in a new country and what should be the relation of the government to it is one that has overshadowed our existence ever since and is not yet completely solved. Undoubtedly the particular solution that was attempted in the 1850s by Hincks' bargain with Messrs. Peto, Brassey, Jackson and Betts, while it eventually produced a great trunk railroad line, had an enormously evil influence in demoralizing Canadian public life and in saddling the country with an almost ruinous public debt.

The *Globe* fought the Grand Trunk from the beginning as a sinister force of corruption and extravagance.[11] It believed it was a

---

[11] See the article of 8 May, 1858: "We are now witnessing the full results of the evil principles introduced by Mr. Francis Hincks. The railway era which he inaugurated brought with it reckless extravagance in the finances of the Province, and an utter disregard of every consideration of public duty."

political railway built for the benefit of promoters and contractors and politicians at the expense of the English shareholders and the Canadian public. The original contract and the successive, almost annual, revisions of it at the demand of the Company, as it sank deeper and deeper into the financial mire, were opposed strenuously by Brown both in editorials and in speeches. Every year when a fresh demand from the Company was presented in the House, and at every general election, the *Globe* teemed with articles giving a detailed review of all the sordid and expensive transactions to date; and on each occasion Brown was beaten. Sadly he had to admit that opposition members were open to Grand Trunk influence as well as the "corruptionists" on the government side.[12] Fiercely he denounced the cabinet ministers who served two masters at once — Cartier who was solicitor for the Company in Lower Canada, Macdonald who was involved with Grand Trunk men in dubious land deals at Kingston and Sarnia, Galt who had unloaded the Montreal–Portland line on to the Grand Trunk at a handsome profit to himself and his friends while serving as a director of the Grand Trunk, Ross whose only function in the cabinet was to look after Grand Trunk interests, etc., etc.,[13] while the smaller fry who got the pickings from the feast came in for the same castigation. Even the Governor-General did not escape.[14]

> The Grand Trunk Company — exclaims the *Globe* on 22 April, 1857 — governs Canada at the present moment. Its power is paramount. The Ministry are mere puppets in its hands and dance to whatever tune the Company pipes. We much fear that the present Parliament is not better than the Ministry. It may require more careful handling, more skilful management of the wires and more oil for the wheels, in order to make things run smoothly; but the Grand Trunk managers have learned how to handle it . . . The Grand Trunk moves by one of two modes or by a combination of both . . . by threatening to use its political power against the refractory member at the next election . . . or by promising per-

---

[12] See e.g. an article of 2 May, 1857.
[13] Details of these charges against ministers and of their connection with the railway may be found in an article of 11 June, 1861. The charges against Galt are given with most particularity on 9 February, 1861. The Sarnia and Kingston cases with which Macdonald was connected are discussed on 24, 26, 28, 30 November, 1860; 1, 19, 27, 28 December, 1860; 18, 25 May, 1861.
[14] See articles on 12 June, 1856 and 7 November, 1860.

sonal advantages, pecuniary or otherwise. In either case the result is more disgraceful to the individual, and more degrading to the country, than the forced acquiescence of the legislature like that of France or Prussia.

In another article about the same time (16 April, 1857) dealing with the extension to Rivière du Loup, it explains the railway's legislative methods with more particularity as to persons:

> We are still ignorant of the capacity of the ministerial omnibus. . . . At all events it is intended to embrace the Quebec members. . . . Were it not to gain votes, what ministry would think of compelling the Grand Trunk to build a line to Rivière du Loup, a line which never will, and never could pay running expenses! . . . It passes no town nor even large village and it ends nowhere. . . . A million of Canadian pounds is to be paid that John A. Macdonald and his precious company may secure the aid of Messrs. Baby, O'Farrell, Chapais, Simard and Thibaudeau.

And when the bill is finally through it burst out, with a slight mixture of historical references: "Oh for a Cromwell or a general election to cleanse the augean stable of this Parliament!" (14 May, 1857.)

Three years later, on a report in the *Leader* which hinted at the taking over of the road by the Government, the *Globe* relieved its feelings in an editorial (7 November, 1860) which is worth quoting at some length as a good example of its general attitude:

> If it has become bankrupt in the hands of private capitalists, working it for their own profit, what will be its condition in the hands of a Government working it as a political machine for the benefit of a party? . . . We had no idea that anything so bold, so gigantic, so utterly ruinous as the scheme which the *Leader* has just announced, would be proposed even by the desperados of the present Cabinet. It is time for the whole country to rouse itself to action, to appoint and instruct its leaders, to put on its armour, and prepare for the conflict. We have seen the previous Grand Trunk bills carried through Parliament under whip and spur; we have seen agents from England hovering around the lobbies of Parliament; we have seen members who denounced the Grand Trunk on the floor of the House taken into a committee room for a few minutes and returning mollified and converted, and ready to vote for everything that was proposed; we have seen the lobby agents of the English speculators rushing off to Government House at one o'clock in the morning to announce to His Excellency the success of the measure to convert the loan of sixteen million dollars by the people of Canada into a gift to their principals.

We have seen millions of dollars voted amidst derisive laughter and drunken uproar; amidst shouting, singing, and cock-crowing for the benefit of certain classes in Lower Canada; we have seen the rules of Parliament, the laws of the land, the obligations of the constitution, and the proprieties and even the decencies which ought to be preserved by a deliberative body, trampled upon without hesitation, and set aside without shame, in order that the corrupt bargains of corrupt men might be carried out.

After 1861 when the management of the company was reorganized with Watkin as president and Brydges as general manager, the *Globe* hoped at first for better things, as the new directorate showed some promise of trying to run the railway as a commercial concern. But Watkin began immediately to pull strings for the building of the long-discussed Halifax-Quebec railroad; and the *Globe* was in arms once more against what seemed to it another scheme for plunder, for getting government subsidies that would all go into the pockets of the promoters. Down to 1864 it treated the whole Intercolonial idea as a Grand Trunk job and nothing more. The demand of the company for increased postal subsidies also led to a long controversy, and soon the *Globe* was as suspicious of the new management as of the old. "Mr. Brydges is still here," its Quebec correspondent writes on 23 March, 1864, at the time of the last crisis but one before the great coalition, "and it is commonly remarked that he is never absent when a political crisis is going on." When finally Confederation and the Intercolonial were both assured the *Globe* returned to the charge. One of its chief arguments against putting Macdonald into power to inaugurate the government of the new Dominion was that to do so would be simply to re-establish a Grand Trunk government. "Shall we surrender to Macdonald and Galt the control of that great work, the Intercolonial? Shall we permit them to construct another edifice of fraud similar to the Grand Trunk?" (26 June, 1867.)

This long fight against the railway octopus in Canadian politics deserves much more attention than it has usually been given in accounts of Upper Canadian Reform. It was the chief fight which the *Globe* conducted against the undue influence of special interests; but it went hand in hand with a vigorous campaign against the efforts of Galt and the Bank of Montreal to monopolize credit facilities, against the efforts of the manufacturers for a protective tariff, against the efforts of Montreal wholesalers and importers to compel the West to deal exclusively with them. All these were attacks upon the interests of the common man as the *Globe* saw them, upon the interests of "the intelligent yeomanry of Upper Canada". So far as railway affairs went the Grand Trunk was too strong for the *Globe*, and Grit political purists could do little more than make unavailing protests. It is part of the irony of Brown's career that, after struggling all his life against the domination of Canadian politics by the Grand Trunk, he passed away just too soon to see the advent of the Canadian Pacific Railway. Perhaps he was happy in the time of his death.

2. The North-West

In another direction the *Globe* was able to make a more positive contribution. This was in regard to the North-West. Speaking in the House after he had got the campaign in his paper for incorporating the West well under way, Brown recalled that he had made the West a part of the very first speech he had delivered in the legislature. (See his speech reported in the *Globe*, 2 March, 1857.) Certainly, from 1856 on, the *Globe* took the lead in Canada in agitating for the removal of the company's monopoly on the Red and Saskatchewan rivers and the opening of the territory to Canadian settlement. More than any other agency it deserves the credit for educating Canadian public opinion up to the conception that the future of Canada depended upon the country beyond Lake Superior.

The Reform convention of January, 1857, made the incorporation of the North-West one of its planks. And from that time on the *Globe* was full of news, articles and editorials on the subject. Conservative papers for a long time pooh-poohed the project as visionary; and the *Globe* characteristically charged them and the government they supported with being in the pay of the Hudson's Bay Company. Cartier, it declared constantly, from his post of vantage inside the cabinet, was thwarting any advance by Canada towards the Red River in his fear that it would upset the political balance of power to the detriment of Lower Canada.[15]

---

[15] An article of 10 January, 1857, refers to "Sir George Simpson and his golden arguments". See also the article of 23 April, 1858: "Are we to be shut out from this territory because Mr. Rose, Mr. John Ross and Mr. John A. Macdonald either by monetary inducements or by well-directed influence,

When a group of leading Toronto business men formed the North West Transit Company to develop the route from Collingwood via Fort William to Fort Garry, the *Globe* was loud in their praises.[16] In 1859, when two Toronto newspaper men, Messrs. Buckingham and Coldwell, went out to start a paper in the Red River settlement, Buckingham wrote special letters to the *Globe* about their trip; and after the *Nor-Wester* was started the *Globe* published extracts from almost every number it printed.[17] With an enterprise which was notable in the journalism of the day, the *Globe* brought out a special supplement on the North-West containing one of the very few maps that appear in the newspapers of those days (18 May, 1857). It watched with interest the struggles of the settlers against company rule; it published extracts from the reports of the expeditions of Hind and Palliser and the others; it teemed with letters from settlers and special correspondents; and when British Columbia began to go ahead it redoubled its enthusiasm because this increased the importance of the Red River settlement as a link in an all-British route across the continent.

The *Globe* also kept its readers well informed about the different phases of the question in the mother country. When the British House of Commons investigated the company's régime in 1857 the *Globe* received special correspondence from Mr. F. W. Chesson, the secretary of the Aborigines Protection Society which was fighting the company on the ground that its rule was bad for the Indians.[18] Chesson continued to supply anti-company news and arguments from London for more than two years. In addition to his letters the *Globe* reproduced every item unfavourable to the company that appeared in any of the leading English papers. It watched the changes of government in Britain, criticized the Whigs in much the same terms as it used about Macdonald and Cartier in Canada for their undue friendliness to the company, even welcomed a Tory government as being more independent of Mr. Edward

---

are more disposed to act in the interest of the Hudson's Bay Company than for the benefit of the people of Canada?" On the opposition of Cartier and the French to western expansion see articles of 6 January, 1857 and 2 August, 1860.

[16] The company was formed in 1856. A review of its operations is given 18 July, 1859.

[17] Buckingham's letters appear in October, 1859.

[18] Letters from "F.W.C." begin to appear in March, 1857.

Ellice.[19] And it eagerly gathered information about the financial deal of 1863 which put the company into the hands of the same group of interests that controlled the Grand Trunk.[20]

What the *Globe* especially insisted on was the great future which was in store for Canada if she would only rise to her opportunity. Here Brown was undoubtedly a magnificent prophet. He tried to stir the ambitions of his fellow-citizens and constantly lamented their lethargy as contrasted with the American energy in pushing westward. Commenting (24 February, 1862) on a news item from Belleville that the explorer Fraser was 86 years old, the *Globe* asks: "Is it not disgraceful to us as a people that in the year 1862 we should have advanced so little beyond the steps taken by the bold fur-trader of 1805 — that the journey across the Rocky Mountains should be nearly as arduous now as it was then? How long are we to bear this reproach upon the enterprise of our race? So long as Mr. Cartier rules but not one day longer, we trust." A little later in the same year (23 April) it declares: "The opening up of the country belongs not to Great Britain but to those who will be most benefited by it, the people of Canada. . . . It is an act of the greatest absurdity for men to advocate our paying between one and two million a year to support Imperial policy on foreign affairs, and, at the same time, to allege that the Imperial Government should bear the expense of opening up and settling our territory."

Again, answering arguments of the *Leader* that Canada already had more territory than it could populate, the *Globe* replies: "If the original thirteen states had been guilty of the narrow-minded policy now recommended to Canada; if they had isolated themselves from the rest of the continent and persistently refused to share in any way the burdens or to provide in any way for the wants of the territories, where would be the greatness to which they have achieved?" (30 June, 1862.) And it continues a little later: "The non-occupation of the North West Territory is a blot upon our character for enterprise. We are content to play the drone while others are working. We settle down quietly within the petty limits of a province while a great empire is offered to our ambition." (15 July, 1862.)

---

[19] See articles of 25 February, 1857; 22 March and 4 August, 1858; 30 June, 1859; 4 March, 1860.

[20] See articles of 8, 18, 27 July, 1863.

"A great empire is offered to our ambition." This was the constant clarion-call of the *Globe*. "When the territory belongs to Canada, when its navigable waters are traversed for a few years by vessels, and lines of travel are permanently established, when settlements are formed in favourable localities throughout the territory, it will not be difficult by grants of land to secure the construction of a railway across the plains and through the mountains. . . . If we set about the work of opening the territory at once, we shall win the race. . . . It is an empire we have in view, and its whole export and import trade will be concentrated in the hands of Canadian merchants and manufacturers if we strike for it now." (6 March, 1862.)

In similar strain is an article of 22 January, 1863: "The public mind has been carefully prepared; the time for argument and discussion is almost past; action is now demanded on all hands. . . . If Canada acquires this territory, it will rise in a few years from a position of a small and weak province to be the greatest colony any country has ever possessed, able to take its place amongst the empires of the earth. The wealth of 400,000 square miles of territory will flow through our waters and be gathered by our merchants, manufacturers and agriculturists. Our sons will occupy the chief places of this vast territory, we will form its institutions, supply its rulers, teach its schools, fill its stores, run its mills, navigate its streams. Every article of European manufacture, every pound of tropical produce will pass through our stores. Our seminaries of learning will be filled by its people. Our cities will be the centres of its business and education, its wealth and refinement. It will afford fields of enterprise for our youth. . . . It is a bright prospect and its realization would be worthy of some sacrifice."

What lent additional fervour to the *Globe*'s appeals was the fear that the West would fall into American hands if Canada delayed too long. This danger forms a frequent subject for editorials. The *Globe* watched anxiously every movement, commercial and political, that seemed to bring the Red River closer to St. Paul. "If we allow it to slip from our grasp and to pass into the possession of the United States, if all the rest of the continent outside of Canada and the Atlantic provinces acknowledges the sway of the Republic, we should be unable to contend with her. Our ultimate absorption would be a foregone conclusion." (12 April, 1860.) "Cooped up as Canada is between lake and river, and the frozen north, should all the rest of the continent fall into the possession of the Americans, she would become of the smallest possible importance. . . . So far as England is concerned, it matters, may be, little to her whether the Nor-West continues to fly the British flag or not; but to us it is of vital concern. There is yet time to make up in great measure for that which has been lost. And if we are not the most stupidly supine of any people in existence, we shall prove equal to the occasion." (27 January, 1864.)

One could go on indefinitely illustrating various aspects of the *Globe*'s campaign. It dwelt upon the argument that with the West a part of Canada our adventurous spirits would go there instead of being lost to the United States; and that the Red and Saskatchewan valleys would make us a rival with the Republic for European immigration.[21] It even appealed to the French Canadians to come out of their self-centred introspection on the lower St. Lawrence and renew the achievements of their great ancestors, the fur-traders and explorers of an earlier generation.[22] It pointed out to the manufacturers that a great market beyond Lake Superior would do them more good than anything protection could accomplish for them in the little settlements of Upper and Lower Canada.[23]   And finally when the Quebec conference included absorption of the North-West in its resolutions, the *Globe* rejoiced at victory after a long campaign. Representation by Population and the absorption of the North-West, it again and again repeated, are the two great boons which Confederation brings to the people of Upper Canada. Today when the citizens of the North-West are looking for suitable methods of commemorating Confederation, it would not be a bad idea, if, somewhere in that vast Red and Saskatchewan territory towards which his eyes were ever turned, they erected a statue to George Brown.

3. Confederation

Suspicion of the Grand Trunk and enthusiasm for westward expansion caused the *Globe* down to 1864 generally to pooh-pooh proposals for closer union with the Lower Provinces down by the sea. It regarded union at some day as inevitable, but thought that it

---

[21] See articles of 5 February, 1857; 27 February, 15 July, 1862; 5 February, 1863.
[22] See article of 3 February, 1863.
[23] See article of 5 February, 1863.

must be a slow work of time; and especially it was convinced that most of the closer-union proposals, in so far as they emanated from any Canadian source, were merely a blind to turn attention away from its agitation for the rights of Upper Canada. When finally, on the formation of the Coalition in 1864, Brown went in whole-heartedly for a general Confederation, the *Globe*'s main arguments for it were that it gave Upper Canada what she had been struggling for — control of her own local affairs and a proper influence, based on her population, over general affairs, together with the great future which the empire of the West would bring. The arguments that union with the Maritimes would give Canada new markets in the East and an outlet to the ocean and would make her stronger defensively against the American Goths and Vandals who (according to British and Canadian Imperialists) were gazing with envy on her fair fields — these arguments never impressed the *Globe* very much.[24]

From his entry into public life Brown had been preaching Representation by Population, a sacred cause which the *Globe* always refused to slight by calling it Rep. by Pop. Simple Representation by Population in a legislative union would, of course, have tended to mean the domination of Lower by Upper Canada; though the *Globe* always put its argument in the form of a demand for the emancipation of Upper Canada from Lower Canadian domination. Every year Brown or one of his friends forced a debate and a division in the Assembly on the question; and they gradually made such headway that it became more and more difficult for an Upper Canada member of either party — at least for a member from west of Kingston — to vote against their demand. When in March, 1864, the last patched-up ministry before the great Coalition was got together, the *Globe* boasted that John A. had had to take into his cabinet the only two representatives from west of Kingston left in the assembly who still voted against Representation by Population — Simpson of Niagara and Isaac Buchanan of Hamilton.[25]

But the Brownites were able to make no inroads on the solid Lower Canadian phalanx opposed to their demand. In the 1856

---

[24] See e.g. an article of Dec. 3, 1864. On June 21, 1862, the *Globe* declared: "We in Canada do not see in the Northern army a horde of Goths and Vandals who are likely to be attracted to this Province, as were the hordes of Alaric to the rich plains of Italy."

[25] April 1, 1864.

debate A. A. Dorion, the leader of the Rouges, suggested some
form of federalism as a solution of the difficulties between the two
sections, [26] and so opened a new phase of the question. The suggestion apparently made little impression on the western Grits who
continued to agitate for Representation by Population or dissolution of the Union. But when the Brown-Dorion ministry was
formed in 1858 the two leaders made some sort of an agreement to
work out a *modus vivendi* which would satisfy both Upper and
Lower Canada and which would include guarantees — whether of
a federal nature or otherwise was not specified — for the peculiar
institutions of Lower Canada. What they might have accomplished
in practice they were not given a chance to prove.

In the meantime Galt had come forward with his proposal for a
wider federation to include all the British North American colonies;
and the Cartier-Macdonald Government which followed the two-
day ministry of Brown and Dorion committed itself to Galt's
scheme. The *Globe* refused to take this sudden conversion of the
"corruptionists" seriously. It was a mere trick intended to divert
public attention from the scandal of the Double Shuffle and from
the past iniquities of the Coalition "desperados". On October 8,
writing about the Cartier-Galt-Ross mission to England, the *Globe*
declared: "Doubtless the Canadian delegates will endeavour to
impress upon the English ministers that the only means of relieving
Canada from the political evils under which she suffers is the federation of the provinces. But we fancy that Sir Bulwer Lytton has
already seen and heard enough of Messrs. Galt and Ross to induce
him to receive with caution anything which they may tell him. They
are notoriously connected with the Grand Trunk Company, and
more especially with its contractors, who will be chiefly benefited
by the extension of that work to the Lower Provinces; and he must
be blind indeed if he cannot see that this sudden love of confederation is far more the result of the necessities of the railway than of a
desire to promote the welfare of British America.... The question
of Representation by Population is an awkward one for the Cartier
Government and they seek to engage the Imperial Government in
a rash scheme of federation in order to avoid the difficulty which
they have not the manliness to face. If Sir Bulwer Lytton will inquire he will discover that there is no desire on the part of the

---

[26] Reported in the *Globe* of April 25.

people of Canada for immediate union with the Lower Provinces. He will discover that there is no communication at present between the various sections sufficient to justify a political union; and let him beware how he endeavours to hasten an event which can only be accomplished by the cordial co-operation of all parties interested. We have every confidence that some time or other the whole of the British North American Provinces will be united in one gigantic confederation; but no one can believe that the moment has arrived for the fulfilment of that scheme. And if the Colonial minister, to help the condemned administration of Mr. Cartier, endeavours to force such a thing upon the Canadian people, the whole effect will be to delay its accomplishment for an indefinite period. . . . The eyes of the Canadian people should be turned not to the East but to the West. The commercial advantages to be derived from a union with the Lower Provinces are hardly appreciable, while in the boundless West there lies open to us a field of enterprise which might cause wealth to flow into every city and village of our land. . . . If the Imperial Government is willing to grant assistance for the development of British power in North America, let her grant it in aid of the Pacific Railway . . . or the founding of a great colony on Lake Winnipeg and the Saskatchewan. . . . That will be a work ten times more beneficial to all these provinces than a railway through the wilderness which divides Canada from New Brunswick. . . . If we must go begging for Imperial assistance, let us ask it for the opening of this magnificent country. . . . This is an enterprise worthy of a statesman's thought; but instead of attending to it our ministers have thrown every obstacle in the way of its accomplishment. They have pandered to the monopoly which has been and is still a barrier in its path. They have done nothing to urge on the Imperial Government the necessity of action, and now they are bending their whole thoughts to the construction of a work which will benefit Messrs. Peto, Brassey and Betts, but nobody else."

Again on 30 October, 1858: "The shape in which the project of a Federal Union has been taken up by Sir Edmund Head's advisers does not permit of misinterpretation. The most superficial of observers cannot be tempted to accord them credit for broad, statesmanlike views in connection with the subject. But the other day all of them, save Mr. Galt, pooh-poohed it as for the present an impracticability. . . . Even Mr. Galt had so little faith in his own proposition that he allowed it to fall to the ground after the faintest possible imitation of a fight. It was evident that his action in the matter was not the offspring of strong earnest conviction, but was merely undertaken with the view of bettering his political position.[27] . . . It is impossible to doubt that even now these men regard a Federal Union as aught else than a scape-goat. An Intercolonial railway is the primary object to be obtained. . . . Messrs. Ross and Galt have studied in the school of the Grand Trunk Company, and they approach the Intercolonial with the keenness and cunning of practised spoilsmen. . . . So the three ministers have gone to England brimful of speculative loyalty and business-like patriotism."

To this attitude the *Globe* remained firm practically until the Coalition of 1864. Again and again in the two or three years after the Cartier-Galt-Ross Mission it pointed out that the ministry had made no further effort to develop or explain its federal scheme, a fact which was proof enough that it was not sincere in taking the scheme up in the first place.[28] Nor had the proposition been welcomed by the mother country or by the other colonies; the Maritime people were afraid to trust themselves to politicians who had the reputation of the railway speculators of Canada. "They decline the offer of our hand when they see the dowry we shall bring them."[29]

In the meantime the Upper Canada Reformers had made an advance in their own political thinking. After the passion aroused by the events of the summer of 1858 had cooled down, the *Globe* began in 1859 to publish a series of very able editorials on the political situation which are remarkable in its pages for their cool philosophical tone.[30] In its analysis it discovered two main evils: (1) the complete failure of the Union to produce an amalgamation of the two races, and the intense bitterness of feeling which had grown up in consequence; (2) the excessive influence of the executive over the legislature which freed unscrupulous ministers with money to spend on railways and public works from all the checks supposed to be provided by Responsible Government. Neither of these evils could

---

[27] The reference is to Galt's motion for a general federation of British North America which was discussed in July, 1858, before the crisis at the end of the month developed.

[28] See e.g. articles of Feb. 7 and 11, Sept. 21, Nov. 30, 1859; April 19, 1860.

[29] Dec. 7, 1860.

[30] See articles of May 10, 11, 12, 13, 14, 18, 23. The discussion continues through the summer in the pages of the *Globe* and there are many quotations from the Reform press of the province.

be cured by Representation by Population alone; and so the *Globe* began to suggest that a federal system be applied to the two Canadas with a written constitution containing definite checks on the power of the executive over the people's taxes. As the year went on it warmed to the subject; and in the autumn, in November, a great Reform Convention was held in Toronto with nearly 600 delegates present from all parts of Upper Canada — though, according to Sandfield Macdonald, only 19 of these came from east of Kingston, and Sandfield himself did not attend.[31] The Convention lasted for three days, and after long discussion and considerable opposition, Brown succeeded in inducing them to accept the proposals which the *Globe* had been advocating since the previous May. The resolutions adopted decided against a general federation of all the provinces as not practicable for the present, against simple dissolution of the Union, and for "the formation of two or more local governments, to which shall be committed the control of all matters of a local or sectional character, and some joint authority charged with such matters as are necessarily common to both sections of the Province", with the addition that representation in the new federal system should be based on population.[32]

It is worth noting that in pleading against the alternative of dissolution of the Union which found much support amongst some of the Grits from the Peninsula, Brown stressed the national argument. "I do place the question on the ground of nationality. I do hope that there is not one Canadian in this assembly who does not look forward with high hope to the day when these northern colonies shall stand out among the nations of the world as one great confederation. What true Canadian can witness the tide of immigration now commencing to flow into the vast territories of the North-West without longing to have a share in the first settlement of that great fertile country? Who does not feel that to us rightfully belong the right and duty of carrying the blessings of civilization throughout those boundless regions, and of making our country the highway of traffic to the Pacific? And how can there be the slightest question with one who longs for such nationality between complete dissolution and the scheme of the Committee?" (*i.e.* the

---

[31] See his speech in the Assembly reported in the *Globe* of June 1, 1861.

[32] Reports of the proceedings of the Convention run in the *Globe* from Nov. 10 to Nov. 16.

federal scheme of the resolutions, which would make it easy for the West to be taken in as a partner in the federation).[33]

Federalism, however, proved no more acceptable to Lower Canada than Representation by Population had been, and the French leaders continued to impose an absolute veto on any change whatsoever. One result of this was that many of the Reformers drifted back into advocating simple Representation by Population instead of the 1859 federal scheme. And in 1862 when a chance came at last to escape from their long wandering in the wilderness of opposition, most of them were persuaded fairly easily by Sandfield Macdonald to drop for the moment both Rep. by Pop. and the 1859 platform in order to form a coalition with a group of the French led by Sicotte. The *Globe* was never more brilliant and devastating than in the editorials in which it tore Sandfield's Double Majority ideas to pieces; but it supported the new government generally because of its platform of economy and because two of its leading members, McDougall and Howland, were known to be enthusiasts for action about the North-West.

By this time Mr. Watkin's diplomacy had so successfully revived the Intercolonial project that in September, 1862, a conference of the three governments concerned was held at Quebec followed by the sending of delegates to London to treat with the Colonial Office.

The *Globe* viewed all these transactions with open hostility and poured heavy sarcasm on the negotiators. "The Halifax and Quebec railway is a large work . . . and it is rather a reputable thing to be connected with it, even while it is in the distant future. No one has any objections to say a word for it and it is quite a pleasant thing to be appointed to go to England to look after its affairs. A visit to the Colonial Office, a dinner at the Secretary's, perhaps a card to Lady Palmerston's Ball, possibly a presentation at Court for Mrs. Bluenose and the Misses Bluenose. . . . Therefore it is that in spite of frequent snubbings there is still another deputation about to visit England. The Grand Trunk and Mr. Watkin have fanned the flame which is always kept burning on the railway altars in Halifax and St. John, and the conflagration has spread through three provinces. That is to say, deputations are found to travel for the scheme and newspapers to write about it. As to the public, they do not care a button about it, either in Nova Scotia, New Bruns-

---

[33] The speech is reported on Nov. 16.

wick, or Canada. . . . We in Upper Canada look westward for communications, not eastward; we have plenty of avenues to the ocean; we have none to the ocean-like prairies of the North-West. . . . The only Canadians who care a straw for the road are the few hermits in the wilderness which lies between Trois Pistoles and the New Brunswick line and the members of the Cabinet who desire to keep Mr. Watkin, the Grand Trunk agent, amused and occupied during his sojourn in this country, and hope that if the home authorities should be fools enough to grant money to the road, the Grand Trunk and themselves will make something in the scramble for the spoils which will follow." (1 October, 1861; this was written before the Macdonald-Sicotte ministry came into office.)

When the Canadian delegates, Howland and Sicotte, by very tortuous methods, succeeded in bringing all negotiations to an end, the *Globe* exulted: "All's well that ends well. The country may congratulate itself on its escape from a railway job of even worse character than the Grand Trunk." (19 January, 1863.) "The affair will be adjourned *sine die*. . . . With the Intercolonial Railway is linked the great question of the federation of all the British North American Provinces, and that question is not yet in a position for settlement. Looking at the matter from an Upper Canadian point of view, the advantages of delay can hardly be overestimated. If our government were to rush into the railway project . . . both the alliance and the road would be carried out for the benefit of the dominant power in this Province at this moment; we need hardly say we mean Lower Canada. The important question to Upper Canada — her connection with the North-West territory — would be altogether ignored, Quebec would be made the capital of the Federation, Representation by Population would form no part of the compact, and instead of having one leech draining her resources, Upper Canada would have three. Before entering into new alliances it should be the effort of Upper Canadians to regulate the affairs of their own province, to obtain Representation by Population, to open the North-West territory so that when the federation of all the British North American Provinces does come it may be formed with Upper Canada as the central figure of the group of states, with western adjuncts as well as eastern." (6 January, 1863.)

It is unnecessary to enter into the troublous politics of 1863 and the first half of 1864, when ministries clung to office by two or three votes and all sorts of combinations of public men were discussed officially and unofficially in the effort to devise a stable govern-

ment. The *Globe* was able to survey these events with a certain un-
wonted detachment since Brown himself was not a member or a
candidate for membership in any of the actual or paper cabinets
which were set up. Brown had been defeated in the election of 1861
and retired temporarily from politics, going on a visit to Scotland
where he was married. After his return to Canada he re-entered
the legislature as a member for South Oxford, and from this time
his speeches and many of the articles in the *Globe* take on a new
note of moderation. The theme of pleading with both parties to
drop partisan quarrels and face the difficulties between Upper and
Lower Canada becomes increasingly frequent. One can see from
the *Globe* of 1863 that Brown's willingness in June, 1864, to bury
the hatchet was no sudden impulsive resolve. Whatever the reasons
for this new moderation, there is no doubt that it begins to be in
evidence after his return with his bride in December, 1862. Perhaps
the real father of Confederation was Mrs. George Brown.[34]

From the formation of the Coalition in June, 1864, the *Globe* is,
of course, full of the subject of Confederation, and it would be impossible here to refer to all the points it raises in its discussions.
What it is most insistent on, however, is that the scheme worked
out at Charlottetown and Quebec embodies the full achievement of
all that the Reformers of Upper Canada had been seeking for the
last fifteen years.

A long article on July 6, 1864, comparing the scheme of 1864
with the platform of 1859, concludes: "The most casual reader can
scarcely fail to perceive that the policy of the Administration is substantially that enunciated in the last two of the above quoted resolutions (of 1859). The remedy for existing constitutional evils is,
according to the ministerial program, to be sought in the federative
principle. So it was sought in 1859. Then, as now, it was deemed
advisable to give local matters to local control, while reserving for

---

[34] The Quebec correspondent of the Montreal *Gazette* on June 25, 1864,
remarks: "Remember that since his return to parliamentary life Mr. Brown
has repeatedly professed a belief in the need for greater moderation." Brown
moved in August, 1863, for a Committee to consider the constitutional
difficulties between Upper and Lower Canada, but withdrew his motion
later in the session owing to the unsettled state of parties. He renewed the
motion in the 1864 session and got his Committee, which reported in favour
of some kind of federalism on the very day that the Taché-Macdonald
ministry was defeated.

general authority matters necessarily common to both sections of the Province. In the same way, both in 1859 and 1864, the same declaration is made, that under the new system representation according to numbers must be conceded. . . . But, says an objector, the convention of 1859 declared that the formation of the larger federation was too remote a contingency to serve as an immediate remedy for the grave difficulties for which that body was seeking a remedy. The best evidence that that was a sound of opinion lies in the fact that no progress since has been made towards the realization of such a federation."

And again on October 13, 1864:

"The public will pay small attention to arguments against us based upon what we said years ago in reference to the question of confederation, when presented as a thing of the future rather than as a scheme immediately practicable, and as a means of defeating our principles rather than causing them to prevail. We never assumed the position of extreme opponents of the confederation of all the provinces. On the contrary we have always believed that the union would some day be realized. But we did refuse to be diverted from the advocacy of parliamentary reform and the opening of the North-West by proposals that we should, at some future time, get confederation; and the more clear did we feel that it was our duty not to join in the premature advocacy of the measure, for the reason that the offer of it was never coupled with any promise or hope that we should get along with it that justice to Upper Canada which we were advocating.

"The scheme which we declined to advocate was — the intercolonial railway first; the confederation next, but at some indefinite time; and justice to Upper Canada last of all, or more likely, not at all. The policy which we are now supporting reverses all this. We are getting, as first and most important, justice to Upper Canada; next, confederation; and last, if at all, the railway."

Finally when at last the British America Act was passed, what was to be the political attitude of the Upper Canada Reformers in the Dominion? Was there not some plausibility in John A. Macdonald's plea that the slate of the past should be wiped clean and that Canada and Ontario should start on their new career with non-partisan, or rather bi-partisan governments? The *Globe* would have none of it. The no-party cry was simply a device to get the old Macdonald-Cartier-Galt gang back in power again. "The intelligent yeomanry of Upper Canada who can look back on the political events of the last twenty years need no instruction as to the meaning of the no-party cry. . . . Can the men fancy that the Reformers of Upper Canada do not comprehend that the main boon secured by the accomplishment of Confederation is the power to bring to an end the outrageous misgovernment of the last dozen years?"[35] And in the midst of the election campaign on August 10, it came out with a characteristic editorial on Galt's banking scheme, headed "The Danger of the Hour", which is a good summing-up of the whole radical position. "With the Grand Trunk and the Bank of Montreal at his back, there is no saying how far the reckless financier of the present government may carry his schemes. These institutions are the enemies of the people and of popular rights. They have special interests to advance in Parliament. . . . It is time that Upper Canadians were united together in resisting these monopolies, and the Government which has created and supported them. It is time that we had a government above being the servant of railway or banking institutions. It is time that we had a government which would consider the interest of the whole people and not of a few wily money-makers who can bring influence to bear upon Parliament. It is above all a necessity that the people of the West should elect men who will be able to prevent the mischief which Mr. Galt is still anxious to do to the interests of the western country."

And so the *Globe* plunged once more into the fray. Alas for its high hopes of reaping the fruits of victory with at least sixty good Reformers in Parliament from Upper Canada! The "corruptionists" came back to power again, and from 1867 till very recent years radicalism has been at a discount in Canada. Confederation did not bring Upper Canada into the Grit land of promise. It was again and again necessary to fight for provincial rights. Railway and other special interests were as rampant as before. The North-West was an unconscionably long time in developing. And in the

---

[35] April 23, 1867. A similar article of Feb. 11 runs: "We are about to reap the fruits of a long protracted struggle . . . . Constitutional changes are but the means to an end; they are but provisions to secure better government and more equitable legislation. Having triumphed in the struggle for constitutional reform, the Liberal party are of all men the most fitted to be trusted with the practical working out of the great reform they have spent so many years in accomplishing. It were worse than folly to commit that duty to those who were so long the bitter enemies of reform."

meantime Ontario itself changed slowly from the pioneer agricultural settlement which had produced the radical Grits of the 1850s and 1860s into the industrialized community of today with its fat and prosperous capital. No good Torontonian of the present generation could possibly read Brown's *Globe* without shuddering. But out in the territory of the Red and Saskatchewan the Clear Grit movement has come to life again in a fresh incarnation; and the farmers of the prairies are unconsciously reviving many of the ideas for which the farmers of what was then western Canada strove two generations ago. With that Upper Canada which read the *Globe* and voted Grit we of the modern West have a natural affinity. It is our spiritual home.

4. Political Ideas
of the Upper Canada Reformers
1867-78

(This paper was read at the annual conference of the Canadian Historical Association, 1942, and published in its Report of that year.)

"But in this country . . . what is there for Conservatives to conserve or for Reformers to reform?" The question came from the By-stander, Professor Goldwin Smith, newly arrived in Toronto and writing his current comment in the newly established monthly journal, the *Canadian Monthly and National Review*, in its issue of April, 1872. "What is there," he went on, "to preserve our parties from gradually becoming mere factions, and our country from becoming the unhappy scene of a perpetual struggle of factions for place? . . . For party without party principles inevitably becomes faction; and faction as inevitably supports itself by intrigue, demagogism and corruption."

Regularly in every issue the *Canadian Monthly* kept up this theme of the evils of party in a country where parties were based upon no distinctive principles. In 1874 it was joined by the weekly journal, the *Nation*, the organ of the Canada First movement. Both these journals of the intellectuals pointed out, with a constant succession of fresh examples from the news of the day to illustrate their point, that Canadian governments kept their followers together and themselves in office by a continuous system of bribes to sectional, class, racial, and religious interests, and that this was all that party policy ever meant in practice. Both of them were especially severe upon the Reform leadership of George Brown and the *Globe*. They denounced Brown for trying to maintain a brutal dictatorship over men and opinions in Toronto and Ontario. "Reputations," said the *Nation* of the *Globe*, "oscillated nervously between its black letter and its small pica."[1] Goldwin Smith, unwearied in his efforts

---

[1] The *Nation*, June 4, 1874.

to emancipate Ontario from a false and degrading partyism, as he saw it, put money successively into new papers — the *Mail*, the *Liberal*, and finally the *Telegram* — in order to break the domination of the *Globe*. His experiments did not work out very satisfactorily from either the intellectual or the financial point of view. "The *Mail*," he remarked, "has saved us from a dictatorship, though much as we might be saved from typhus by having the small-pox."[2]

These criticisms of the nature of Canadian party which appeared in the columns of the *Canadian Monthly* and the *Nation* were no doubt caviar to the general, and in the long run they were almost completely ineffective in modifying the course of Canadian party politics. The *Globe* and the *Mail* and their cohorts of local papers across the province were steadily bringing it about that every little Upper Canadian boy and girl should be born into this world alive as either a little Liberal or else a little Conservative. And no Reformer would have admitted for a moment that the struggle between his party and John A. Macdonald's "corruptionists" was merely one of outs versus ins.

Reformers recalled that it was only through party that Responsible Government had been established in Canada; and they believed that the Reform party was still a party with a mission. George Brown was fond of comparing his function as publisher of the *Globe* and leader of the Grits in the House with that of Cobden and Bright in England, the radicals who brought new ideas into English politics and gave expression to the aspirations of new classes. It was the Cobdens and the Brights who were the creative influences in politics, he said, as distinguished from the mere humdrum administrators or time-servers who occupied the front benches in Parliament.[3] Edward Blake, the rising hope of the Reform party, had this same sense of a mission in politics. He told his audience in his Aurora speech that he preferred to be a private in the advanced guard of the army of freedom; and he concluded that famous "disturbing" address by quoting Tennyson's ode about freedom slowly broadening down from precedent to precedent, and declaring that the political heresy of today, with which his speech

---

[2] *Canadian Monthly*, Nov., 1874, 459.
[3] See, e.g. editorials on Nov. 28, 1873, and Dec. 29, 1874.

was somewhat crowded, might become the political creed of tomorrow.[4]

What then were the ideas and principles which Upper Canadian Reformers regarded as their distinct contribution to the politics of the new Dominion? I propose to discuss first their attitude on purely political and constitutional issues, and then to go on to their conception of Canadian nationalism in its various aspects. The two parts of my paper may be entitled *Parliamentary Government* and *The New Nationality*.

1. Parliamentary Government

First of all we may list a group of reforms which all tended to make more effective the machinery of government by public opinion. Representation by population was achieved in the B.N.A. Act, and this Reformers claimed, rightly enough, as a great Reform victory. They were alert to attack Macdonald's breaches of the principle when he gave the new western provinces of Manitoba and British Columbia more seats than their population warranted; and they indignantly pounced upon him when he made use of these pocket-borough seats for his own party purposes.[5]

In order to make the electoral system fair and honest, Reformers also fought for the introduction of the ballot, for the system of having all elections in a general election take place on the same day, and above all, for the trial of controverted elections by judges instead of by packed election committees in the House of Commons. In all these campaigns they were triumphant by 1874 against Macdonald's opposition. They insisted also on the franchise being fixed by each province for itself because the provincial legislators were the best judges of who were fitted to vote in their own provin-

---

[4] *"A National Sentiment!" Speech of Hon. Edward Blake, M.P., at Aurora, with the comments of some of the Canadian press thereon* (Ottawa, E. A. Perry, Elgin Street, 1874).

[5] "Those six British Columbia constituencies — those six wretched outrages on justice and decency — created in 1871 by Sir John Macdonald for precisely such work as the present," exclaimed the *Globe* (Sept. 2, 1872) on the news that Sir Francis Hincks, defeated in eastern Canada, had been provided, through the intervention of the Lieutenant-Governor, with a seat in British Columbia.

cial community. In Ontario they added an income franchise to the already low property franchise, and gave the vote to farmers' sons who lived at home and couldn't qualify otherwise with either income or property. That is, they established a system pretty close to manhood suffrage. Some Reformers were prepared to go still further. Edward Blake in his Aurora speech proposed compulsory voting and minority representation based on the Hare system as two reforms which he thought the party should take up. David Mills crusaded against the appointed Senate and in 1875 persuaded the House of Commons to agree with him, though his party, then in office, did nothing about the matter. And George E. Casey was beginning his long campaign for Civil Service reform.

The two supreme constitutional issues, however, on which Reformers saw themselves as fighting to the death against John A. Macdonald and his system were those of the strict interpretation of the new federal constitution and the securing of the independence of the legislature from undue executive influence.

To the Grits Confederation, from the constitutional point of view, meant primarily two things — representation by population; and provincial autonomy, with a clear-cut separation of provincial from federal affairs. After 1867 they were constantly in arms against any interference by Ottawa with matters of local Ontario concern, and against all policies which tended to blur the distinction between general federal affairs and local provincial affairs. Their main indictment of John Sandfield Macdonald was that he permitted himself and his government in Toronto to become mere adjuncts of the Ottawa government. They instituted at once an assault upon the system of dual representation by which the same individual could sit in both provincial legislature and Dominion Parliament, and they succeeded in abolishing it. John A. Macdonald's interference with Ontario legislation through the disallowance power was watched with a hostile eye.

"There is as yet no satisfactory way of disposing of cases of dispute as to the authority of Federal and local legislatures," said the *Globe* on December 24, 1868. "It is not desirable to have such questions settled by the Minister of Justice. He is by no means a safe depository of so much power." "There is need for a court to deal with unconstitutional or illegal legislation ...," it said on November 11, 1869. "If Confederation is to be a success the present arrangements must be changed."

But the Reformers were politicians looking for votes as well as constitutional purists. Their "hands off" attitude towards federal interference in Ontario affairs did not deter the provincial government from interfering in Dominion affairs. Blake persuaded the Ontario legislature to pass a resolution calling for justice upon the murderers of Scott at the Red River, and his government offered a reward for their apprehension. While they denounced John A. in Ottawa for intervening to assist John Sandfield's government to get elected in 1867 and 1871, still when the Dominion elections came on in 1872 Oliver Mowat felt no constitutional scruples in adjourning the Ontario legislature in order that its Reform majority might go out and campaign for Mackenzie and Blake. "The true lover of his province," remarked the *Globe* with some unction (January 19, 1874), "must love the whole Dominion on the principle that true patriotism begins with home and kindred, and radiates from thence in ever widening circles till the whole nation is embraced."

The fact was that the Reform constitutional philosophy, with its demand for a clear-cut separation of Dominion from provincial affairs, neglected the most important element in the situation, the party system. Federal Reformers and provincial Reformers depended upon one another for strength and success; they had a common interest in weakening John A. and his supporters in the federal or in the provincial field as the case might be. The party system made mutual interference by province and Dominion with one another's affairs inevitable.

A major issue in this controversy over Dominion-provincial relations during this first decade was raised by the question of "better terms" to Nova Scotia. The Reformers as strict constructionists opposed Macdonald's procedure in granting relief to Nova Scotia.[6]

---

[6] The *Globe*, in an editorial of June 15, 1869, entitled "The Constitution in Danger", declared: "The doctrine [of the government] proclaims a new era of jobbery and log-rolling. . . . The effect of the vote is to destroy the federal character of the Union. . . . The question in debate was not even whether or not these new advantages should be conferred on Nova Scotia; but it was whether so grave a reversal of the fundamental conditions of the Union Act could be effected by an Act of the Dominion Parliament, or must emanate from the Imperial Parliament. . . . Throughout the whole debate not one reason was advanced why this latter course should not have been followed. . . . The Ministers had deliberately resolved to break down the constitution . . . and were chuckling in anticipation of keeping themselves in office by buying up Constituencies and their Representatives. . . . An impudent attempt to bring back all the evils and discordancies of a Legislative Union."

Blake, defeated at Ottawa, carried his efforts so far as to get the Ontario legislature to pass a resolution for an Address to the Crown requesting an amendment to the B.N.A. Act which would make clear that the Parliament of Canada should have no power in future to disturb the established financial relations as between the Dominion and the several provinces.

"Better terms" was only one instance of what Reformers found to be a chief vice of Macdonald's system of government, his practice of spending federal revenue for purely local purposes in order to keep the members from Quebec and the outlying provinces lined up on the right of Mr. Speaker. And all this improper expenditure might be prevented, as the *Globe* was constantly pointing out, if the Ontario delegation at Ottawa would only stand firm. It was chiefly with Ontario's taxes that Macdonald was bribing the other provinces, and Ontario had almost half the seats at Ottawa. But inevitably to these other provinces this reiterated appeal of the Grit organ for Ontario solidarity appeared only as an acute case of selfish Ontario sectionalism. Alas, it has not been only in the 1870s that the citizens of the different provinces of Canada have found that the most congenial method of contributing to a national spirit is to denounce the sectionalism of their neighbours.

The second great constitutional issue was the independence of the legislature, a good Whig cause which Reformers in Canada had long made their own. Ever since the 1850s the Grits in opposition had felt that the British Cabinet system, as applied to a government busy with the construction of railways and public works, gave too much power to the executive. At the Quebec Conference in 1864 George Brown proposed a constitution of checks and balances for Ontario based on that of an American state.[7] In the end Ontario and the other provinces got miniature responsible governments. But Reformers still remained suspicious of undue power and influence in the hands of the executive. Blake introduced a series of bills both at Toronto and at Ottawa for the independence of Parliament. The issue on which he finally defeated Sandfield Macdonald in 1871 was Macdonald's policy of taking power to his government to distribute a lump sum for the assistance of local railways without allowing the legislature to pass on the details of how much was to be allocated to each railway.

---

[7] Joseph Pope, *Confederation, being a Series of Hitherto Unpublished Documents Bearing on the British North America Act* (Toronto, 1895), 74.

But it was at Ottawa, of course, that the great crisis in the relations of executive and legislature developed, in connection with the Pacific railway enterprise. The Macdonald government in 1872 took blanket powers to choose between two rival companies seeking the charter, to create a new company if necessary and make a contract with it, to fix the terms on which cash and land subsidies should be transferred to the company, and all this to be done without further consultation of Parliament. In vain did the Reform opposition draw attention to the abuses that might take place when the executive was granted such unchecked discretionary powers. In vain did they point to past scandals in the relations of Macdonald & Co. with the Grand Trunk and the Intercolonial. In vain did they move that no directors or shareholders in the new Pacific Railway Company should be allowed to hold seats in either House of Parliament. The issue, as the *Globe* put it, between them and Macdonald was that between "government by Orders in Council and government by the representatives of the people".[8]

"The present is not merely a selfish struggle between ins and outs. It is the old constitutional question of the people's right through its representatives to control the national legislation and the national expenditure; to prevent Orders in Council and Star Chamber decrees taking the place of Acts of Parliament."[9]

"Railways," said David Mills in the *Canadian Monthly* (November, 1872), "create new political and social forces, which may affect injuriously Parliamentary Government. . . . It may be that it will yet be found necessary for reasons political as well as commercial to make all such works the property of the State. Great railway corporations are the most dangerous enemies popular government has ever had. . . . They have marched their *employés* to the polls as an ancient baron did his vassals to the battlefield. . . . They endanger if they do not destroy the independence of Parliament."

Reform indignation boiled over when the rumours about a corrupt bargain between the government and Sir Hugh Allan were confirmed by the revelations of 1873. The material details of the Pacific Scandal need not concern us here. What is important to note is the constitutional stand taken by Reformers on the way in which the investigation into the whole business should be carried

---

[8] *Globe,* May 21, 1874.
[9] *Ibid.,* Aug. 3, 1872.

on. Macdonald's delaying manoeuvres succeeded in preventing investigation by the Committee set up by the House of Commons, and in August he used the Governor-General's prerogative to transfer the whole case from Parliament to a Royal Commission of nonentities appointed by himself. Blake and Dorion, the Reform members of the Parliamentary Committee, refused to serve on the Commission. Huntingdon and the Opposition witnesses refused to appear before it. On the unconstitutionality of Macdonald's actions and on the critical nature of the issues raised by it the *Globe*, Goldwin Smith, Blake, and the Reform orators, were all agreed. Blake talked of Sir John Eliot and his struggle against the despotism of Charles I; he quoted the Bill of Rights. "There is no parallel in English history," he declared, "for the audacity of the ministers in breaking up the trial and on the same day creating a tribunal to suit themselves for their own prosecution.... It is a high contempt of Parliament.... The privileges of Parliament are the privileges of the People, and the rights of Parliament are the rights of the People."[10]

2. The New Nationality

One of the things which most impresses a reader of the newspapers and periodicals and pamphlets as well as of the debates in Parliament during the first decade of Confederation is the immense volume of discussion that took place on the implications, practical and theoretical, of the new Canadian nationality. The respective parts to be played by French and English in the building up of the new nation; the problems of extending the nation-state from ocean to ocean; the three great nation-building policies of Pacific Railway, immigration and settlement, and tariff; the character of Canadian civilization as distinguished from British and from American; the future of Canada's relations with Great Britain and the United States, whether the Dominion was to achieve a higher position in the Empire through Imperial Federation or some form of alliance, or whether it was to become a separate independent state, or

---

[10] *Three Speeches by the Hon. Edward Blake, Q.C., M.P., on the Pacific Scandal* (Toronto, 1873), Number Two, Speech at London, August 28, 1873.

whether separation from Britain meant inevitable annexation to the United States; all these questions were debated vehemently and endlessly. Canadians have indeed been arguing about them through most of their subsequent history; but one has the impression that they never argued so well as in that first decade, and that nothing new on any of these topics has ever been said since.

The *Globe* was always proud of the fact that from the early 1850s it had been the leader in the campaign for the westward expansion of Canada. It never ceased to preach that the future of Canada depended upon its success in genuinely incorporating the West into the Dominion and developing its resources. It always had more news from the West than from the Maritimes, and generally even more than from Quebec, for it regarded the West as Ontario's proper sphere of influence. It watched with suspicion every step taken by the Macdonald government in its North-West policy. It criticized the first proposed form of government by an appointed council as the setting up of another Family Compact system on the Red River.[11] It was on the alert for every bit of evidence that French Catholic influences were trying to construct another little Quebec in Manitoba. At one moment it referred to them as Mrs. Partingtons trying to sweep back the tide of English immigration.[12] "We hope to see a new Upper Canada in the North-West Territory — in its well-regulated society and government, in its education, morality and religion."[13] At another moment it was proclaiming Manitoba as the Kansas of Canada and hoping that the struggle starting there would not be long and sanguinary as it had been in the United States.[14]

From first to last the *Globe* emphasized the vital importance for the future of the Dominion of railway connection on Canadian soil between East and West. "With the construction of the railway the country will be populated by Englishmen; without it by Americans."[15] But at the same time it denounced Macdonald's extravagant bargain with British Columbia. The promise to build a transcontinental railway within ten years over territory that had never been surveyed, with an eastern terminus in a community of only

---

[11] *Globe*, Aug. 31, 1869.
[12] *Ibid.*, Nov. 17, 1869.
[13] *Ibid.*, June 2, 1869.
[14] *Ibid.*, May 3, 1870.
[15] *Ibid.*, March 23, 1870.

four million population, and a western terminus in a community with practically no population at all, and with hardly any population in between to provide local traffic, seemed to Reformers an insane policy. And the revelations of the Pacific Scandal convinced them that Macdonald had been more intent on a conspiracy to entrench himself in office than on a business-like enterprise of nation-building.

When Mackenzie took over the wreckage of the Pacific scheme the *Globe* supported him steadily in his policy of advancing gradually, always insisting that the essential step was to establish communication over Canadian soil with the Red River and that the rest, rail communication with British Columbia, could come later as circumstances would permit. A group of Reformers, of whom Blake was the chief, became even more cautious than this. The financial difficulties caused by the depression after 1873 alarmed them as to the future financial stability of the country if the Pacific enterprise should be persisted in. "If under all the circumstances," said Blake at Aurora in 1874, "the Columbians were to say: 'You must go on and finish this railway according to the terms, or take the alternative of releasing us from the Confederation,' I would — take the alternative!" Blake had also earlier expressed willingness to release Nova Scotia if she remained obdurate in her opposition to Confederation. In the end it was not the opposition of the Blake group but the depression which prevented the Mackenzie government from getting very far forward with the Pacific enterprise. But their failure left an impression that Reformers were not quite so keen as they ought to be on the project of a Dominion from sea to sea.

The tariff issue did not, of course, come into Canadian politics with Confederation. But almost immediately after Confederation, from 1870 on, the magic phrase "A National Policy" began to appear in tariff discussions. The *Globe* always emphasized that pure free trade was not an issue in Canada, since some kind of revenue tariff was a necessary feature of the Canadian fiscal system. In its view the real issue was whether Canada was to grow and attract settlers by making herself a cheap country to live in as contrasted with the United States, and by devoting herself to the agricultural, lumbering, fishing, and mining industries which were natural to her. When the extra duties of 1870 on certain commodities were taken off in 1871, the *Globe* repeated with approval

David Mills' epitaph: "Died, aged 11 months, the National Policy!"[16]

Brown's attitude on tariff questions came out most completely in the discussion of his own Draft Reciprocity Treaty of 1874 with the United States. The Brown treaty, in fact, while it never came into force, caused or coincided with a crystallization of Canadian opinion about the tariff. Before 1874 nearly everybody in a vague general way had been in favour of Reciprocity. But Brown's negotiations showed that no new treaty would be considered by the Americans unless it included a wide range of manufactured goods in addition to natural products; and the announcement of the schedules in his proposed treaty brought the organized manufacturers into the field against it. Significantly enough they were supported by the *Canadian Monthly* and the *Nation*.

The *Globe* pointed out (July 23, 1874) that Canada's agricultural industry surpassed in importance all other economic interests put together, and that next to it came lumbering, fishing, shipping, and mining, and that none of these objected to the treaty. "All these great branches of industry will be benefited by having a market of forty million thrown open to them. . . . The alarm has come entirely from the manufacturers, and these are more frightened than hurt. . . . Will it [the treaty] give a new impetus to our national industry? Will it increase our foreign commerce? . . . Will it set at rest all troublesome questions with our great neighbours for a quarter of a century and give peace in our time? We have not the shadow of a doubt that it will do all this." "The manufacturing interest may not be small hereafter," replied the *Canadian Monthly* (September, 1874). ". . . we are in a state of development and we must guard and cherish the acorn for the sake of the future oak." But this conception of a "national tariff" as a dynamic instrument for national development seemed to most Reformers only a camouflage for the most selfish kind of protection of special interests. In 1876 the Mackenzie government almost took the plunge of raising the tariff in order to balance their budget, but having drawn back then, they tended thereafter to become more and more dogmatic in their free-trade utterances. It was Macdonald and the Conservatives who capitalized on the national idea in the tariff.

Industrialization raised some other problems in the new nation besides that of the tariff, problems to which the *Globe*'s response is

---

[16] *Ibid.*, April 15, 1871.

interesting. As Upper Canada passed out of the pioneer stage, differentiations in economic functions became more obvious, and class divisions began to emerge. In the 1870s Ontario farmers began to form Granges to look after their social and economic interests, in imitation of their neighbours in the mid-western states. The *Globe* was not too sure about the Granger movement.

"The denunciation of middlemen may have some reason in the Western States . . . but we are not aware that the same thing can be said of Canada. . . . Let the Grangers point out the 'tyrant monopolies' against which they propose to make war and we shall help them with all our hearts and all our energy."[17]

"The farmers of Ontario have, so far as we are aware, no special grievances. So large a portion of the real government of the country is controlled by municipal organization that the people may be said to have it almost literally in their own keeping." Still, it concluded that the movement might have good effects socially in making farm life more attractive, and it bestowed a qualified blessing on it.[18]

Quite otherwise was it with the movement amongst the industrial workers in the towns. Trade Unionism raised the *Globe*'s suspicions from the start. *Globe* editors were well grounded in all the arguments of the orthodox economics proving that unions couldn't in the long run raise real wages which were determined by the impersonal operation of the laws of demand and supply.

In the spring of 1872 Brown had to deal with this problem in a practical way, in a famous dispute with his own printers which caused much unholy glee amongst his enemies and made both political parties for the next few years anxious to pose as the friend of the working man. The trouble came as part of a nine-hour movement which was sweeping over the industrial workers in eastern Canada and of which the chief leader was a man named Trevellick, an English trade-unionist. "It is," said the *Globe*, announcing the printers' strike, "in obedience to foreign agitation carried on by paid agents who have nothing to lose as the result of their mischievous counsels that the printers of this city have succumbed."[19]

---

[17] *Ibid.*, June 8, 1874.
[18] *Ibid.*, Sept. 25, 1874.
[19] *Ibid.*, March 26, 1872.

It can hardly be said that in this country there is such a thing as a capitalist class, much less, like that of England, a capitalist class socially separated from the working man, closely united with a territorial aristocracy, and in conjunction with that aristocracy wielding overwhelming power. . . . Oppression of the working class such as was revealed in England by the Mines and Factories reports, is in Canada morally impossible. The only thing that here threatens the kindly relation between employer and the employed, and the industrial prosperity of the country, is the gratuitous introduction from the old country into Canada of those industrial wars which were the natural consequence of the antagonism of classes and the depressed condition of the working men of England but which have no justification here. . . . We may destroy our happiness by inoculating our industrial system with the maladies of a distant country and an alien state of society.[20]

The *Globe*, as a liberal paper, does not perhaps show up too well in these early incidents of the class struggle in Ontario. It should be added, however, that its news despatches and editorials on the Paris Commune show a remarkable detachment from bourgeois prejudices, and that, during the early 1870s, it printed occasional articles on Karl Marx, his doctrines and his International Association of Workingmen, which, if they were read, must have given the *Globe*'s readers of those days a considerably better understanding of Marxism than their grandchildren could have obtained from its successor in the 1920s and 1930s.

What was the bearing of the new nationality upon the relations of colony and mother country? This was the question which caused most trouble to Reformers amongst themselves, for on this question they were deeply divided and they fought out their differences in public. The differences divided the party into two wings, a Brown wing and a Blake wing, and the two groups remained imperfectly reconciled long after the 1870s.

During the first years after 1867 the spirit of nationalism seemed to many thoughtful Canadians to be likely to supply the dynamic force which would make one great people out of several little parochial provincial communities. "Nationality," said Goldwin Smith in his presidential address at the first dinner of the National Club of Toronto, "will bind the members of the Confederacy together by stronger as well as nobler ties than Sectional Cabinets

---

[20] *Ibid.*, April 1, 1872.

and Better Terms."[21] The *Globe* itself in the early years frequently took a holiday from vituperative attacks upon John A. Macdonald to reflect pleasantly upon the growth of national spirit in the new Dominion. But by 1874, when Goldwin Smith's address was delivered, it had for some years been attacking nationalists with all its artillery. Nationalists tended to propound doctrines of independence. In the first two or three years after Confederation they had been most prominent in Montreal. Sir Alexander Galt, John Young, L. S. Huntingdon, all advocated Canadian independence. The *Globe* sneered at these Montrealers and said their zeal for a new state of existence was chiefly stimulated by the bad state of trade in Montreal (as in 1849).[22] The *Globe* itself was fervently and fanatically devoted to the integrity of the British connection. What raised its ire more than Montreal heretics was the constant tendency of Cobdenites and Gladstonians in England to announce unctuously that Canada was perfectly free to leave the Empire if she wished. Separation from Britain, it repeated over and over again, could mean only annexation to the United States. Furthermore, and this was also a much-repeated point, it was undesirable to be constantly suggesting doubts about Canada's position just at the time when all efforts should be devoted to making the new experiment of Confederation work.

But the Treaty of Washington in 1871 raised outspoken criticism all over Canada about the handling of Canadian interests by the British government and the British plenipotentiaries. And nowhere were the criticisms more trenchant than in the *Globe* itself. Just after this came the arrival of Goldwin Smith in Toronto, the founding of the *Canadian Monthly* and the *Nation*, and the launching of the Canada First movement. Talk of a change in imperial relations now found its centre in Toronto. Edward Blake concluded from the Treaty of Washington that if Canada must defer in her external relations to imperial interests, she must have a voice in determining what those imperial interests were; and he began to draw the moral of Imperial Federation. Goldwin Smith was for out-and-out independence. The *Canadian Monthly* and the *Nation* were full of articles about the need for a change, for working out the full implications of nationality. "The authors of Con-

---

[21] As reported in the *Nation*, Oct. 15, 1874.
[22] *Globe*, May 3 and 5, 1869.

federation," remarked the *Nation* in disgust, "once appealed to the spirit of nationality. . . . Now some of them tell us that their object was limited and that they set the forest on fire only to boil their own pot."[23] To all this the *Globe*'s reaction was to take as violent a loyalist stand as any Tory could have wished. To the *Nation* and the Canada First group this seemed an admirable opportunity for the launching of a new Liberal party which would appeal to the incipient nationalism of the country and make both Brown Grits and Macdonald Tories obsolete. And the leader whom they nominated for the new party was Edward Blake. Blake disappointed their hopes in the end, but it was just when all this discussion was at its height that he made his famous Aurora speech (October 3, 1874), which received more discussion in the Canadian press of the time than any other utterance of that generation.

> Our government [he told his Aurora audience], should not present the anomaly which it now presents — a government the freest, perhaps the most democratic in the world with reference to local and domestic matters, in which you rule yourselves as fully as any people in the world, while in your foreign affairs, your relations with other countries whether peaceful or warlike, commercial or financial, or otherwise, you may have no more voice than the people of Japan. . . . It is impossible to foster a national spirit unless you have national interests to attend to. . . . The time will come when that national spirit which has been spoken of will be truly felt among us, when we shall realize that we are four millions of Britons who are not free. . . . Tomorrow, by the policy of England, in which you have no voice or control, this country might be plunged into the horrors of a war. . . . The future of Canada, I believe, depends upon the cultivation of a national spirit. . . . We are engaged in a very difficult task — the task of welding together seven Provinces which have been accustomed to regard themselves as isolated from each other. . . . How are we to accomplish our work? How are we to effect a real union between these Provinces? Can we do it by giving a sop now to one, now to another, after the manner of the late Government? . . . Not so! That day I hope is done forever, and we must find some other and truer ground for union than that by which the late Government sought to buy love and purchase peace. We must find some common ground on which to unite, some common aspiration to be shared, and I think it can be found alone in the cultivation of that national spirit to which I have referred.

---

[23] *Nation*, Feb. 26, 1875.

Blake's speech was delivered on a Saturday. It was not accidental that on the following Monday the *Globe* had only a few words about it but devoted its leading article to a long, blistering attack on Canada First. When it did get round to discussing Blake it dismissed his ideas on the position of Canada in the Empire as "interesting and harmless speculation".[24] Alexander Mackenzie, the Reform Prime Minister, congratulated Blake in a private letter on his "disturbing" speech; but writing to another correspondent he was more frank and declared that speeches of this kind were unnecessary and that all unnecessary speeches did harm.[25] The *Globe* proceeded to discourage such unnecessary speculation by concentrating its heaviest artillery upon Goldwin Smith, and doing its best to commit the Reform party to its own emotional loyalist position. The controversy was to continue at intervals for several years.

> Mr. Smith has come into a peaceful community to do his best for the furtherance of a cause which means simply revolution. . . . If national life pulses with any measure of vigour there will be some things instinctively put out of the category of open questions. . . . In Canada we have got so far on the road to nationality that we *have* settled that Queen Victoria is our sovereign, and that the allegiance we owe her is not an impalpable something which may be rendered or withheld according to the determination of any club. . . . The advocacy of Canadian Independence touches every individual in the Dominion in all his dearest and most important relations. It puts all his material, social and religious interests into possible jeopardy. . . . They [the advocates of independence] might be the fathers of a new nationality but they might also . . . be voted simply mischief-makers, whose insignificance and powerlessness were their sole protectors, as these made the community feel that they were not important enough for the traitor's trial or the traitor's doom.[26]
> The truth is that Mr. Smith is a dreamer, not a statesman. . . . Another Don on another Rosinante. . . . Very many [people] have settled in Canada because they wish to live and die under the British flag. When the time comes that it shall be proposed to haul that flag down, the contest may be fierce — aye, and with all respect to Mr. Smith, bloody. . . . Mr. Smith fancies, in the honest

---

[24] *Globe,* Oct. 7, 1874.
[25] Public Archives of Canada, Alexander Mackenzie Letter Books, Oct. 28, 1874, Mackenzie to John Cameron of the London *Advertiser.*
[26] *Globe,* Oct. 27, 1874.

simplicity of his heart, that men in ordinary life can be played with as safely as their representatives on a chessboard.[27]

How deeply did all this discussion of the meaning of the new nationality sink into the mind of the ordinary Canadian of the 1870s? By the end of that decade it was petering out. It appealed primarily to intellectuals like Goldwin Smith and Blake, and to the small group who found journals of the quality of the *Canadian Monthly* and the *Nation* good reading. But the long severe depression killed off whatever tendencies the average Canadian may have had to play with general political ideas. "It must be owned," said Goldwin Smith sadly in 1877, "that in industrial communities the economic motives are stronger than the political, and that the movement in favour of Canadian nationality had only political motives on its side."[28] What he failed to discern was that the national spirit which he was seeking to foster in Canada was being canalized into economic rather than into political channels. A newspaper critic of Blake's Aurora speech had said: "He does not show that it [Imperial Federation] would remove any hindrance to material development or add one dollar to the capital of the country."[29] That was it. Material Development. Canadians, big and small, Grit and Tory, were chiefly intent on material development. The big ones had plunged into the great business enterprises of developing the resources of half a continent. And the little ones, as the seventies passed into the eighties and the depression still continued, were finding that the business of making a living absorbed their energies.

---

[27] *Ibid.*, Nov. 7, 1874.
[28] Goldwin Smith, "The Political Destiny of Canada" (*Canadian Monthly*, June, 1877).
[29] London *Free Press*, quoted in "*A National Sentiment*," 25.

5. Goldwin Smith

(This article first appeared in the *University of Toronto Quarterly*, April, 1933. I have tacked on to the end of it five paragraphs which formed the conclusion of a talk on Goldwin Smith that I gave over the C.B.C. on 6 December, 1950. Since my article appeared in 1933 two large-scale studies of Goldwin Smith have been done, one in the form of a Toronto Ph.D. thesis by Ronald McEachern (unpublished), and the other a book by Elisabeth Wallace, *Goldwin Smith: Victorian Liberal* (Toronto, 1957).)

It is now twenty-three years since Goldwin Smith died. During his career, both in England and in Canada, he was engaged in almost continuous controversy; and during the last thirty-nine years of his life he resided in a city which, while it respected him highly for his attainments, abhorred his political views and never made much attempt to understand him. Though he had been a Regius Professor of History, his own writings were mostly in the nature of journalism, and they are already largely forgotten by Canadians, who, as inveterate newspaper readers, are a people with short memories. His secretary, Mr. Arnold Haultain, who was his literary executor, has left us the only attempt at a full-length portrait that we have; it was painted when Mr. Haultain was smarting a little from a sense of ill-treatment, and it shows much more concentration upon the warts than upon the rest of the face. Besides, no man was ever more completely unfitted by temperament for understanding the real elements of Goldwin Smith's greatness than was Mr. Haultain. He had a naive instinctive admiration for everything which his chief detested. He bubbled with enthusiasm for the Chamberlainite imperialism of the late 1890s and early 1900s, and he believed firmly that Rudyard Kipling was a poet.

It seems, therefore, worth while, even though the issue between Cobden and Chamberlain is not yet settled in the British Empire, to survey afresh the development of Goldwin Smith's ideas. The more difficult task of estimating his influence in Canada I shall not attempt. I suspect that his real influence is yet to come, and will be exercised upon those Canadian historians who settle down to study the Canada of 1867 to 1914, who fall under the spell of the Bystander and come to see how shrewd were his comments upon current events, how enlightening his criticism of the nature of

Canadian nationality, and how far-reaching his conception of the place of Canada in the English-speaking world.

Goldwin Smith was born in 1823, the son of a well-to-do physician in Reading. He received the typical training of the English scholar and gentleman of his day. He was sent to Eton in 1836, went up to Oxford in 1841, and won his B.A. in 1845. A brilliant classical student, he became on graduation a candidate for a fellowship at Queen's. But already he was marked out as a coming man in the little group of reformers in the university, and he was defeated for the fellowship by an obscure rival who was supported by the ecclesiastical party in the college.

This was the beginning for him of a struggle in which he was to play a part for the next twenty years in the university. Oxford was then almost entirely under clerical control, and it was only beginning to awake from the long intellectual torpor of the eighteenth century. Academical duty, Goldwin Smith tells us in his *Reminiscences*, was lost in the theological fray. The great question in his student days was, of course, the controversy over Newman. Looking back on it in his old age he declared that "the confluence of Newmanism with Romanism seems as natural as the confluence of two drops of water on a window-pane, and perhaps fraught with consequences little more momentous to humanity". But in the 1840s and 1850s he threw himself vigorously into the efforts of the little group of liberal reformers who were fighting against both Newman and his opponents, who were striving to emancipate Oxford altogether from its ecclesiastical atmosphere and its clerical control, and as he put it himself, to restore it to the nation. After the failure at Queen's he won a fellowship at University College. In 1850 he was appointed assistant-secretary of the Royal Commission of Inquiry which the reformers succeeded in having set up; and he served also as secretary of the later Parliamentary Commission which drafted the legislation of 1854 and so made the first breach in ecclesiastical monopoly. The long and bitter struggle against the ecclesiastical party in the university coloured all his later thinking. He became a zealot for the removal of privileges and especially of religious privileges; he preached the separation of Church and State, and he continued to be a passionate anti-clerical all his life.

His connection with the Royal and Parliamentary commissions introduced him to London society and to public life there. For some time he read law. In 1855 he became a member of the staff of the newly founded *Saturday Review* and began to distinguish himself as a political and literary controversialist. An admirer of Peel, he went with the Peelites to the liberal side of politics after the great disruption over the Corn Laws. In 1858, while still a young man of thirty-five years, he was appointed Regius Professor of Modern History at Oxford; and he returned to active work in the university, already a marked man on the liberal side both in the internal academic politics of Oxford itself and in the wider field of national affairs.

How Goldwin Smith conceived his function of professor of history is somewhat difficult to judge. His inaugural lecture in 1859 presents the honours History school as a discipline in preparing young men of the upper classes for public life. That it should be also a discipline for the training of scholars, of historians, does not seem to have been part of his ambition. He himself never settled down to research, and he has left behind him no great work which recreates and reinterprets for us a past period of history. Sometimes one is bound to wonder whether he would not have been a happier man had he devoted his life to his favourite period of early seventeenth-century Puritan England and anticipated the work of those later heroes of research, successors of his in the Oxford chair, Professors Gardiner and Firth.

In 1861 the American Civil War broke out. It is evident now that the Civil War was the turning point in Goldwin Smith's life. As a leader among the Liberals at Oxford he was already tending apparently to become more and more immersed in current controversies; perhaps he was finding the ecclesiastical and conservative tone of the university more and more uncongenial and was beginning to long for a wider sphere of activity. The American struggle produced a sharp cleavage of opinion in England. "Society" in general, the governing classes and the Church, violently espoused the cause of the South; and their chief journalistic organ, the London *Times*, set itself to stir up ill-will between England and the North. On the other side stood Cobden and Bright and the Manchester Liberals, a few prominent intellectuals like John Stuart Mill, and the industrial masses of northern England. Goldwin Smith with a small group of Oxford, Cambridge and London dons, joined the Manchester men. But they were a very small minority in the society among which they moved.

Smith, who perhaps had a congenital tendency for finding himself on the minority side, was stirred as he had never been before. He became a pamphleteer. He began to deliver lectures before great public audiences in London and in the North. This activity brought him into personal contact with Cobden and Bright and the other members of the Manchester School, and he quickly found in their midst, rather than at Oxford, his spiritual home. In 1864 he went out to visit America, more or less as an official delegate from those sections of the English public who had taken the side of the North. The Regius Professor of Oxford, bearing a message of goodwill from the English democracy to the Northern democracy of the United States, was fêted and received with honour wherever he went in the States. He came back to England confirmed in his belief that in America was the hope of the English-speaking race. The tremendous popular success of his American visit and the revelation of the intensity of anti-American and anti-democratic feeling among the English governing classes caused him to look more and more longingly across the Atlantic.

The direction in which his mind was moving during these Civil War years is shown in his private letters. Thus in 1864, before his American visit, he writes to Charles Eliot Norton: "For my own part I have fairly thought my way out of social and political Feudalism and out of the State Church which is its religious complement; and my intellect and heart are entirely with those who are endeavouring to found a great community on the sounder as well as the happier basis of social justice and free religious convictions." He gives a fuller revelation of his mind in a speech which he delivered at Boston in the course of his tour. It shows a Goldwin Smith to which later Canadians are hardly accustomed, not the sarcastic and destructive critic but the preacher expounding his faith in a mood of the highest exaltation.

"To America, though an alien by birth, I am, as an English Liberal, no alien in heart. . . . England bore you, and bore you not without a mother's pangs. For the real hour of your birth was the English Revolution of the seventeenth century, at once the saddest and the noblest period of English history. . . . In England the Revolution of the seventeenth century failed. It failed, at least, as an attempt to establish social equality and liberty of conscience. The feudal past, with a feudal Europe to support it, sat too heavy on us to be cast off. . . . The nation had gone a little way out of the feudal and hierarchical Egypt; but the horrors of the unknown wilderness and the memory of the fleshpots overpowered the hope of the Promised Land; and the people returned to the rule of Pharaoh and his priests amid the bonfires of the Restoration. . . .

But the yoke which in the mother country we had not the strength to throw off, in the colony we escaped; and here, beyond the reach of the Restoration, Milton's vision proved true, and a free community was founded. . . . Yet in England the party of Cromwell and Milton still lives. It still lives; and in this great crisis of your fortunes, its heart turns to you. On your success ours depends. Now as in the seventeenth century the thread of our fate is twined with the thread of yours. An English Liberal comes here, not only to watch the unfolding of your destiny, but to read his own. . . . The soldiers of the Union are not Puritans, neither are the planters Cavaliers. But the present civil war is a vast episode in the same irrepressible conflict between Aristocracy and Democracy. . . . The England of Charles and Laud has been against you; the England of Hampden, Milton and Cromwell is on your side."

While his mind was full of conceptions such as these, there occurred an event in his personal life which was decisive for his future. In 1866 his father, who had long retired from practice and was living as a country gentleman near Reading, suffered an injury in a railway accident, which produced a mental derangement. Goldwin Smith, a devoted son, was the only member of the family free and able to look after him. He threw up his professorship at Oxford and for two years was in almost daily attendance upon his father. Then he was compelled to leave home for a couple of days to attend to some business. While he was away his father committed suicide. The shock prostrated the son, and it was a long time before he fully recovered from it. The tragedy made all his old associations in England seem unbearable. Just at this time he met Andrew White, who invited him to join his staff in the newly created Cornell University. Smith accepted the invitation and came to America in 1868.

Life in the little rural village in northern New York confirmed him in his belief in the essential soundness of the American democratic experiment; and he was often accustomed in later years to contrast his own experience of the American people with that of the hypercritical English visitors who saw only the unlovely side of American democracy in the big cities. But apparently he found the task of teaching the very immature students of Cornell not altogether congenial. At any rate in 1871 he moved north to Toronto and settled here amongst relatives, continuing to go back periodically to Cornell to give courses of lectures. In 1875 he married

Mrs. Boulton, the mistress of the Grange, and became a Torontonian for the rest of his life.

Several times during his early years on this side of the ocean he was invited back to England to enter politics on the Liberal side, and was offered safe constituencies in the North. He was invited to come back to Oxford as Master of University College. Later on, when the Home Rule struggle was at its height in the 1880s, the Unionist Liberals invited him to come back and lend his voice in Parliament against the dismemberment of the United Kingdom, a cause about which he became almost as passionate as he had been in his preaching against the dismemberment of the American Union. But he resisted all temptations and remained in Canada. He must often, when being bitterly reviled in Toronto for his political views, have looked back with some regret to the career that a man with his intellectual abilities might have had in Oxford and in England. He was keenly conscious of the narrow stage upon which Canadian actors must play their part and of the limited audience before whom they perform. He was to learn to his sorrow that the influence which an intellectual can exercise in Canadian public affairs is severely limited. For in Canada there is little of that personal intercourse between practical statesmen and university dons which is a unique and charming feature of English life, raising the intellectual level of politics and saving the universities from becoming the breeding ground of Ph.D.s.

Before he left England Goldwin Smith had published another work, which, on the whole, seems to me to be the finest thing he ever wrote and which has been rather undeservedly forgotten. The Trent incident at the end of 1861, with its threat of war between England and the Northern States, raised the question of how Canada should be defended. In the spring of 1862 the Canadian legislature unceremoniously threw out a Militia Bill which had been drafted under the advice of Imperial staff officers; and the sequel was a long and acrimonious controversy between colony and mother country, which was carried on both in official despatches and in newspaper editorials. The defence crisis, coming on top of Canada's protective tariff of 1859, accentuated the tendency in England to discuss separation as the ultimate goal to which the colonies were inevitably drifting. Goldwin Smith entered the discussion with a series of letters to the chief liberal London paper, the *Daily News*. He gathered the letters together in a book entitled *The Empire*, which he published in 1863. They form the most perfect embodiment that we have of the imperial, or rather anti-imperial, doctrines of the Manchester school. They are written in what is for him a buoyant and high-spirited tone; for the writer believed that he was expressing the opinions of the most intelligent Englishmen whose minds were not biased by special interest.

The Empire is full of the usual Manchester arguments about the extravagance of maintaining colonies who close their markets to the products of the mother country and make no contribution to imperial defence. But it is more interesting to us today for the leading idea which runs through the book, the conception of Canada as potentially a new nation in a New World. "England," he writes, "has long promised herself the honour of becoming the mother of free nations. Is it not time that the promise should be fulfilled? . . . We are keeping the Colonies in a perpetual state of political infancy, and preventing the gristle of their frames from being matured and hardened into bone. . . . We have given them all that we really have to give — our national character, our commercial energy, our aptitude for law and government, our language. We have given them the essence of our constitution — free legislation, self-taxation, ministerial responsibility, personal liberty, trial by jury. The accidents of that constitution — the relics of the feudal world in which it was wrought — we can no more give them than we can give them our history or our skies. England is a European aristocracy, Canada is an American democracy. . . . I am no more against Colonies than I am against the solar system. I am against dependencies, when nations are fit to be independent. . . . But grant that Canada cannot stand as a nation by herself, it is with a nation in America, not with a nation in Europe, that she must ultimately blend. . . . And while she remains a province, Canada is, in fact, insensibly blending with the United States. . . . As a province she cannot form the independent character or assume the clear lineaments of a nation. . . . There is but one way to make Canada impregnable, and that is to fence her round with the majesty of an independent nation."

Was it not a cruel joke of fate that the man who dreamed this splendid vision of an independent Canadian nation should have been destined to live thirty-nine years in Toronto, the home of the United Empire Loyalists and the Loyal Orange Lodges?

But while he called upon Canada to undertake the responsibility of nationhood, Goldwin Smith did not mean that colonial nationality should involve the complete breaking of the tie with the mother country. "What is proposed is, not that Canada shall cease to be a Colony of England, but that she shall cease to be a dependency . . . Is there any reason why, after the separation of the Governments, natives of Canada should not still be allowed, on coming to reside within the pale of English law, to become British citizens, to acquire all kinds of property, and to exercise, if otherwise duly qualified, all political rights? Is there any reason why Canada should not keep the old flag, with such difference as the Heralds' College may require? . . . These cravings for a grand unity are destined to find their fulfilment in the moral and intellectual, rather than in the political sphere."

The truth is that the new British Commonwealth of Nations which we have been working out since 1914 bears a remarkable resemblance to the ideas of the Manchester men in the 1860s. They saw far more clearly than their successors, the Imperialists of the 1880s and 1890s, the one essential fact, the fact of colonial nationality; and they welcomed it gladly. They did not believe that the young colonial nations could indefinitely remain within the political orbit of Great Britain. They did not believe that colonial nationality was compatible with the political centralization of the empire. We have retained more of the political and legal ties than they thought possible, especially the tie of the Crown. But most of these are now the harmless playthings of constitutional lawyers. The despised Manchester men have turned out to be much better prophets of the future course of imperial development than either Disraeli or Chamberlain.

Though he preached the gospel of Canadian nationality as against a colonial dependence upon England, it is clear from several passages in *The Empire* and in other writings that already before he left England Smith was impressed with the idea that the natural destiny of Canada was absorption in the United States. But he arrived in Canada in 1871 just when the country (or rather perhaps that part of it which centred about Toronto and Montreal) was in the first flush of national enthusiasm after the achievement of Confederation. Several leading public men, among them Alexander Galt on the Conservative side and L. S. Huntingdon on the Liberal side, were talking openly about independence. There was a feeling in the air, which was quickly sensed by the Oxford professor still alert for the potentialities of the New World, that great deeds were about to be performed, that all things were possible now that Canadian public men had shown their capacity to rise out of the muck of party politics and to join hands in creating "a new nationality".

The first result of this national impulse in the literary field was the launching, in January, 1872, of *The Canadian Monthly and National Review*. "It is hoped," said the publishers, "that the effort to give an organ, in the form of a periodical, to the intellectual life of Canada, is now made under better auspices than before. There has been of late a general awakening of national life, which has probably extended to the literary and scientific sphere, and special circumstances have favoured the publishers in obtaining literary assistance in the conduct of their Magazine." The special circumstances consisted in the arrival of Goldwin Smith in Toronto. He joined heartily in the new venture. In the second number of the *Canadian Monthly* appears the first article under the pen name which was to become so famous in Canada — "A Bystander". Very soon he was contributing a regular feature in the journal, a monthly commentary on current affairs, which he kept up, along with other contributors, till the end of 1874. He assisted in other ways also. We find him writing to Professor Max Müller of Oxford, asking him to procure some German stories which could be published in translation in the new magazine. "They hope," he writes in explaining the new venture to his friend, "to stop the process which is at present going on of intellectual annexation to the United States."

More important than this activity was another with which Goldwin Smith soon became connected. In Toronto a group of young romantics launched the "Canada First" movement, and sought the counsel and guidance of the Oxford professor who had so distinguished himself in England by his advocacy of Canadian nationality. The young men of "Canada First" were never quite sure whether their watchword meant political independence or not, and whether their function was to liberalize the Liberal party, or to found a new third party, or merely to help in creating a deeper consciousness of the implications of the new nationality among the community at large. But in 1874 they founded the National Club in Toronto, and Goldwin Smith became its first president. Edward Blake seemed to be their obvious political leader, and his great Aurora speech of 1874 with its declaration that we are "four millions of Britons who are not free", was taken up by them with enthusiasm. What they welcomed especially was Blake's tendency to discuss the broader issues of Canadian affairs and to emancipate himself from mere party warfare.

In April, 1874, appeared the first number of a new weekly journal in Toronto, the *Nation*, started as the organ of "Canada First" to preach the new nationalism. In January, 1875, Goldwin Smith dropped his connection with the *Canadian Monthly*, which now seemed fairly launched, and joined the *Nation*, becoming one of its chief editorial writers. But already the "Canada First" movement had been causing alarm in the minds of the regular party leaders and journals; and the *Globe* and the *Mail*, the two party dailies in Toronto, united to crush it. The *Globe* was especially ferocious in its attacks because it feared that Blake, if he listened to the blandishments of "Canada First", might lead off a large section of the Reformers in a break from the Brown-Mackenzie fold. A convenient method of intimidating Blake was to attack the Oxford professor; and upon Goldwin Smith through 1874 and 1875 it poured out its wrath. He was accused, when he discussed independence as the manifest destiny of Canada, of furthering a cause which meant simply revolution, of advocating a policy which would put in jeopardy the material, social and religious interests of every individual in the Dominion; and his accuser announced that he was worthy of "a traitor's trial and a traitor's doom". Smith and his friends replied vigorously in the *Nation*, claiming the right to free discussion, denouncing the attempt to crush political independence by personal slander, and vaunting their determination to rescue Toronto from the journalistic despotism of George Brown. In the spring of 1875 the Blake section of the Reformers started a daily paper, the *Liberal*, in opposition to the *Globe* in Toronto, and Smith lent his pen occasionally to this journal also. But the *Globe*, or some other influence, was effective. The *Liberal* petered out after a few months. Blake returned to party orthodoxy and became a member of the Mackenzie cabinet. And the "Canada First" movement gradually disintegrated. The *Nation*, its organ, ceased publication in the fall of 1876.

Goldwin Smith was discouraged and disgusted. He was never afterwards quite able to forgive Blake for what seemed to him, as he looked back, the desertion under fire of the one political movement in Canada that showed promise of raising the intellectual and moral level of Canadian public life, and of turning the country's attention to something more significant than the ignoble struggle of party machines for the spoils of office. Smith, as all his life showed, was easily discouraged and disgusted. After the failure of "Canada First" he reached the conclusion, which was fortified by all his later experience, that the Canadian people simply hadn't in them the capacity for making a nation.

Nevertheless, he still looked forward to playing an active part in the community of which he was now a citizen. In the middle of the 1870s he was thinking seriously of seeking a seat in the Ontario Legislature so that he could get into closer touch with the real daily life of the ordinary Canadian. Sir John Macdonald, with whom, in spite of the Pacific Scandal, he was on terms of friendly intimacy through the 1870s, encouraged him in this idea and held out hopes that he might become Minister of Education when the Conservatives succeeded, as John A. Macdonald was sure they were just on the point of doing, in ousting Oliver Mowat from office. In 1878 Smith supported Macdonald in the campaign for the National Policy, and spoke at one of the campaign meetings. It is significant that he welcomed the National Policy, though he was a good disciple of Adam Smith and Richard Cobden, because it was a declaration of national tariff autonomy in opposition to the tendency, of which he thought Brown and Mackenzie were guilty, to curry favour with British industrialists and the British Government.

In the meantime he was still active in journalism. Apparently he ceased to write for the *Nation* early in 1876, several months before it gave up the ghost. But in April, 1876, he was helping John Ross Robertson to start the *Evening Telegram*. "The *Telegram*," its editor announced to his readers, "is a newspaper. It has no political axes to grind. In the bickerings and animosities of factions it takes no part. In the schemes and plots of politicians it has no share." To the *Telegram* in its early months the Bystander contributed frequent long letters which were really special articles on various subjects of Canadian public interest. Goldwin Smith and Sir Alexander Galt were the *Telegram*'s two chief heroes in those days because of their independent stand in politics. Volume One, Number Fourteen of the paper devotes almost one page (five solid columns) to reproducing an article of Goldwin Smith — on "The Immortality of the Soul". In September, 1876, the Bystander was writing letters to the editor entitled "Is Protection the Real Remedy?" and arguing for closer trade relations with the United States.

There is an interesting letter from Goldwin Smith in the *Telegram* of October 2, 1876, on the occasion of the demise of the *Nation*, in which he gives his somewhat gloomy conclusions about native

Canadian periodicals. He points out what he was to repeat very often later on, that Quebec severs Ontario from the Maritimes not only in a political but also in a literary sense, and that the only market to which a high-class Canadian journal can look is Ontario and the English district about Montreal. The *Nation* had failed because it could not command a large enough market to meet the competition of English journals, and, what was far more formidable, of the periodical literature of the United States, under the most spirited and skilful management in the world. "Nothing can sustain the Canadian publishers against such competition except the prevalence of a patriotic feeling, of pride and interest in native productions; and if such a feeling exists neither I nor the publishers with whom I have been connected have been able to discern it."

Nevertheless, he continued to the end of his life in his stubborn effort to foster high-class independent journalism in Canada. In 1880 he began his own little personal magazine, *The Bystander*, with its motto "Not party but the people", in which perhaps is to be found his best Canadian writing. *The Bystander* ran as a monthly through 1880 and the first half of 1881, was dropped then, while he went on a visit home to England, and was revived as a quarterly for the year 1883. On December 6, 1883, appeared the first number of *The Week*, "an independent journal of Literature, Politics and Criticism", edited at the beginning by Charles G. D. Roberts. Goldwin Smith was part owner of *The Week* and he ceased publication of his *Bystander* at the end of 1883 to take up under the same pen name a weekly feature of the new journal, two or three columns on *Current Affairs*. Like its most distinguished contributor *The Week* stood in favour of Canadian independence and was highly critical of both Canadian political parties, though not as despondent about party government in general as was *The Bystander*.

Later in the 1880s *The Week* came under new control and turned against Goldwin Smith's ideas about the political destiny of Canada. So in 1889, when the campaign for better trade relations with United States was at its height, he revived his *Bystander* to fill what he thought a dangerous gap in the advocacy of Commercial Union, and twelve numbers of a new series of *The Bystander* appeared from October 1889 to September 1890.

But this was not the end of his journalistic efforts. In 1896, now an old man of seventy-three, he was induced by a group of young radical friends to join in yet another venture. The *Weekly Sun*, the organ of the Patrons of Industry, was in financial difficulties owing to the disintegration of patronism amongst the Ontario farmers. Goldwin Smith already had a connection with Ontario farm movements through his part in the Commercial Union campaign which had been much more popular among the farmers than among the protected industries of Toronto and other urban centres. He bought a controlling interest in the *Sun* and the familiar pen name of the Bystander appeared once more. From 1896 he continued to write from one to three columns regularly for the front page of the *Weekly Sun*, until his wife's death at the end of 1909 and his own accident early in 1910 made further writing impossible.

What effect did all this journalistic writing have upon Canadian intellectual life? We must remember that at the same time Goldwin Smith was writing books of one kind or another, his *Cowper* and his *Jane Austen* in the English Men of Letters series, his *Canada and the Canadian Question*, his *Essays on Questions of the Day*, his *Irish History and the Irish Question*, his political histories of the United States and of Great Britain, various booklets on religious questions, not to mention a host of articles in English journals like the *Fortnightly* and the *Nineteenth Century*, letters to the London *Times* and the New York *Sun*, letters and book reviews in Godkin's New York *Nation;* and a good part of this material must also have reached many of his Canadian audience.

No one today can read for long in Canadian journalism from the 1870s to the early 1900s without realizing how much higher a standard of writing the Bystander provided than most of his Canadian contemporaries. His comments on current affairs have behind them a rich store of historical knowledge upon which the writer constantly draws, and they show a range of interest which was lamentably lacking then, as it is lacking today, in Canadian journalism. He took his readers not only into Canadian politics but into American and British and continental European affairs as well. He could discuss Gladstone and Salisbury familiarly as men whom he had known as equals, and could deal with men like Morley, Chamberlain, Rosebery, Asquith and Balfour as mere juniors. He lived to write obituary notices of all the great Victorians, and some of these magisterial criticisms, perhaps more than anything else in his writings, make one feel what a difference there was between the imported standards of London and Oxford and the native standards of Toronto. But the outstanding feature of his political writing is that he saw contemporary politics as only part of a world-wide intellectual movement. The breakdown of the old religious beliefs, the rise of science, the movement of feminism ("the sexual revolution", as he used to call it), the onward sweep of new socialistic movements in Europe, the slow drift of his own peaceful Victorian civilization into the madness of a world war, all these deeper undercurrents of human affairs drew his interest; and over against them he set the dismal pettiness of our parochial Canadian politics. To a modern reader the Bystander's writing shines out amidst the Canadian journalism of his day in somewhat the same way as Burke's speeches shine out amidst the windy oratory of the late eighteenth century in England. Let us put down at least this to his credit, that he paid his Ontario audience the compliment of believing that they were capable of appreciating the highest English culture.

About the style of his writing, as distinct from the matter of it, one need not say much. "Style," he said once, when asked how he achieved the austere simplicity and clarity which is the mark of his prose, "Style! I have no style, I merely wait for the mud to settle." There is not much Canadian journalistic writing which shows any sign of its author's having waited for the mud to settle.

But, of course, what Goldwin Smith is best remembered for in Canada, is the body of doctrine as to Canada's destiny which he preached month in and month out. There are three or four main ideas around which all his journalistic writing is built. One is that of Canadian independence from Britain, to which reference has already been made. After 1870 this Manchester doctrine was gradually replaced in England by the movements for Imperial Federation and an Imperial Zollverein. Smith would have nothing to do with either movement. Again and again he called upon the Federationists to produce a concrete scheme so that it would be possible to discuss it. Again and again he pointed out that there was no hope of Canada's being induced to give up her control of trade to any imperial body and that she showed no signs of being willing to undertake the greater defence obligations which closer imperial union would involve. Especially did he object to the anti-American tendencies of these projects. "There is a federation which is feasible, and, to those who do not measure grandeur by physical force or extension, at least as grand as that of which the Imperialist dreams. It is the moral federation of the whole English-speaking race throughout the world, including all those millions of men speaking the English language in the United States, and parted from the rest only a century ago by a wretched quarrel."

In a closer imperial union, then, he saw no future. Every year he became more convinced that the real destiny of Canada lay rather in a closer union, commercial and political, with her neighbour upon this continent. The failure of "Canada First", the continuing cleavage between French and English, the geographical sectionalism of the country, all combined to make him pessimistic about the possibility of our achieving a separate nationality of our own upon this continent. Curiously enough, the development which made this a fixed idea in his mind was the building of the C.P.R., an exploit to which we look back now as the most magnificent expression in our history of our national faith in ourselves. Goldwin Smith, on the contrary, believed that the taking into Confederation of the great distant stretches of western prairie and of the still more distant province of British Columbia had produced a geographical structure in which no real unity was possible, and that the attempt to bind these vast territories together by the C.P.R. would bankrupt the country, and was only an over-ambitious scheme of imperialist knights to carry out the project of attaching Canada to the Old World and making out of her an anti-American, anti-democratic Empire.

And this inescapable sectional and racial division of the country had its effect, as he was forever pointing out, in the party politics which developed after 1867. Macdonald kept things going by an unscrupulous policy of corruption, bribing first one section and then another, with special grants and public works. Unfortunately, such a policy was the only one possible in a country whose sections had so little in common. In his *Canada and the Canadian Question* Goldwin Smith quotes with relish the reply of a citizen of British Columbia of whom he had inquired what his politics were, and who answered promptly "Government Appropriations". "Not Cavour or Bismarck," he writes of Macdonald in another place, "is more fitted for his special task than he (Macdonald). He has always had to deal with what have happily been called sinister interests. When he is gone, who will take his place? What shepherd is there who knows his sheep or whose voice the sheep know? Who else could make Orangemen vote for Papists and induce half the members for Ontario to help in levying on their province the necessary blackmail for Quebec? Yet this is the work which will have to be done if a general breakup is to be averted. When the shears of fate cut the thread of Sir John Macdonald's life what bond of union will be left?" Briefly, of course, the answer to this pessimistic analysis of the means by which Canadian unity was maintained was that when Macdonald disappeared the Providence which watched over the destinies of the Canadian people could be trusted to produce a Laurier who was equally adept in the politics of "Government Appropriations".

So he stood for Continental Union because geographical sectionalism and racial and religious divisions made the smaller national union of Canada impracticable. Always, be it remembered, he repudiated the word "Annexation" with its suggestion of compulsion. The union he wished was one which would be freely and voluntarily entered into by both parties, like the Union of Scotland and England, and one to which he believed the mother country would give her blessing. That the disruption of the existing union with Great Britain would mean a breaking of old associations and a destruction of the continuity of our national life such as Canadians were not willing to contemplate he never grasped. "I look forward," said Principal Grant of Queen's, "to the happy reunion of our race with as much longing as Dr. Goldwin Smith, but to begin it with a second disruption is out of the question." That was the point which Goldwin Smith could not appreciate.

The controversy with Principal Grant, the last of many such controversies on this subject, took place in 1896, in the pages of the *Canadian Magazine*. By this time Goldwin Smith was an old man and had become more and more melancholy. He saw his own native country drifting, as it seemed to him, into the lowest type of demagoguery under Gladstone and then under Chamberlain, and the English democracy of which he had once had high hopes turning to confiscatory socialism. He called in vain for a Peel to appear and rally all the moderate elements of the community about him. At the same time the United States drifted into bimetallism and Bryanism. "The American Commonwealth," he told his farmer readers in the *Weekly Sun* in 1896, "is the greatest experiment ever made in popular government. The fate of popular government in all countries, notably in our own, must be largely decided by its result. . . . Bimetallism, even repudiation is not the greatest factor in this crisis. All the elements of distress, disaffection, revolution and anarchy have for the first time banded themselves together against the life of a Commonwealth which is founded on property and the vital principle of which is liberty under the law." But when the republic escaped the peril of Bryanism it was only to plunge into a greater evil, the imperialistic adventure of the Spanish American

War. "The American Republic was the hope of democracy. . . . It promised to do something more than the Old World towards correcting the injustice of nature, equalizing the human lot, and making the community a community indeed. . . . Shall the American Republic follow its own destiny and do what it can to fulfil the special hopes which humanity has founded in it, or shall it slide into an imitation of European Imperialism?" At the same time Britain became entangled in the Boer War; and, to his infinite disgust, Laurier allowed Canada to be entangled also. The two great branches of the Anglo-Saxon race, to whose ultimate reunion he had dedicated his life, seemed to be uniting only in a career of unscrupulous imperialism.

And when the Boer and the Spanish-American wars were over, there began to loom up the prospect of a still more terrible war between Britain and Germany. The last contributions of the Bystander to the *Weekly Sun* were mainly taken up with warning Canada not to let herself again be involved in the adventures of British Imperialism. "What a close to the Peelonian era!" he wrote to an old English friend in 1900, "I well remember the Reform Bill of 1832 with its golden hopes of a reign of reason and peace." The sun of humanity was behind a cloud, and perhaps the Bystander was not altogether sorry to leave the world before his worst fears as to the future could be realized.

The problem of our Canadian nationality, of the conditions which have determined its development in the past, of the possibilities which lie before it in the future, is the fundamental question that confronts any student of Canadian affairs. It is because Goldwin Smith's mind was exercised about this problem for so long a time and because he brought to it such a store of experience and philosophy from an older civilization that he is so much worth studying. Why has the growth of nationality been so slow and uncertain? In the first number of the *Canadian Monthly* of 1872 there is a long editorial discussing why British America had up to then produced no literature worth speaking of and pointing out that it was still a pioneer community from which the finer fruits of civilization could not yet be expected. We are still making the same defence of ourselves in 1933. For our political history shows the same perplexing lack of growth as our cultural history. The gristle of our frame has never matured and hardened into bone. As Sir John Willison remarked cynically at the close of his life, with every change of government in Canada we are made into a nation over again. And the student of Canadian history, as he puzzles over these conditions, gets an overpowering feeling that he is going round and round inside a squirrel cage. He begins to wonder whether Goldwin Smith's interpretation of events was quite so wide of the mark after all. I expect that when the definitive history of the Dominion is at last written it will contain long and frequent quotations from the Bystander.

He died in 1910. I was an undergraduate in the University of Toronto at that time, and I can still remember well the day of his funeral. It was in June at the time of Convocation. The City of Toronto, which had long repudiated with loathing most of the opinions of its most distinguished citizen, decided to give him a public funeral; and the service was held in Convocation Hall at the university. Officials from various government bodies attended. The federal government sent its young Minister of Labour, the Hon. W. L. Mackenzie King. A few of us students were recruited to serve as ushers. But the day of the funeral dawned cold, windy, and rainy. Gusts of rain swept across the university lawn as the funeral cortège arrived and as it left. And we ushers were hardly needed, because so few of the public attended. I have always thought that that gloomy funeral day symbolized most fittingly the relations of Goldwin Smith with his fellow-citizens of Canada. They remained aloof from each other and estranged to the end.

What are we to say now, today, about Goldwin Smith's opinions? Canada has become an independent nation, as he originally wished. But we have achieved our independence without the breach in the British connection that he thought to be necessary. We have not united politically with the United States, as he later wished, though he was right in foreseeing that the lives of the two North American peoples would interpenetrate each other more and more closely every year. So closely, in fact, that many of our intellectuals today are deploring our dependence upon the United States just as he in his day deplored our dependence upon Britain. Like him, they seem to have lost faith in our Canadian capacity to live an individual, autonomous, self-respecting Canadian life of our own. We spent the century from the Rebellion of 1837 down to the outbreak of war in 1939 in achieving our independence of Great Britain. We are going to spend the next century, from the Ogdensburg and Hyde Park agreements of 1940 down to somewhere about 2040 in maintaining our independence of the United States. And, no doubt, the second century is going to be a tougher experience than the first.

But there is no need for us to wring our hands in despairing defeatism or to start on witch-hunts looking for the traitors who have led us into this dire peril. The trouble with Goldwin Smith, his root weakness, the reason for his loss of faith in his fellow Canadians, was that he lived too far aloof from them. As he grew old, he sat there in his library in the Grange, insulated by his bookshelves from the teeming life of Toronto all around him and from the life of Canada beyond Toronto. What he needed was to get out and meet a few ordinary Canadians and become intimate with them — not intellectuals from the university but just ordinary Canadians. And this is what our critical university intellectuals of today need to restore their faith in the capacity of Canada to survive as a Canadian community. Faith is something that comes from living and not from purely intellectual processes.

Sursum corda! Let us lift up our hearts. We have come a long distance since Goldwin Smith's day, and there is no need for us to sink once more into his despair. Obviously Canada is no longer just the four northerly extensions of the American fertile belt, which was all he could discern in 1891. Our statesmanship has proved anything but bankrupt. Now that we are trying ourselves out on the stage of world power politics, we can afford to be proud of the skill with which our spokesmen are giving expression to a Canadian point of view and the wisdom with which they are looking after Canadian interests. *Sursum corda!*

But at the same time, as I hope I have shown, many of Goldwin Smith's criticisms have a remarkably up-to-date ring about them; and it will not do us any harm now and then to go back and restudy the picture of our weaknesses as he painted it at the end of the nineteenth century.

PART II
Political Controversy in the
1930s and 1940s

1. On Professors and Politics

(*Canadian Forum*, March, 1936.)

One of the signs of the slowness of Canada in emerging from the frontier stage of civilization is the shocked surprise with which so many worthy people regard the intrusion of university professors and students into current political discussions. Anyone who reads the history of the nineteenth century in Europe knows that there the universities have always been in the thick of politics; this, in fact, is one of the reasons why European writings on jurisprudence, history and economics have tended to be so much more vital than the parallel productions of North American scholars. But to the business men of this country universities are still very much like Dutch paintings; they are things to which you point with pride as the proof of culture, especially of its expensiveness; but they have no part in the world of practical affairs.

The intrusion of professors into politics is, as a matter of fact, an old-established British institution. And this should be pointed out repeatedly in such communities as Toronto, which are always boasting of their devotion to British precedents. At the first election to the new reformed Parliament after the Reform Bill of 1832 one of the burgesses from Cambridge was George Pryme, professor of political economy in Cambridge University. His successor, Henry Fawcett, was elected M.P. for Brighton and professor of political economy in the same year, 1863, and continued to combine both activities to the end of his life. A long list of other academic men who have played a part in public life could easily be made out — classicists like Jebb of Cambridge who sat for his university in Parliament without losing his Greek serenity, and Gilbert Murray of Oxford who would have done the same for his university had the Anglican parsons not refused to elect him; historians like Sir John Marriott and Sir Charles Oman; and a host of younger men who are active in contemporary politics. Far from being regarded as something unusual (and therefore improper), this habit of Oxford and Cambridge and London men through the past century was only one aspect of that more intimate relationship of the English universities with public life which has tended to make them schools of statesmanship rather than the breeding grounds of Ph.D.s such as our universities sometimes pride themselves on being.

Nor in times past has the spectacle of the academic man taking some part in public affairs been entirely unknown in Canada. We have yet to produce a greater university head than Principal Grant of Queen's, who during his principalship was, as his biographers remark, a sort of "consulting publicist". In the 1880s Dean Weldon of the Dalhousie Law School was a prominent Conservative member of Parliament at Ottawa. As to more recent times, Professor Stephen Leacock has just been reminding us that he and some of his McGill colleagues at the time of the Reciprocity election of 1911 were in politics "up to their necks". I am unaware of any volume of protest having been aroused by such examples.

Why then the outraged indignation of so many respectable people at the present activities of a few professors in politics? Can it be that the real offence just now consists of the fact that the professors concerned have mostly taken the radical side? . . .

The most curious reaction to the spectacle of professors in politics has been the holy scientific horror of some of their colleagues. The idea that the university is the seat of an esoteric culture which can never be shared with the multitude and that politics is only dishonest demagoguery is, of course, mostly held by intellectual snobs rather than by genuinely educated men. The university professor who conceives of himself as an aloof impartial objective scientist, living in an Olympian detachment from human passions and prejudices, seldom in these days deceives anyone but himself. It is the duty of the academic man, in so far as he aims at being scientific, to make himself aware of his own biases and predilections, of the system of values within which his thinking goes on, of his "inarticulate major premises". Any social scientist, if he is honest with himself, will acknowledge that he never quite succeeds in living up to this duty. And most of those academic Pharisees who have of late so sanctimoniously been thanking God in our learned quarterlies that they are not as other men, soon display by their own remarks that they are subject to the same weaknesses of prejudice and partisanship which they denounce in the professor-politician.

In our modern large-scale democracies party is the necessary instrument through which the process of persuading and educating the public is carried on. It is the only device that we have yet discovered through which the participation of the people in making decisions on public policy can be assured with a reasonable degree of continuity. No professor who gives advice in any form on controversial issues can avoid taking sides sometimes on matters about which parties are engaged in controversy. The professor who aligns himself with one party certainly runs the risk that his own intellectual integrity will suffer from the habit of partisanship and from the still more dangerous habit of getting involved in transitory ephemeral issues. These are serious risks. But in trying to avoid them it is not necessary to go to the other extreme and become a fussy academic old maid always in terror lest the virginal purity of one's scientific mind be exposed to indecent assault if one ventures out into the rude world.

At any rate, when he is castigated by the Brahmins of the academic world for his sins, the low caste politician-professor may comfort himself by reflecting that there are certain vices to which the Brahmins themselves are specially prone. One of these, a much more insidious danger in the long run than partisanship, is the vice of never making up your mind. We are all familiar with the professor who is so solicitous about his scientific purity that he never comes down off the fence on any issue, that he sees all sides of every question and never commits himself, delaying decision until all the facts are in, in the serene knowledge that all the facts never will be in. This kind of intellectual jugglery is not science, it is a caricature of science. The scientist reaches conclusions if his mind is not paralyzed by indecision, but he is bound to hold his conclusions as hypotheses and not as dogmas.

The other danger which confronts the intellectual integrity of the academic man is the danger of respectability. It is one to which economists in this country are especially exposed. For all Canadian economists are divided into two classes: there are, firstly, those who have already served on Royal commissions; and there are, secondly, those who are still hoping to do so. Now to serve on a Royal commission one must have achieved a reputation for respectability. But for any reader who is familiar with the inside of our Canadian universities there is no need to develop this point further.

2. A Letter
to the *Winnipeg Free Press*
on Academic Freedom

(1 August, 1934, on the Regina School Board and Mr. M. J. Coldwell.)

To the Editor, — I was shocked to read on the editorial page of the *Free Press* of July 19 an article by K.M.H. approving of the ruling of the Regina school board by which it forbids teachers to take part in political party activities. The *Free Press* has an honourable record in the consistency with which it has stood for freedom of speech in the past, and many more readers than myself must have been disturbed to find it bringing out all the old familiar sophistries to support what is in essence simply a brutal attack by one political party upon the freedom of teachers who do not happen to agree with it. For, of course, the Regina ruling, while officially that of the school board, is actually a device of the Liberal party machine in Saskatchewan to eliminate its ablest and most dangerous opponent from public life. It was the more surprising to find arguments of this kind in the *Free Press*, since of recent months it has been so busy deploring the tendency of Conservatives and Socialists to introduce into Canada a régime of authoritarian regimentation and has been holding up the Liberal party for our admiration as the last bulwark of freedom in this country.

It may be granted at once that there can be no absolute freedom to teachers or to any other group to speak and act as they please. The root fallacy of K.M.H.'s argument, however, is contained in her statement that they are under "a definite moral obligation" to their educational institutions and to their colleagues not to speak or act in an embarrassing way. The difficulty in this field, as in so many fields of human conduct, is that, while there may be an obligation, its extent and limits cannot be definitely and precisely laid down by any written rule. Surely it is a good liberal principle that prohibitions should not be put upon the freedom of teachers in their exercise of the ordinary rights of the citizen until it has been clearly proved in practice that such freedom has evil social consequences.

I have never heard of any charge that Mr. Coldwell's political activities have interfered with his efficiency in his educational work. Teachers quite properly use their spare time in many different ways. Some devote it to art or music, or amateur dramatics, some to religious work in church organizations, some to social service work, and some merely play bridge. So long as they do not use up too much energy which might more properly be devoted to their professional activities, nobody objects. Why should those who are interested in politics be singled out for prohibitions and regulations?

K.M.H. admits very handsomely that the teacher has a trained mind which may give very useful service to the community in the discussion of the social, economic and political questions perplexing our generation, and that the community will suffer if it is deprived of such a contribution. The teacher is not a civil servant engaged in administration and cannot be bound by the rules which apply to the civil servant. But, says K.M.H., if the teacher goes beyond mere discussion and engages in active political work, he is in danger of losing that impartiality and detachment which make his opinions so valuable.

It may be granted at once that such a danger does exist. But detachment by itself is not the supreme virtue, and the temptation to undue partisanship on the one side is equalled by the temptation to pure futility on the other. The besetting sin of the academic man is his tendency to achieve that extreme detachment which results in his adopting an agnostic attitude towards every issue, in balancing the pros against the cons with the skill of a juggler, in seeing all sides of every question and never committing himself to any, in delaying action until all the facts are in because he knows that all the facts never will come in, with the result that by the time that middle age is approaching his powers of action have atrophied and his social sympathies have decayed. Somewhere between these two extremes every teacher must find the satisfactory mean for himself. But, and surely this is fundamental to the liberal faith, the mean will not be attained unless the teacher is left perfectly free to attain it for himself. And in practice it is a sound liberal rule that while some may go too far to one extreme and some too far to the other, the best general social results will be obtained if each individual is put upon his own responsibility and left to the guidance of his own conscience and to that supplied by the approval or disapproval of his professional colleagues.

Furthermore, let us not exaggerate the dangers to detachment and objectivity which result from participation in political activity. In Canada it is a new phenomenon for teachers to want to take part in politics, but in England they have been accustomed to this for years. And surely no one is going to argue that the educational standard of English schools and universities is lower than our own because of the deplorable drift of English teachers into public life. Did Sir William Anson lose his objectivity as a student and teacher of English constitutional law because he became Conservative member for the University of Oxford and played a leading rôle in the exciting debates on constitutional questions which marked English politics in the early years of this century? Did Sir Richard Jebb lose the serenity and detachment which belong to the great Greek scholar by becoming Conservative member for Cambridge? Or, in our own day, did Sir Charles Oman cease to be a reliable historian because he sat as Conservative member for Oxford? Or has Professor Gilbert Murray become any the less the greatest Greek scholar in the English-speaking world because of his frequent (if unsuccessful) efforts to be elected as a radical representative of Oxford?

Moreover, detachment, while it is valuable, is not the only virtue of the teacher. What makes a great teacher is vitality, and the secret of vitality is not yet discovered. But surely it is worth remarking that in the field of social science today much of the most vital teaching and thinking is being done precisely by those men who are most immersed in current controversial and political activity. In England, for example, if one were asked to name the university men in the studies of political science and government who are doing the most creative thinking and having the most vital influence upon their students, one would naturally think first of such men as Laski, Cole and Tawney, who are notoriously very active in the Labour party.

These men, also, it should be observed, serve in universities which are now dependent upon public funds just as our Canadian educational institutions are. For the universities of Oxford and London get from 20 to 30 per cent of their revenue today from the public treasury.

If English experience has proven that it is possible for teachers to take part in politics (and I have only named a few outstanding cases) without particular damage to the teachers or to education in general, and perhaps with some important positive benefits, should we not beware in Canada of restricting their liberty upon hypothetical grounds? Surely, at any rate, all liberals should adopt the attitude of tolerance until it has been clearly proven by experience that the Canadian teacher cannot preserve his virtue except in a cloistered seclusion.

We live today in a generation in which great decisions have to be made. All the values of our civilization are being questioned. It is difficult to determine what is the true function of education in relation to society at large in an age, such as ours, in which society is passing through a painful process of transition from one era to another. Educationists themselves differ strongly on this matter. But every teacher who is worth his salt is in indignant revolt against the way in which the best efforts of the school are so often frustrated by the other social institutions which surround the school. If some teachers feel themselves driven into politics in order to change those social institutions surely it is not the part of Liberals to order them back into the school-room or to refuse them the opportunity of trying to carry their ideas into practice. The very urge which sends them into politics is their passion for a more effective educational system.

The mere right of free discussion by itself is not enough. Discussion in a democratic community is the necessary preliminary to action. But if discussion does lead to organized action by the democratic community, that action takes place through political parties. It is parties in the end which put legislation upon the statute book. If you deny to teachers, or to any other group of citizens, the right of taking part in political party activity you are, in the long run, effectively denying them the right of free discussion.

FRANK H. UNDERHILL

Toronto

3. W. L. Mackenzie King

a. The Close of an Era: Twenty-five Years of Mr. Mackenzie King

(*Canadian Forum,* September, 1944.)

On August 7, 1919, Mr. Mackenzie King was chosen by his party, in convention assembled, as their national leader. A few months previously, in November, 1918, his book, *Industry and Humanity*, had been published. And now, in August, 1944, party and leader have been celebrating twenty-five years of successful leadership. It is foolish for critics to deny the success, or to refuse to admit that it must have been due to some great qualities in the leader. They only show their own pettiness and bad temper when they act in this way. But we all find it hard not to snort when Mr. King himself claims that the success was based upon the great principles laid down in *Industry and Humanity* and worked out in practice through the great policies of the platform of 1919. Let us pause over this claim for a little while.

Mr. King came to the leadership because of his supposed expert knowledge about questions of industry and labour. He had been deputy minister and then minister of labour before 1911. These were the questions that formed the subject of his famous book. Yet it is clear that it is in this field that he has been the greatest failure. His government is detested by organized labour. His book was full of noble sentences about the need for industry becoming a partnership between capital, management, labour and the community; but his practical application of these lofty principles at the time was to organize a company union for the Rockefellers in their Colorado mines. And since he came back to Canada, what has he done in his eighteen years of prime ministership to bring closer the day when industry shall be worked by a constitutional system instead of by the centralized irresponsible despotism to which he was so verbally opposed in his book?

In his book and in many of his speeches Mr. King pats himself on the back for two of his pre-1914 legislative achievements, the Indus-

114

trial Disputes Investigation Act and the Combines Investigation Act. They have not been useless, but how little have they accomplished in dealing with labour disputes and with concentration of control in modern mass industry! When we look around at the monopolies and near-monopolies in Canada which dominate so much of our economy, the Combines Act resembles nothing so much as the bleating of a pathetic vegetarian lamb in the midst of a carnivorous jungle. That is just it. Mr. King never quite got it into his head during his economic studies at Toronto and Harvard that our civilization is dominated by carnivorous animals. He was meant to be a professor safe in the study, not a statesman out in the jungle. For sooner or later the statesman must clear out the jungle and make it habitable.

Next to labour and industrial questions, Mr. King prides himself on his early interest in the social services. As usual, he can quote passages from his book. And the Liberal convention of 1919 committed itself to a very modern social service structure, "that in so far as may be practicable, having regard to Canada's financial position (note that they say 'financial position' and not 'federal constitution'), an adequate system of insurance against unemployment, sickness, dependence in old age, and other disability, which would include old age pensions, widows' pensions, and maternity benefits, should be instituted by the federal government in conjunction with the governments of the several provinces." What is his record on these promises, which, like all the sections of the 1919 platform on labour and industrial questions, were drafted by Mr. King himself? Old age pensions were instituted in 1927 under pressure from Mr. Woodsworth at a time when Mr. King very badly needed the votes of the western Progressives. And that is all he did until 1940. It was Mr. Bennett who brought in unemployment insurance in 1935 and so forced the issue on that question.

Why this strange inaction on Mr. King's part during all these years? His apologists say that he could not act in advance of public opinion or the opinion of Parliament. How did he know that he was in advance of opinion? When did he ever introduce any resolutions to test opinion? What campaign did he ever start to educate opinion on the need for social services or for more progressive labour legislation?

And even if public opinion on social questions was very backward, has a leader who professes certain principles never any duty to risk his career for those principles? We judge from the admiring pages of the *Winnipeg Free Press* that Mr. King, having waited patiently for twenty years until Canadian opinion caught up with him, is now hastening to make up for lost time. The *Free Press* would rather like us to share its admiration for this inspiring spectacle of the elderly statesman now at last on the road to realize the dreams of his youth. No doubt Mr. King himself, when he sits down to write his memoirs in the exile to which the electorate will shortly retire him, will tell us, using Napoleon's apologia, that he asked for thirty years and destiny gave him only twenty-five.

It is the same story in the field of constitutional reform. For years everyone acquainted with our Canadian problems has known that we cannot get forward unless we revise the relations of federal and provincial authorities. What lead has Mr. King ever given in this direction during the eighteen years he has been in a position of responsibility? The only constitutional question on which he ever showed any personal interest was reform of the Senate. That was away back in the election of 1925, when he had a strong Tory majority in the Senate against him. Once enough Tories had died to enable him to appoint a Liberal majority, his interest in Senate reform died also. He did, it is true, in more recent years appoint the Rowell-Sirois Commission, which gave a thorough examination to our federal system; but he allowed the whole of its work to be wasted because he wasn't willing to take the lead against the Hepburn gang. And all through these twenty years his government has steadily used the constitutional difficulty as an excuse for not getting on with the social and labour reforms in which the author of *Industry and Humanity* was supposed to be specially interested. Can we be blamed for snorting when we read about the patience of the great Liberal leader?

The 1919 platform contained one plank in which Mr. King has certainly seemed to be interested: "Resolved, that we are strongly opposed to centralized Imperial control." He has won famous victories in this field and completed the work of Laurier before him. Yet as time goes on the purpose of these struggles becomes less and less clear. We are approaching the day when the inevitable little girl will ask her grandsire what they fought each other for, and he will only be able to assure her that at least it was a famous victory. For under Mr. King we have followed the British lead in all essentials. If we had been really pursuing an autonomous Canadian policy we should have had to make up our own minds about conditions in Europe and in the world at large; but we have been content to look out on the world through British spectacles, and to accept the commitments which British statesmen make for us. The British deal with events when they are still in fluid form; we never touch them until they have hardened into a form in which only one course of action is possible. So Mr. King applauded British statesmanship at Munich, followed it into the war, and is following it today in the decisions it makes about the future of Europe and Asia. . . .

If the ritualistic fools like Lord Halifax had only sense enough to see that, though Mr. King doesn't go in for the bowing and the censer-swinging of their particular form of worship, still he is a good reverent member of the Imperial church, they would keep their mouths shut and leave him to act in his own way. Fortunately, perhaps, their Laudian determination to realize the beauty of holiness in their own day drives them to persistent attempts towards uniformity. And the quarrels among the faithful bring joy to the ungodly.

To discuss all these topics, however, is not to explain Mr. King's long success in Canadian public life. Part of this, a great part of it, has been due to his luck in the opponents he has had to meet. He has towered up like a mountain in the House of Commons because of the flatness of the landscape opposite him.

Just consider the list of Conservative leaders in his day. First, there was Meighen, the lean and hungry Cassius, the bitter fanatic who lost votes all across the country every time he won a debate in the House. In 1926 he had Mr. King at his mercy on the customs scandal, and he threw away his chance completely. If Mr. King had been caught out then, we should only remember him as a rather colourless and ineffective party leader who wrote an unreadable book and got involved in a malodorous scandal. But Meighen muffed an easy catch, and King went on to bat up a century.

Then there was the preposterous Bennett of the booming voice and the beetling brows, the lord of the iron heel. Mr. King had only to sit back quietly in opposition for five years and let Bennett hang himself. Then there was the lightweight Manion, followed quickly by the old muzzle-loading blunderbuss from New Brunswick. And now, just when Mr. Bracken was beginning to make Mr. King nervous by never committing himself to anything except pious abstract platitudes such as might have come from the author of *Industry and Humanity* himself, and just when the strains of a long war seemed to make it certain that even a government of archangels could not survive the next election, along come the two

Georges from Toronto.[1] They have equipped themselves with a battle-cry that is sure to turn everyone outside Ontario against them; and Mr. King must be beginning to think that once again his old ally, Providence, is on his side.

There are two ultimate reasons for Mr. King's long success in Canadian politics. They both rest upon marked characteristics of our Canadian community. One is our Canadian preference, in spite of the clearness of our physical climate, for living constantly in an atmosphere of mental haze. We never make issues clear to ourselves. We never define our differences so that they can be understood clearly or reconciled. Our Fathers of Confederation created a Dominion of Canada without ensuring that there should be any clear understanding of the respective limits of federal and provincial jurisdiction. Contrast the way, moreover, in which Confederation was put across in 1867, in the midst of a vague general feeling that it was a good thing, with the vehement discussion which took place among the Americans when they decided upon their federal constitution, and which produced some of the imperishable classics of political science. The Americans make every issue clear in this way. That is why their politics seems to us so noisy and violent. We prefer to leave issues undefined, with an assumption that all right-thinking people would agree about them if ever they were defined. And the public man who devotes his life to seeking clear definitions, like Mr. Bourassa for instance, is regarded by most Canadians as an unmitigated nuisance. Mr. King is obviously the most complete personification of this national Canadian characteristic who has ever appeared in our public life.

... The other main reason for Mr. King's long predominance is Canadian disunity. We have never been in any deep sense a united people. We have not yet overcome the difficulties of geography, and we are as far from reconciling the differences of race as we were a hundred years ago. If Mr. King had not been the high-souled idealist, which we must believe he is on his own story, but simply a low, cunning politician basing his actions upon day-to-day calculations of expediency, he would have acted throughout his career exactly as in fact he has acted. For the politician who knows that he governs a community that is really only a loosely bound aggregation of rival sectional communities, carries on by balancing one

---

[1] Messrs. Drew and McCullagh.

pressure-group against another, making new balances every morning, and going to bed every night with a pattern in his mind of still newer balances to be tried out tomorrow morning. This work never ends, and it is eternally fascinating; and Mr. King has been immensely more skilful at it than any of his contemporaries.

So historians of the future will look back to a King era just as present-day historians look back to a Macdonald and a Laurier era. But Macdonald and Laurier tried to do something more than merely balance section precariously against section. They tried to give Canada a national policy which would bind the country together into a really national unity. Macdonald by his geographical expansion, his railway building and his "national" tariff; Laurier by his railway building again, and his immigration, leading up to the great wheat boom; both were trying to hold certain national purposes before the Canadian people in which all could join, and in the achievement of which they could sink their differences. Mr. King in the 1920s and 1930s found no such nation-building policy. He contented himself with the day-to-day work of seeking balances among sectional interests. But the experience of those two unhappy decades has shown that we cannot afford so negative and unconstructive a policy as this. We must again set out on the hard road which Macdonald and Laurier first surveyed, and try to find a new national policy which will bind us all together as Canadians. Mr. King is not the leader for this enterprise, and the King era is coming to a close.

b. Twenty-five Years as Prime Minister

(*Canadian Forum*, July, 1946.)

In August, 1919, Mr. Mackenzie King was chosen national leader of the Liberal party; and in August, 1944, he and his party celebrated twenty-five years of successful leadership. Now he is celebrating either the beginning or the end of his twentieth year in office as prime minister — we forget which. He has, it seems, held the office of prime minister longer than any other prime minister in the history of the British Empire, except Walpole. Will the next celebration come when he sings his *Nunc Dimittis*, or is there some other record at which he is aiming? In the September, 1944, issue of the *Canadian Forum* we had an editorial on his twenty-five years of leadership; and reading it again today, we cannot see that much needs to be unsaid or much to be added to it. But we must confess that we hate to recall how often in our editorial wisdom we have discerned the inevitable course of events as bringing to an end the King era in Canadian history, and how regularly we have been premature in our predictions. Evidently Mr. King meets the needs of the Canadian people much more satisfactorily than we and other critics have been willing in the past to admit. So we may as well frankly admit that fact now.

Mr. King is our most completely typical Canadian. Obviously, from the respectful attention which he receives when he speaks for us abroad — in London, Washington, San Francisco, Geneva, and elsewhere — the Canadian qualities which are summed up in his character do meet with considerable approval from the peoples of the world with whom we have business to transact. There is some solid worth in them. And we should be willing to pay cordial tribute to him for this fact.

But at the same time it must be said that Mr. King has been prime minister for so long because he has been able without much effort to take advantage of the fundamental pattern in which the Canadian people vote. This is a pattern of which most Canadians seem blissfully unaware. Yet the remarkable thing is that it repeats itself generation after generation. Broadly speaking, it is that the other provinces combine against Ontario. Compared with this unvarying instinctive habit in our national politics, the differences in our history between the so-called Liberals and the so-called Conservatives have been superficial. Even the differences between English and French accommodate themselves to this pattern.

After 1867 Macdonald kept himself in power pretty steadily by getting a majority from Quebec assisted by majorities in the smaller outlying provinces. The Grits, recovering from their unexpected defeat in 1867, soon gained control of the premier province and kept it until after the turn of the century. But to their dismay and indignation they could never collect enough votes elsewhere to unseat Macdonald, save on the extraordinary occasion of the Pacific Scandal in 1873–4. It is amusing today to read their denunciations of the way in which Macdonald spent federal funds to bribe the other provinces, in subsidies, railways, public works, etc.; and especially to read their outcries at the way in which he made a milch cow of Ontario for the benefit of the rest of the country. Though they know it not, Messrs. Hepburn and Drew in our own day have been repeating exactly the same cries against Mr. King; the only difference is in the inelegant twentieth-century language through which they give expression to their agony.

An even more striking parallel between the Macdonald and the King eras can be traced in the behaviour of the Ontario electorate itself. In the 1870s and 1880s and early 1890s many a good Ontario citizen would vote Grit in provincial politics, and then, appalled at the thought of Grit domination of the whole of Canada, he would turn round and help re-elect Macdonald in federal politics. Just so today. Thousands of Ontario voters last summer, after putting Mr. Drew into office, turned round within a week and helped the rest of Canada to make sure that Ontario Tories should not dominate the Dominion.

When Laurier came into office in 1896 this fundamental pattern soon began to reassert itself, though with the parties reversing the rôles that they had played in the Macdonald period. By 1900 Laurier had lost the Liberal hold on Ontario but had solidified himself in Quebec; and he kept himself in power henceforth by combining Quebec with the Maritimes and the West against Ontario. Mr. King has merely taken over this pattern from the Laurier period.

The remarkable thing about this pattern of voting is, of course, that the supposed English-Canadian dislike of Quebec does not express itself in the ballot-boxes save in Ontario. The other provinces always in the end seem to come round to voting with Quebec. It is not French domination that they instinctively fear, it is Toronto domination. Their actions speak more loudly than their words. The 1917 election was an exception to this rule; in that year Ontario for once found an issue on which the rest of Canada agreed with it. But the *damnosa hereditas* of Ontario favour has kept the Conservatives out of office almost continuously ever since. If Mr. King wants to stay in politics, as far as we can see, there is nothing to prevent him from doing so indefinitely. The two gorgeous Georges are comparatively young men, full of the zest of life. As long as the Drew-McCullagh combination dominates Ontario Mr. King is assured of office at Ottawa.

One little point is worth noting in this connection. It has often been made an occasion for sneering against Mr. King that he could not hold a seat in his own province, and this has been said to prove his weakness as a public man. On the contrary, the fact that he had to seek election in Prince Albert was a symbolical expression of the most important factor in his strength. He came unto his own, and his own received him not. His great appeal to the rest of Canada was precisely that he was rejected in Ontario. This was part of Macdonald's strength also. If Mr. King is the far-seeing man that we think he is, he will look for a nomination out in the West or down in the Maritimes before the next election comes on.

Mr. King has been lucky in another respect also. All over the western world the advance of industrialism has resulted in the crushing out of the nineteenth-century middle-class Liberal parties between the old Conservatism on the one side and the new proletarian working-class movements on the other. Only in North America do these nineteenth-century Liberal parties (called Liberal in Canada and Democratic in the United States) survive and still manage to collect votes from all groups in the nation, including industrial workers as well as farmers. And in the United States this middle-class Liberalism came through the crisis of the 1930s in the control of an effective political party only by adopting the New Deal. In Canada there was no New Deal during the depression, and the C.C.F. came into being. But it is remarkable that the Canadian C.C.F. has yet to win the successes which have come to similar labour movements in Great Britain, Australia, New Zealand, and to social-democratic parties all over western Europe. What is there about our Canadian make-up that explains this strange phenomenon? What is it that causes most Canadians to be surprised and slightly indignant when they are told that this is a strange phenomenon in the modern world? What is it that makes government by a party completely dominated by big business and viciously anti-labour in its practical policies so continuously acceptable to the Canadian public, and so successful in its pose of benevolent liberalism (with a small "l")?

In North America, since we have no feudal conservatism to contend with as in Europe, the essence of liberalism should be that it is a protest against the domination of social institutions and ideas by the business man. Such protests are likely to come primarily from two social groups, the farmers and the industrial workers. An effective liberal movement will combine both these groups with sympathizers from among the urban intellectuals. This has been shown most recently by the experience of the Roosevelt New Deal party in the United States. The leadership of such a party will be execrated by the business men, their wives and their kept editors — as was the late President Roosevelt. Before this recent Roosevelt era the United States went through the same experience under President Wilson; and the tradition goes back to Jacksonian Democracy. We have nothing similar to that in our Canadian history.

If we search back into our history, we find that the reason for this is that the first great liberal democratic upheaval in nineteenth-century Canada, the movement of Papineau in Lower Canada and of Mackenzie in Upper Canada, the movement which was our Canadian version of Jacksonian Democracy, was a failure. Ultimately, the reason why William Lyon Mackenzie King has been our highly respectable prime minister for twenty years is that the anything-but-respectable William Lyon Mackenzie was beaten in 1837.

c. Liberalism à la King

(*Canadian Forum*, February, 1948.)

One of the pleasant things about our country at the present moment is that we have a prime minister who is also an author. This affords the final proof that we have achieved complete equality of status with Britain. The intellectual level of our Canadian politics would be considerably higher if we had a nucleus of leading politicians, such as Britain has always enjoyed, who find time to write books on politics or economics or history. What gives the British Labour party its easy superiority over the Tories is that the Labour cabinet is full of authors, whereas the opposition can only boast of one, even if he is a big one. But it must be said that this particular book[1] of Mr. King's does little to raise the intellectual standards of our public life.

Mr. King first published his *Industry and Humanity* in 1918 when he was not an active politician. In its original edition, with a large equipment of footnotes, it showed that he had been a genuine student of labour problems and was conversant with all the current discussion of the subject by experts in Britain and America. Even so, the book that emerged from his studies was mostly a collection

---

[1] *Industry and Humanity*: The Right Honorable W. L. Mackenzie King; Macmillan; pp. xxix, 270; $4.00.

of uplifting abstract moral platitudes; and it stood in striking contrast with a work such as that on *Industrial Democracy* by the
Sidney Webbs which got down to concrete cases and discussed
practical problems in a practical way.

The original *Industry and Humanity*, however, did devote a good
deal of space to particular illustrations of the general principles
which the author thought so important. There was a long account
of how he had himself applied his principles to the Colorado Fuel
and Iron Company. There were discussions of the Whitley Coun-
cils in Great Britain, of schemes of "scientific management",
"profit-sharing" and "co-partnership" in industry. And there was
a very optimistic explanation of the workings of the Industrial
Disputes Investigation Act. All these sections have been deleted
from the present revision or drastically reduced. Is Mr. King no
longer proud of what he accomplished in Colorado, which was
denounced at the time by labour as an application of the company-
union technique? Why doesn't he tell us more of the constitutional
difficulties which his Industrial Disputes Investigation Act en-
countered, and which makes it appear much less significant now
than it did in 1918?

What is left is a series of sermons on the so-called Law of Peace,
Work and Health which Mr. King derived from a somewhat
rhetorical passage of Pasteur. (According to press despatches he
made a point of visiting Pasteur's grave again on his recent European trip.) That capital, labour, management and the community
are all partners in industry is an admirable starting-point for a
series of sermons; but like most sermons, Mr. King's never commit
the preacher to anything much beyond abstract general principles.
It is difficult to understand why a book of this kind can have gone
through so many editions, unless it is widely collected by parsons as
a source for sermon material on the labour question. Almost any
of its chapters could be delivered verbatim most acceptably any
Sunday morning from any Protestant pulpit. And like that too,
too famous sermon on sin, these sermons also would leave their
audience uncertain about most points except that the parson was
against sin.

Perhaps remarks of this kind should be put down simply to
the unreasonable bad temper of the reviewer. For the book has
undoubtedly found a certain considerable market over the past
twenty-five or thirty years. But a reviewer of a book by a prime
minister is bound to raise another point. Since the first edition of

this book was published Mr. King has been in office for some twenty years; he was chosen in 1919 as the Liberal leader partly because of his expert knowledge of labour questions. What has he done since then to apply these noble principles in action? . . . Where is the Canadian Wagner Act? Of course, constitutional difficulties under the B.N.A. Act have been in the way. But what effective initiative has Mr. King's government ever taken to awaken Canadian public opinion or to get Canadian public men to face up to these constitutional difficulties and to do something about them?

Mr. King makes an admirable point in his book that the solution of industrial relations depends upon the same principles as the solution of international relations. The whole thesis of the book is that in both fields we must strive constantly to substitute reason for force. Now every Liberal will agree that a healthy society is one in which reason plays an ever-increasing part and force an ever-decreasing part. But realistic Liberals know that there will always remain some element of force as long as human beings are the imperfect creatures that they are. Labour leaders have always known by instinct that this beautiful liberal process of round-table discussion is not likely to yield them much fruit until they come to the round table with as much effective power in their hands as is possessed by the employers; and so they have set to work to make their unions as strong as possible. Collective bargaining has become a standard process not merely because of appeals to sweet reasonableness but because the labour bargainers now have power in their hands as well as the employers. And in all the bargaining and discussion by which social decisions are made, this element of power, of force, of coercion, is never very far in the background. The liberalism which abhors power politics so thoroughly that it spends its time dreaming (or writing books) of a world from which power will have been eliminated is a liberalism fit only for Sunday sermons.

In the international field in our day this element of power and force has been even more evident than in the field of industrial relations. And Mr. King has gone through what should have been an enlightening experience in this international field since he wrote his book in 1918. It was all very well then to talk nobly about substituting reason for force in human relations. We were all naïvely optimistic about the League of Nations in those days, and everybody in North America was going to abolish the Balance of Power by joining the League or by going into isolation. But since then Mr. King has led his people into a second world war. And today, as the prospects grow dimmer of getting a second international round table that will work, Mr. King's Minister of External Affairs and his responsible officials have been hinting broadly that Canada is prepared to join a closer mutual-security organization within the United Nations, the members of which would pool their national military forces for common protection. This does not mean abolishing force but using it in a more effective way.

In international relations since September, 1939, Mr. King's actions as a responsible statesman (for most of which this reviewer has the highest admiration) bear little relation to the naive Utopian liberalism of *Industry and Humanity*. He has been quite prepared to use force when necessary. In industrial relations, since he was chosen leader on the far-reaching platform of 1919, his activities have been mainly negative. He has not extended even the limited participation of the Community in the "Partnership of Industry", which was achieved in his early Industrial Disputes Investigation Act, to the bulk of Canadian industry. As for social legislation, after twenty years in office his government still has a considerable part of the platform of 1919 to carry out, and most of the legislation it has passed has resulted from the lead given by Mr. Woodsworth or Mr. Bennett. When a politician's literary performance diverges so widely from his practical achievement one is compelled to revise one's first thoughts and to doubt whether Canadian politicians should go in for authorship at all.

d. The End of the King Era

(Canadian Forum, August, 1948.)

Political historians of the future will refer to the last twenty-five years as the King era, just as we now speak of the Macdonald and Laurier eras. And as time goes on, they will point more and more to features in the statesmanship of Mr. King that resemble the statesmanship of the two earlier national leaders. The essential task of Canadian statesmanship is to discover the terms on which as many as possible of the significant interest-groups of our country can be induced to work together in a common policy. It is to make them conscious of what they have in common rather than of what divides them. No one can deny, now that he is retiring, that

Mr. King has been the only political leader of the last generation who has understood in its full implications the nature of this, the fundamental responsibility of Canadian leadership. So he will go down in our history in the select company of Macdonald and Laurier, while his contemporaries and rivals fall back into the comparative obscurity of sectionalists and particularists.

In the long run of history it will not matter much that he never won the passionate personal devotion of his followers and associates, as Macdonald and Laurier did of theirs. Whatever they may have said of him individually, when they tried to give articulate expression to their feelings, the majority of the Canadian people have instinctively recognized that Mr. King is the leader who divides us least, and they have voted accordingly.

This seems to be the furthest point of growth that the Canadian national spirit was capable of reaching in our day. At such a phase in its history nationalism is not a very exhilarating phenomenon. Canadians who demand more stirring emotions in their politics have attached themselves to other isms. But since a united nation of some sort is the necessary framework within which all these other isms must be realized, we have all of us, however qualified our enthusiasm, acquiesced more or less willingly in the fact that Mr. King for twenty-five years should be at the head of His Majesty's Government. His statesmanship has been a more subtly accurate, a more flexibly adjustable Gallup poll of Canadian public opinion than statisticians will ever be able to devise. He has been the representative Canadian, the typical Canadian, the essential Canadian, the ideal Canadian, the Canadian as he exists in the mind of God.

Two specific achievements will always be associated with Mr. King's name. He brought us out of Dominion Status, the half-way house in which Laurier and Borden had left us; and we face the 1950s as an independent nation, making our own policy, prepared to undertake the responsibilities of an adult people in world politics. He carried us through the strain of a second world war without precipitating an irreconcilable split between French and English Canadians; he avoided the kind of mistakes which, repeated in the 1940s, would have had more fatal consequences than they had in 1917.

Laurier defeated the earlier efforts of British imperialists to construct a British Empire holding-company with a single foreign policy directed from London. Mr. King's long period of office has given him the opportunity of leading us to the goal towards which

Laurier's policy pointed, of an independent Canada within a British Commonwealth which is no longer an exclusive association, which has no central organs for making military or economic policy, and which tends more and more to merge itself into the larger more comprehensive Atlantic Community that is developing under our eyes. Mr. King has always been aware that no form of international organization could meet Canada's needs in which the United States is not a full partner. In peace and in war he has remained firm in this understanding of the realities of our situation. And now today this Atlantic Community under American leadership provides the solution for the difficulties of both the older British Commonwealth and the newer West European Union.

Canada has been able to play a significant part in these recent developments because during the King era we have been gradually equipped with a well-staffed Department of External Affairs. We can now participate in the hard day-to-day practice of international diplomacy. Before we had a diplomatic service of our own, most of the talk of the Laurier and Borden days about our equality of status with Britain was largely in the nature of rhetorical flourish. We have not solved all our practical problems by any means. Evidently there are elements in the British Foreign Office who still labour under the delusion that it is the function of Downing Street to provide the policy and the function of Canada to provide the transport planes; and there are still a few colonial Canadians who agree with them. But these are mere vestigial survivals.

Also it should be remarked that the usefulness of Mr. King's clear-cut conception of the nature of the British Commonwealth has been weakened in recent years by his going soft over the Monarchy, at the very time when the Commonwealth is expanding to include members such as India and Pakistan for whom the Monarchy will never mean what it means to us sentimental Canadians.

However, his essential achievement remains. He has led us irrevocably past the stage at which it was possible to think of Canada as a junior partner in some Britannic firm. And he has assisted us to some of his own understanding that neither Canada nor Britain can get along in the twentieth-century world except in close cooperation with the United States. His successors will still have plenty to do in emancipating us from our inherited anti-American phobias. One of Mr. King's incidental successes is that he has brought us through a couple of decades without an outbreak of the fever of 1891 and 1911. If we can get through another twenty or thirty years without some impassioned patriots winning a general election by saving us from the United States, this will afford the ultimate proof that we have at last grown up.

One of the fashionable criticisms in academic circles of Mr. King's external policy is that it was isolationist in the 1920s and 1930s, and therefore adolescent and irresponsible. This is to miss the essential conditions under which Canadian policy is carried on. In the inter-war decades we were isolationist in the same way that Great Britain and the United States were. We refused commitments in a collective-security system just as they did. At present we have committed ourselves to far-reaching actions in world politics just as the British and American peoples have done. If the world comes to show signs of a little more stability, the Canadian people, like the British and Americans, will become more absorbed in their own local concerns. In whatever direction we move, it will be along lines already being traced out by British and American policy.

To keep French and English in Canada working together has been the basis of Mr. King's policy, both in external and in domestic affairs, as it must be the basis of the policy of every responsible-minded statesman. The division between these two communities is the deepest division in our national life.

Now, the classical institutional procedure by which French-English co-operation has been achieved in Canadian history has been that of a national political party. For the decade before Confederation and for two decades after Confederation Macdonald worked through the Liberal-Conservative party. Laurier succeeded him, after a transitional period of bitterness and confusion, with the Liberal party till 1911. The ten years from 1911 to 1921 form a unique period in our history when an attempt was made to govern Canada without the effective co-operation of Quebec. Mr. King's life has been devoted to the restoration of a working national harmony of the two racial communities through a revived Liberal party. He has had to face conditions that did not confront Macdonald and Laurier, and he cannot be said to have been as successful as they were. When he goes, the Liberal party which he reconstructed after 1919 will probably disintegrate.

Out of the confusion of political groups in the 1950s, who will be the statesman to construct another national party capable of government, as Macdonald did one hundred years ago in the 1850s?

This is the great question that faces Canadian politics at the end of the King era.

The essence of a national party which is capable of government in Canada is that it should have a substantial following from all the main groups and sections of the country — geographical, racial, religious, and economic — and especially that it should unite enough of the French and the English within its ranks to make possible a stable and continuous administration of the country for a decade or a generation. In the past it has always had an opposition party striving with it which was also potentially national in the comprehensiveness of its appeal and which was always threatening to win away from the governing party a sufficient number of interest-groups to supplant it in office. . . .

If our political history means anything for the future, there are apparently two conditions that cannot be established for any length of time in Canadian politics. One is a union of the English-speaking provinces under the leadership of Ontario, with Quebec in opposition. At least it is to be assumed that a long time will pass before any politicians will be so stupid as to try over again the experiment which the Conservative party tried during the first world war and from which it has never recovered. The other is a political union of Ontario and Quebec to dominate and exploit the rest of the country. But we have always enjoyed some relief from this by the fact that the voters of Ontario and Quebec cannot be induced for any long period to support the same federal political party.

Mr. King has ruled, to a greater extent than either of his two great predecessors, by depending upon an overwhelming majority of seats from Quebec, with enough support from the outlying English-speaking provinces, so that he has not had to worry much over the slings and arrows of outrageous fortune directed against him from Ontario. But, like Laurier in his later years, he has had to worry about a violent French nationalist movement in Quebec. If his successor can overcome this nationalist particularism by holding Quebec federally within the Liberal fold, then it may be premature to speak of the end of the King era. But I should guess that, as we approach the 1950s, we are on the eve of a radical up-heaval in Canadian politics such as marked the 1850s, with Quebec shifting her political allegiance, with new movements more alarming to the orthodox than ever were the Rouges and the Grits of the 1850s, and with a new pattern of political groupings emerging which will make many of the successful King techniques look very old-fashioned.

Two great developments in Canadian democracy have occurred during the King era. To them Mr. King contributed nothing whatever. So far he has managed to deal with their political repercussions rather successfully, but they will confront his successor in far more serious form. These are the growth of co-operative movements among the farmers, especially among the prairie wheat-farmers, and the growth of trade unionism among the industrial workers of the urban centres. Mr. King's first problem when he became prime minister was to meet the challenge of the agrarian uprising which in 1921 sent 65 Progressives to Ottawa to a House of a total membership of 235. The Progressive movement was confused in its political philosophy and weak in its political organization. By the end of the 1920s Mr. King had successfully headed it off, and he was leading a revived Liberal party which had absorbed most of the Progressive rebels on the Prairie and in Ontario. Yet the co-operative movement among the farmers, of which Progressivism was the first political manifestation, went on and has continued to grow despite this political set-back. And the 1930 funeral service over the Progressives had barely been performed (Mr. Bennett assisting Mr. King at the rites) when a new movement, the C.C.F., emerged from the same discontented farm areas, reinforced this time by support from some politically alert trade unionists and a growing body of white-collar middle-class people. Mr. King has never really solved the problem of the C.C.F.

Mr. King's type of Liberalism is not so well fitted for dealing with these new twentieth-century emanations of Canadian democracy as it was for dealing with the old sectional and racial issues for which Macdonald and Laurier had worked out such efficient political machinery. Nor has Mr. St. Laurent ever so far shown any understanding of the political problems presented by organized labour and organized agriculture, by the demands which face the modern state from all sides for economic planning to guarantee an equitable standard of living to all members of the community. The party, in any case, will not be allowed 27 years to carry out the social planks of the platform of 1948, as Mr. King's party was allowed 27 years, from 1921 to 1948, to carry out some of the planks of 1919. The pattern of Canadian democracy has been changing in the meantime, and new politically conscious groups are pressing for their interests with a new urgency.

The great charge which the history books of the future will make against Mr. King's statesmanship will be that he did practically nothing to adjust his Liberal party to this new emerging situation. Macdonald and Laurier could keep the country reasonably well united on a national policy which consisted of railway-building, tariffs, and immigration, and which offered expanding opportunities to all the social groups that mattered in those days. The weakness of Mr. King is that he has presented to the country no such positive, constructive, nation-building policy for our days. He has sat at Ottawa skilfully measuring the strength of the various competing group-interests and skilfully keeping the balance among them, but that is all. Liberalism in his day has not meant any concrete positive programme which could stir the enthusiasm of the young and the energetic. He has done nothing whatever to educate his party or the public to the new functions of the social-service welfare state. His party has no resemblance to the Labour party in Britain or the Rooseveltian New Deal party in the United States. And as the party arteries have hardened with age, Liberal spokesmen have become increasingly apprehensive about the dangers of socialism. A Liberalism whose chief mark is fear and timidity has no future.

What makes these sins of omission on Mr. King's part the more reprehensible is the fact that he was offered in the 1930s, by some of the leading Liberal intellectuals, the outline of a new flexible pragmatic liberalism that might have headed off a socialist movement. The late Norman Rogers, in his presentation on the Fiscal Disabilities of Nova Scotia in 1934, began to speak a new language about planning our economy so that all sections of the Dominion might benefit more evenly from the national effort. He pointed out that the protective tariff as adopted at the end of the 1870s was only the first step in a programme of national planning which needed to be carried further. The experts of the Rowell-Sirois Commission gave a detailed blueprint of the kind of federal governmental structure which was needed to bring Confederation up to date. A Roosevelt would have taken up such ideas and presented them in a dramatic, dynamic appeal to the people. All that Mr. King did was to get into an interminable controversy with provincial demagogues, a controversy in which the case of the federal Liberal government has never been presented with any force or conviction by Mr. King or any of his present lieutenants.

Everything is fluid now in Canadian politics as the King era comes to an end, and the whole situation is uncertain as it has not been since 1921. The writer who commits himself to predictions about the party which will emerge in the 1950s to fill the rôle that the Macdonald, Laurier, and King parties have filled for the last century, is likely to reveal more about his own preferences than about anything else. The essential task of the national leader remains what it has always been, to discover the terms on which as many as possible of the significant interest-groups of our country can be induced to work together in a common policy. Today the task is much more difficult than it used to be, because there are more interest-groups conscious of their own particular interests and organized to protect them. The Prairie and the Pacific and the Atlantic sections are no longer willing to let Ontario and Quebec get such large slices of the national pie. Farmers are organized to look after their production and marketing interests, trade unionists are organized to secure their place in the industrial sun.

This means that the public discussion of social and economic questions will probably be a good deal more bitter than it has been in the past, when the dominant business group could always count on getting pretty much what it wanted. But it also means that for the first time there is a real chance for a combination of the anti-big-business groups coming into power in Canada, as they first did in the United States under Jackson in the days of Mr. King's grand-father, and as they have recently done in Britain in the form of a Labour government. If this should happen, it would be a develop-ment in Canadian democracy that would very definitely mark the end of the King era.

e. Concerning Mr. King

(*Canadian Forum*, September, 1950.)

Now that he is dead the unpleasant and the abusive things that we all said about him sound rather mean and cheap. And it must be confessed that the *Canadian Forum*, in editorials and signed articles, from the moment that the first King government was elected in 1921 right down to 1948, has as unbroken a record as any Canadian journal of continuous hostile criticism of Mr. King's personality and politics. The significant fact, however — and we should all be reflecting upon this now — is that he defeated all his critics. He defeated the Dafoe-Sifton-Crerar-Hudson group in Winnipeg, the ablest group of Liberals who have appeared in Canada in the twentieth century; and they ended by becoming his supporters. He defeated the Progressive revolt and won most of its voters back into the Liberal fold. He defeated the C.C.F. And incidentally he defeated the Conservatives, who functioned in this last generation largely as passive instruments assisting him to ward off these other much more serious challengers to his leadership. His conception of the lines that Canadian policy should take was in due course accepted by the great majority of Canadians.

Mr. King's career should therefore be very enlightening to all students of history and politics who are interested in the conditions that determine successful political leadership in Canada. And as we look back now, his interpretation of the way Canada should be governed seems in many respects so self-evident that we wonder why we didn't see it all more clearly before. Certainly the C.C.F., now that it is sitting down to reconsider its own past, should devote a great deal of quiet study to the man who was chiefly responsible for the fact that we have so far failed to make more impact on the Canadian public.

The first thing to understand about Mr. King is that he was not the traditional kind of parliamentary leader that you read about in the textbooks on British representative democracy. He obviously disliked Parliament. The representative side of democracy he did not find congenial, and he worked out a much more direct but also much more indefinable relationship between himself and the Canadian people. He was not a great parliamentarian like Lloyd George or Asquith or Churchill, or like Macdonald and Laurier. He avoided the dialectic of parliamentary debate as an instrument for clearing his own and his fellow-citizens' minds, for reaching decisions and for presenting issues to the electorate. But he had an unparalleled intuitive capacity for sensing what his fellow Canadians wanted and what they were about to want, how much a majority would demand and how much a minority would tolerate. And without any of the apparatus of mass hypnosis and police coercion to which vulgar practitioners of the art like Hitler and Mussolini had to have recourse, he succeeded with hardly a mistake for twenty-five years in giving expression, by way of that curious cloudy rhetoric of his, to what lay in the Canadian sub-conscious mind.

This is the kind of leadership, evidently, that modern mass-democracy welcomes and appreciates. But it is not the kind that will ever be very palatable to the more intellectual elements of the community; that is, to the kind of people who write for and who read the *Canadian Forum*.

The commonest criticism of Mr. King was that he never gave a definite lead in any direction or committed himself in advance to anything concrete and tangible. In domestic affairs it would be tiresome to marshal again all the cases which support this charge. But we can afford to admit now that there is more to be said in his defence than we thought there was in the three decades of the twenties, thirties and forties. For we are not a homogeneous or united people in Canada; and only a very cautious leadership will avoid splitting us into bitterly contending groups — racial, religious, geographic, or economic. The successful national leader will always have to feel his way slowly, and will always be acutely conscious that his main task is to carry as many groups as possible along with him, to keep them moving in the same direction at about the same pace without too much strife and division. Mr. King for twenty-five years was the leader who divided us least. Perhaps this is as much as we shall ever be able to say, for a long time to come, about Canadian unity.

But there was one field in which he did give a definite lead — external affairs. And it is in this field that we can now see most clearly that intuitive quality of Mr. King's mind to which I have referred. He grasped what Canadians wanted better than they did themselves, and he was very clear-headed and persistent in moving towards a goal which he saw from the start, but which a good many of his fellow Canadians are not quite sure about yet. He was primarily a North American. He resisted all attempts to make a political or economic or military unit out of the British Commonwealth; in fact, he completed Laurier's work of carrying us past that goal. He realized that a separate exclusive British-Empire alliance is not a workable idea in the contemporary world. Even in the emotional atmosphere of the war he declined all Churchillian invitations into an Imperial War Cabinet. Instead, he was vigorous both in peace and war in strengthening our American ties. Before the war he had already undermined the Bennett-Beaverbrook economic empire of 1932; and after 1939 his alacrity in making American commitments, economic and military, was remarkable. He never consulted parliament or people about these steps; he simply kept us informed.

The significant thing about all this is that Mr. King managed to follow this policy without ever arousing that anti-American fever to which we are so susceptible in Canada. Nothing is easier than to excite Canadians against their great North American neighbour or to get English-speaking Canadians feeling sentimental about their British ties. Yet today most sensible Canadians recognize that the idea of the British nations operating as a kind of "Third Force" apart from the United States is only a dream without basis in the realities of world politics. Both we Canadians and the British have no choice but to work in the most intimate collaboration with the Americans. This is the settled policy of the responsible leaders of the British Labour party; and here in Canada our American ties are so vital that we cannot even aspire to be America's Tito as some of the left-wing Labour intellectuals would like Britain to be. Our fundamental interests are identical with American interests; and such separate individual interests as we may have can best, in the present state of the world, be protected not by trying to stand aloof from the United States but by presenting our point of view vigorously from within the North Atlantic Alliance.

It was Mr. King who led us to this point. And his leadership has been so completely accepted that today only the Communists and a diehard remnant of Tories go about talking of "American Imperialism". Well, no, this isn't quite correct. There are also those academic intellectuals in our universities who are still thinking up nasty wisecracks about American imperialism regardless of the fact that most of their own pet research projects are apt to be financed by money from Rockefeller or Carnegie or Guggenheim.

Mr. King's leadership in domestic matters was based upon two fundamentals, both of which need to be pondered deeply by us in the C.C.F. One was that Canada cannot be governed without the consent and co-operation of the French Canadians; and the other was that in a loosely knit continental community like ours, with all its diverse interest-groups, a political party that aspires to the responsibility of government must not be a class party but must be a loosely knit representative collection of voters from all groups, such as the Liberal party has generally been under himself and Laurier. In other words, the federalism which is the essence of both North American countries must be reflected in their political parties.

The C.C.F. has so far failed to make much impression upon the French Canadians. We started with the thesis that the most pressing problems of our country were economic problems, and we have never been sufficiently aware of the French-Canadian belief that our concentration on achieving uniform economic solutions may endanger their cultural interests as a minority group in the country. In particular we have never understood their conception of themselves as a special kind of minority with deep-rooted peculiar national institutions. A century ago, in the United States, Calhoun worked out for his Southern minority community a political and constitutional theory of "concurrent majorities", according to which the South must not be coerced but must be a consenting party to all major national policies. In its extreme form this was to give the South a *liberum veto* about slavery, and Calhoun's interpretation of his principle was too rigid and legalistic. But the coercion of the South by the North in the Civil War did not settle the issue; and it is remarkable how often in American books and articles you will come across the conclusion that a complex continental community like the United States can only be satisfactorily governed by a general adherence to Calhoun's principle of "concurrent majorities". Statesmanship consists in achieving an interpretation of this principle flexible enough to satisfy all significant groups. We do not need to accept the most extreme version of the French-Canadian principle of "concurrent majorities" in our Canadian national politics, but it is high time that more C.C.F. spokesmen showed that they are aware of what the French are talking about. Mr. King was always aware, as were Macdonald and Laurier. Which is why these three overshadow all other Canadian statesmen.

Quebec is only the chief and most insistent example in Canada of this problem in democratic politics of how to carry all major groups along together in some kind of loose unity. The essence of democratic government is that the rule of the party in power for the time being must be acceptable to those who voted against it as well as to those who voted for it. In the United States this has led most students of politics to agree that a country whose unity is so imperfect and precarious cannot afford class parties. The price of union is that you must get along with parties without principles, like the Democratic and the Republican, parties which can each make a plausible appeal to every interest-group in the country, even if the appeals made to different groups are mutually contradictory. National unity is preserved by having every interest-group effectively represented inside the party which controls the government. The failure of parties like the Populist or the Progressive or Norman

Thomas' Socialist party to make any permanent headway seems to show that the ordinary American voter agrees with the students who have made this analysis. Canadian C.C.F.ers should read some of the best American books which have been written around this theme in recent years.

We C.C.F.ers presumably do not agree with this predominant trend in American political thinking. We think of ourselves as a party with principles and doctrine. The C.C.F., in fact, was an attempt to introduce the British structure of politics into Canada, with a party of the Left and a party of the Right, each adhering to definite principles. Similar attempts had been made earlier by the Progressives of the 1920s, and a similar attempt was also made by the Winnipeg Dafoe group which aimed at turning the Liberal party into a genuinely liberal party (liberal with a small "l"). Mr. King's main contribution to the working of Canadian politics was that he defeated all these attempts (made by men who had been studying English history) and successfully maintained his Liberal party as a typical North American party. Do we have to follow his example if we are ever going to reach office in Ottawa, or can we adjust our British experiment to the North American environment?

The latest of these American books is *The Price of Union* by Herbert Agar, published this year. Some of his remarks in his introduction and conclusion are worth quoting here. "The special problems of the American government derive from geography, national character, and the nature both of a written constitution and of a federal empire. . . . The government must accept the fact that in a country so huge, containing such diverse climates and economic interests and social habits and racial and religious backgrounds, most politics will be parochial, most politicians will have small horizons, seeking the good of the State or the district rather than of the Union; yet by diplomacy and compromise, never by force, the government must water down the selfish demands of regions, races, classes, business associations, into a national policy which will alienate no major group and which will contain at least a small plum for everybody. This is the price of unity in a continent-wide federation. Decisions will therefore be slow, methods will be cumbersome, political parties will be illogical and inconsistent; but the people remain free, reasonably united, and as lightly burdened by the state as is consistent with safety. . . . The American political system has learned to circumvent threats of secession (the mortal illness of federalism) before they arise; it has learned to evade class warfare (the mortal illness of liberty), and to the dismay of its critics it shows no sign of moving towards class parties. Once in the midst of the long period of learning the system failed totally. The result was civil war. The system must always fail partially, since politics cannot rise above the mixed nature of man. . . . A federal nation is safe so long as the parties are undogmatic and contain members of many contradictory views. But when the people begin to divide according to reason, with all the voters in one party who believe one way, the federal structure is strained. . . . The faults of such irrational parties are obvious. Brains and energy are lavished, not on the search for truth, but on the search for bargains, for concessions which will soothe well-organized minorities. . . . Part of the price is the absence of a clear purpose, since the sum of sectional and class interests is not equal to the national interest, and the exchange of favours between blocs or pressure groups does not make a policy. . . . But the United States, until she abandons her federal structure, will continue to be governed by concurrent majorities, by vetoes and filibusters, by parties which take both sides of every dangerous question, which are held together by the amusements and rewards of office-seeking."

This was the kind of politics which Mr. King practised, and in it he showed a virtuosity which even the great American master, Franklin Roosevelt, could not surpass. Evidently, to judge from the election returns, it fitted Canadian conditions better than the kind of politics which the Progressives and the C.C.F. have been trying to introduce. At its worst it can sink to much lower grounds than Mr. Agar is ever quite prepared to allow. The process of "group diplomacy", of making bargains and deals, may become so cynical that it is only adequately described in another famous definition: "Politics is the art of collecting money from the rich and votes from the poor on the pretext of protecting the one against the other." But to charge that this is its inevitable result would be grossly unfair.

The C.C.F. was launched at a moment when both capitalist economic institutions and North American political parties appeared to be finally bankrupt. It was easy then to conceive of the socialist heaven as shortly about to be inaugurated by a new political party. And there still seem to be a good many Seventh Day Adventists left in the British Columbia wing of the party. But eighteen years of experience since 1932 should have made us mature enough to realize that other political parties will continue to keep alive by helping themselves to all of our planks that turn out to be good vote-getters, that some kind of mixed economy is all that there is any likelihood of seeing in our time, and that indeed too much power concentrated in the hands of the state without some new centres of power to balance it would be very dangerous. A party that is mature enough to understand these truths could learn a great deal from studying the career of Mr. King.

4. J. W. Dafoe

(This essay appeared in the *Canadian Forum,* October, 1932, as one of a series by various authors on "Canadian Writers of Today".)

That the *Winnipeg Free Press* is the only newspaper in Canada which exercises anything approaching to a national influence; that its editorial page forms the one indispensable item of daily reading for everyone who professes to take an intelligent interest in Canadian public affairs; and that its editor, J. W. Dafoe, is our outstanding Canadian journalist, are facts which are now known to all and need not be enlarged upon here. Indeed Mr. Dafoe's pre-eminence in Canadian journalism has been so frequently proclaimed by his fellow newspapermen that one is led to wonder why so few of them pay him that sincerest form of compliment which consists in imitating his example.

The position which the *Free Press* has made for itself affords another disproof of the almost universal superstition among modern journalists that what people want nowadays is not editorial guidance but news. As a collector of news the *Free Press* ranks fairly high according to Canadian standards, though that is no great praise. Its press gallery correspondence from Ottawa has always been very good; and it is not altogether accidental that in the new field upon which Canadian papers have been venturing recently — that of special correspondence from Washington — the despatches that come to the *Free Press* and the other Sifton papers are easily the best received in Canada. But it is not its news which has made it pre-eminent, it is its editorial page. The long leading article which appears every morning has made it the moulder of the public opinion of western Canada. For the past generation it has been generally true that what the *Free Press* thinks today western Canada will think tomorrow and the intelligent part of eastern Canada will think a few years hence. This is an influence which has never been enjoyed by any other Canadian newspaper save by George Brown's *Globe* in the 50s and 60s and 70s of the last century.

No one is ever in any doubt as to where Mr. Dafoe stands on public issues. And anyone who makes a practice of reading several

Canadian newspapers will testify how he has got into the habit of waiting to see what the *Free Press* says on a subject, whether he agrees with it or not. The quality which makes its editorial page unique in Canada is its straight-forward, clear-cut definiteness of statement, its abhorrence of rhetoric and cant, and its editor's ability to say what he thinks in the fewest possible words. One doesn't seek in it the graceful style, the lightness of touch, or the subtle irony which made the *Manchester Guardian* of Scott and Montague the finest of all English-speaking newspapers. But it displays the same persistent and fearless championship of liberal principles, and the same unfailing ability to sweep aside the irrelevancies which may obscure a question and to go straight to the heart of the matter.

Moreover, Mr. Dafoe has been a fighter all his life. He is more mellow now than in the days when he was assailing the Roblin-Rogers gang, but it has always been his practice to hit straight and hit hard and keep on hitting. In journalism, as in other walks of life, the man who is afraid of making enemies will never make followers. This simple fact goes a long way to explain why Mr. Dafoe has more followers among the younger generation than any other living Canadian — journalist, politician, author, or preacher.

The secret of a good style is to have something to say. And to have something to say on public affairs one must have developed the habits of the student. Any reader of the *Free Press* who keeps in touch, however imperfectly, with the succession of books and periodicals which appear on English, American and international politics must have been struck by the frequency with which he finds that the writer of its leading article has been reading the most recent authoritative study on some particular question. This is an experience which one seldom enjoys in reading any other Canadian paper. Broadly speaking, our Canadian editors do not read anything except the products of their fellow-editors' pens; their intellectual life is a monotonous process of taking in one another's washing. And Canadian newspaper reporters almost without exception think that they have found out everything that there is to know on any assignment when they have nosed around a few offices and picked up some "inside" gossip. This is the ultimate reason why Canadian newspapers are the worst in the English-speaking world. And it is because they have never been guilty of this intellectual laziness that the only two living Canadian journalists whom an intelligent man can read with unfailing enjoyment and profit are Mr. Dafoe writing in English and M. Bourassa writing in French.

It is because he is a student (incidentally, he is not a university graduate) that Mr. Dafoe has been able to contribute to the literature of politics the series of books which will keep his name familiar to students long after he has ceased to write editorials. His little book on Laurier seems to me the most penetrating study that has been written of Laurier or of any other Canadian public man. His three lectures on Canada in the Harris Foundation series are likely to remain the best and fairest expression of Canadian nationalism in our generation. His biography of Sifton has already taken its place among the small handful of really first-class studies of the art of politics which we have produced in Canada. And everyone hopes that before he lays down his pen for good Mr. Dafoe will find leisure to give us his own reminiscences of the past generation in Canadian public life. He has been behind the scenes in most of the critical events of our era from Reciprocity to the constitutional crisis of 1926, and has played a part in the making and unmaking of more than one government. He owes the Canadian people a book like Mr. J. A. Spender's *Life, Journalism and Politics*.

The sociological historian would at this point remark that the particular qualities of mind and the particular attitude towards public questions which Mr. Dafoe's career has exemplified would never have developed so strongly nor reached such perfect expression save in the favourable environment of western Canada at the beginning of the twentieth century. And undoubtedly the *Free Press* has been so influential just because it has expressed so completely all that is best and most characteristic in the community of which it is a part.

The position of Winnipeg for the past generation affords an interesting parallel to the position of Toronto in the generation after 1850. Like Toronto in those days, it has been in our day the intellectual as well as the commercial and financial capital of the young, vigorous, self-confident, ever expanding, wheat-farming West. The *Free Press* of Mr. Dafoe, like George Brown's *Globe*, found itself in the part of the country which was growing most rapidly and living most intensely, and which was conscious (perhaps over-conscious) that the contribution which it was making to the national life had more than anything else to do with determining the future destiny of the country. Like the *Globe*, the *Free Press* in becoming the champion of the interests and the aspirations of its constituency stood nearly always for causes which were, in the truest sense, national as well as sectional. It fought for the equalitarian social democracy of the wheat-farmer against plutocratic domination by privileged interests in the East. Just as the *Globe* looked beyond the sectional limits of Upper and Lower Canada in the 1850s and became the first champion of westward expansion, so the *Free Press*, speaking for a community which sells its product in world markets, has preached the gospel that Canada must again expand her outlook and become conscious of her membership in a world community. And like the *Globe* in pre-Confederation days, the *Free Press* has led the campaign for autonomy from the Colonial Office and for friendship with the United States.

But that organic relationship of Winnipeg with its prairie constituency is gradually being broken down. New transportation developments destroy its dominance as a distributing centre; and rivals spring up in Regina, Saskatoon, Calgary and Edmonton. Transportation also finds new outlets for wheat in Vancouver and Fort Churchill. Most significant of all, the new radical movements among the farmers which find expression in the U.F.A. and the U.F.C. look for leadership not to Winnipeg but to Calgary and Saskatoon. The *Free Press* is not very sympathetic to them and remains detached and critical.

As for Winnipeg herself, she begins to dream not of wheat but of the untapped resources of the pre-Cambrian belt in northern Manitoba. She has visions of becoming rich from mining and manufacturing, just as Toronto grew fat and comfortable upon the wealth of northern Ontario. And as the visions are realized in the next generation the mind of Winnipeg will gradually change. No longer the alert aggressive champion of agrarian democracy, she will acquire the mentality of a community of stockbrokers and company promoters. In due course, combining this with the Scotch moral unction that she inherited from the Selkirk settlers (which is not essentially different from the Anglican moral unction that Toronto inherited from the U.E. Loyalists), she will become another Toronto. Her streets will be wider but her mind will be as narrow as the mind of that Ontario metropolis which was once also in her day the Queen City of the West. For, as Rupert Brooke pointed out twenty years ago, it is the sad fate of every Canadian town, as it grows older and bigger, to become more and more like Toronto.

And the *Free Press*? Will it go the way of the *Globe* as its city repeats the history of Toronto? Not as long as Mr. Dafoe is in charge. Yet it must be confessed that there is a vein of sentimentalism in Mr. Dafoe just as there was a strong element of romantic sentimentalism in George Brown. For the terrible results of an inheritance of sentimentalism see the *Globe* of our day.

In his early years, apparently, Mr. Dafoe used to write poetry. A little while ago, while working through the files of *The Week*, the organ of Canadian intellectuals in the 1880s, I came across a tender ballad by J. W. Dafoe of Montreal. It was about a fair maiden who waited sadly by the seaside for the return of her beloved, who alas would never return, for the ocean waves had buried him. As an admirer and friend of Mr. Dafoe I shall never reveal the date of the issue of *The Week* in which that youthful effort lies hidden. Yet should it not be remarked that, like the young lady of his poem, he himself is today waiting rather sadly for the return of his beloved — Cobdenite liberalism — which is also irrevocably dead? I fear that this sentimental yearning of his may make him subject to hallucinations as he grows older. One of these days he will be assuring us that at last he recognizes his beloved, returned to life again in the Liberal party of Mr. Mackenzie King.

4a. A Reply by J. W. Dafoe

(Mr. Dafoe wrote me this private letter in comment on my article about him.)

Winnipeg, October 8, 1932

My dear Underhill,

This is to acknowledge to you that I have read your much too kind article about me in the *Forum*. Of course that revelation of one of the skeletons in my closet — that I used to write poetry — calls for forgiveness which is herewith freely extended.

I shall have to admit that as charged I am a Cobdenite, using that term as a mark of identification for people of a certain attitude of mind towards problems of government and society. I agree pretty completely with what Dr. M. J. Bonn said in his Dunford House lecture when he pointed out that last century the western world was given the choice of alternative policies of international relationships: one that could be identified with the name of

Cobden, and the other with the name of Disraeli. The world plumped for the Disraelian ideal and is now getting its fill of the fruits of imperialistic and nationalistic bounce.

Of course Cobden's failure arose from his too naive faith in the applicability of his doctrines to a world not even able to understand his views let alone to apply them. How could *laissez-faire* operate in a world of profound inequalities of status and power, the result mainly of institutionalized privilege? The economic writings of today are filled with parrot-cries of "*laissez-faire* is dead". But it never was really alive. Yet at that, it was the feeble approximation to *laissez-faire* that was possible in the pre-war times which built the world that survived the war and is still staggering along in spite of the efforts of post-war innovators to tie it up with all kinds of strangleholds and knots, in experiments in the new-fangled idea of "managed nations", and "managed currency" and "managed trade". I should say that the business of liberalism everywhere is to work to bring about the conditions which would make possible the largest possible exercise of individual talent free from anti-social practices. I have hopes of Canadian Liberalism along these lines. I have some hope as well of Mackenzie King. He is, of course, not an ideal leader — I have, by the way, never met one, not even R.B.B. — but he has a better intellectual grasp of the fundamentals of Liberalism than most of his colleagues. Since his leadership for the time being is unquestioned, it is the part of wisdom for Liberals who are more advanced to try to bring him along with them instead of starting a faction fight that would leave R.B.B. in a position of unchallenged dictatorship.

The practical political difficulty that you and your associates, in the movements which you have started, will encounter is the hard fact that Mr. Bennett will be the "boss" of Canada — unless he is retired by a palace revolution which is perhaps possible — until he is beaten by the Liberals. I think Mr. Woodsworth's idea of exercising power by controlling the balance of power is an illusion. He looks back to 1925. So do I; and what I see is that the "balance of power" group by refusing to co-operate with the Liberals along the lines of reasonable compromise upset the cart; and brought about a new situation in which the "controllers" were practically powerless, which is still the situation, so far as they are concerned. The idea that a minority can take the majority by the neck and make it do things that it doesn't want to do sounds a little like dictatorship to me. I don't think it will work in this democracy.

However, you must not think me unsympathetic to the L.S.R. and the kindred Co-operative Commonwealth Federation. Anything that will stir up the stagnant waters and force consideration of current problems is all to the good. If you will permit me to say so, the Liberal party will, or at least should, be the chief gainer from your activities. The Liberal party is bound to move to the left without getting over the line which divides Liberalism from State Socialism; and if it does this, under moderately progressive leadership, it will have a chance to pick up all those members of your radical organizations who want some progress right now, instead of contenting themselves with a demonstration against things as they are and a hope for posterity. If the Liberal party in the West doesn't pick up at least fifty percent of the farmer vote that has been steadily Progressive for the past twelve years I shall agree with you that the Liberal leadership is hopeless. These farmers, I should say, cannot be turned into Socialists. They are native individualists and their "spiritual home" is the Liberal party.

To some extent these matters tend to become academic to me. I grow old; and before the movements now setting in clearly reveal their tendency I may well be in final retirement or in seclusion writing those Reminiscences which you think I should set down before I pass on. I have some such idea myself though I have made no plans. I hope after the New Year to get at some writing which I have long had in mind — bringing the constitutional articles which I wrote in 1925 down to date and preparing them for publication. Once I get this off my mind I might begin to take advantage of my age to indulge in "I remember" stuff. But at the moment I am pretty busy at the job which I have held down for 30-odd years and looking forward to at least one more battle when we shall all meet at Philippi some two or three years hence.

With many thanks, my dear Underhill, for many kindnesses at your hands, I am as ever,

Yours faithfully,

J. W. DAFOE

5. J. S. Woodsworth

(This was an address given at a dinner to inaugurate the Ontario Woodsworth Memorial Foundation in Toronto on October 7, 1944.)

I am proud and grateful that the task was assigned to me in this evening's proceedings of speaking about Mr. Woodsworth's life. I am proud to have been a friend of his for some twenty years. To enjoy his friendship was a moral education in itself. He was the most completely honest man that I have ever known; and the most completely selfless man, free from merely personal ambition, never indulging in selfish intrigues or struggles for personal power. It is a great source of strength to the C.C.F. that its first leader was J. S. Woodsworth, and in the movement which he founded it is our duty to keep alive the values which he held dear and to which he devoted his life.

So I am going to preach a little sermon about his life and work. If there is a text it will consist of a quotation from John Bunyan which I shall give at the end. Mr. Woodsworth himself, in a pamphlet which he published in 1926, spoke of his life as a modern pilgrim's progress, and I can think of no description that is more fitting. Hence the Bunyan text. The general theme of my discourse will be that he came from an environment which was most typically Canadian but that he developed qualities of character which are for the most part un-Canadian or which at least are found far too rarely in our Canadian community.

First of all, as to the environment. James Shaver Woodsworth was born in 1874 near Toronto, the son of parents who both came of loyalist stock. His forbears were men and women who moved up to British soil in Upper Canada from New York and Pennsylvania after the American Revolution. His paternal grandfather, Richard Woodsworth, who was a local Methodist preacher in Toronto, served on the loyalist side in the Rebellion of 1837. All those who ever visited the Woodsworth home in Winnipeg will have seen hanging on the study wall the sword which was carried by grandfather Woodsworth when he turned out to help preserve the British connection against the grandfather of the Right Honourable William Lyon Mackenzie King. The Woodsworths were Methodist;

Richard Woodsworth, as I have said, a local preacher here in the Toronto district; his son, James Woodsworth, the father of our James Shaver Woodsworth, a pioneer missionary in the North-West who rose to be the Superintendent of Methodist missions there and played a great part in the building up of our Canadian prairies.

This double inheritance of pioneer loyalism and pioneer Methodism needs to be emphasized. For there is nothing that is more distinctively and essentially Canadian than that combination. We are accustomed to think of the loyalists in Upper Canada as having been mainly Anglican. But the Anglican part of loyalism has left to us mainly a tradition of stuffiness and snobbery. It was the Methodists (with some considerable help from the Scotch Presbyterians) who formed the creative element in early Upper Canada, and who did most to make us what we are today in Ontario.

I remember a few years ago sitting one evening in the chapel of Victoria College when Ned Pratt was giving a recital of his poem *Brébeuf and His Brethren*. The audience consisted of the cream of the graduates of that great Methodist college. Everywhere one could see faces of men who were prominent in the professional and business life of Toronto. The chairman was the titled head of one of the most famous Methodist families of Ontario. And as I listened to those austerely beautiful lines about the struggle of Brébeuf and his companions to convert the Indians to Christianity, and my eye wandered over the members of the audience (with here and there the careworn face and threadbare garments of some university professor sticking out incongruously in that comfortable gathering), I could not help reflecting that, after all, it was neither the Jesuits nor the Iroquois who eventually won Ontario, and who set the imprint of their character upon the life of this province; it was the Methodists.

The Woodsworth family moved to the West in 1882 and young Woodsworth grew up in that great new prairie community whose settlement and expansion were main factors in the making of our twentieth-century Dominion of Canada. He received the best education that was available to the young Canadian of his day. He went through Wesley College in Winnipeg, then came down to Victoria College in Toronto to study theology, and completed his academic training by a year at Oxford. When he graduated at Wesley in 1896 he was elected Senior Stick by his fellow students. No one who is familiar with Canadian college life needs to be told that the Senior Stick is the man who is considered by his fellows to be outstanding for his ability and energy, but who is also known by them to fit most perfectly into his environment, who accepts most implicitly the values of his generation, who can be trusted never to think dangerous thoughts. It is interesting to speculate what some of James Woodsworth's respectable, right-thinking classmates of the class of 1896 must have thought of their Senior Stick in later years when he turned out to be the leading non-conformist of his country. No doubt he must have already shown those strong individual characteristics of his; and his evangelistic background would have made him critical of the society in which he lived. But most Canadian evangelicals have settled down long before they are middle-aged to a very comfortable acceptance of their environment. And this was just what James Woodsworth failed to do.

Perhaps Oxford had a good deal to do with this. He went to England in the fall of 1899. This was the very moment of the outbreak of the Boer War, and he must have become familiar with all the fierce discussion which went on at that time in England (but which was not reproduced in Canada, though we also took part in the Boer War) about the moral values of imperialism. It was in the next year, 1900, that the Labour party was founded, and he must have heard a good deal of talk on this subject too. Oxford must have accentuated whatever tendencies he already had to emphasize the social gospel of Christianity as distinct from its theological dogmas. It was full at that time of the new humanitarian and social-reform ideas which were bringing about far-reaching changes in English politics. Woodsworth did what many another young Oxonian was doing and spent part of his time living in a settlement in the east end of London.

Whether it was Oxford that did it or not, at any rate he came back to Canada with his mind full of a social philosophy which was hardly yet familiar to most of his fellow Canadians, who were still dominated by the nineteenth-century individualistic ideas of a pioneer community. He was the first of those radicals whom Oxford has sent back to us, the forerunner of the Frank Scotts and Dave Lewises and Ted Jolliffes of our own day.

Back in Canada he entered upon the career for which he had been preparing, that of a minister in the Methodist Church. He became assistant minister in Grace Church, Winnipeg. The city of Winnipeg at the opening of the twentieth century was the most dynamic spot in Canada. It was the reception centre through which poured the thousands of new immigrants to be distributed across the whole of western Canada, and it was the collecting centre from which were shipped the millions of bushels of wheat that formed the basis of the new Canadian economy. And it was in dealing with problems of this new civilization that J. S. Woodsworth was to show those distinctive qualities that made him so unusual a Canadian.

What were these qualities which we think of most readily when we look back over Mr. Woodsworth's life? We may note four of them which made him different from most of his fellow Canadians who had come from much the same environment.

First and most important of all was moral courage. We may as well admit that this is not a quality which is very common in Canada. Physical courage we have in abundance. But the man who is willing to stand by himself when he disagrees with his society, who insists, whatever the cost, on proclaiming the truth as he sees it, is somewhat rare in our history. This kind of courage is one of the things that makes English history so inspiring. But Canadians, both English Canadians and French Canadians, are far too devoted to group solidarity and far too fond of the material success which comes from unquestioning acceptance of the prevailing standards of their group. J. S. Woodsworth showed from the beginning to the end of his career a willingness to make sacrifices for his principles. He never failed when this test was applied to him. That nation is most fortunate which produces the highest proportion of sturdy individualists of this kind. Liberty is safe only in a society in which such individuals are fairly common. This is the secret of English history. And we shall no doubt have frequent occasion to thank heaven that the founder of our Canadian socialist party was the most stubborn individualist of his generation.

A second outstanding quality was his sympathy with the underdog, with the downtrodden and disinherited. Such sympathy is part of the tradition of Christianity and of the tradition of democracy, and its existence should not require comment. Yet again, this is a quality which has been displayed much more in English than in Canadian history. We do not exactly pass by on the other side in Canada when we see a man who has fallen amongst thieves. But we have schooled ourselves to believe that in this land of opportunity there are no people needing help. James Woodsworth's life was one long process of identifying himself with the unfortunate and the exploited.

To both of these qualities of moral courage and social sympathy we do, however, pay lip service. Mr. Woodsworth displayed a third quality in which we hardly even profess to believe. That was a passion for clarity. In Canada, in spite of the clearness of our physical atmosphere, we prefer to live in a mental atmosphere of haze and mist. We never make issues clear to ourselves. Our national instinct is against defining differences so that they can be clearly understood or reconciled. We prefer to leave issues undefined, with an assumption that all right-thinking people would agree about them if ever they were defined and that in the meantime all problems can be solved by indulging in emotions of vague Rotarian goodwill. We prefer not to face the fact that our national society is divided vertically into sections and horizontally into classes. At its worst this attitude becomes a dangerous hyprocrisy. We need a constant supply of Woodsworths to keep plaguing us into the unpleasant duty of facing up clearly to the issues that confront us.

And this leads to a consideration of the fourth Woodsworth quality to which I should like to draw attention. He was an intellectual pioneer in an era in our history when a new understanding of and a new approach to our national problems was becoming necessary. He began his work in Winnipeg in the period of the great wheat boom. Canada was growing and prospering as she never had done before. And all that was needed, so far as most Canadians could see, was to shovel in more immigrants, to grow more wheat, to build new railways and new manufacturing plants, to develop our real estate, to make two subdivisions grow where only one had grown before. But what was really happening to us was that we were becoming an integral part of the great society of the industrial revolution; and this meant that our phenomenal growth of which we were so proud was reproducing in our midst conditions with which older countries had long been unhappily familiar. J. S. Woodsworth was one of the first to draw attention to our new problems such as that of the cultural assimilation of the European immigrants and that of the growth of urban and rural slums. These are the themes of the two books which he published in these early years — *Strangers Within Our Gates* (1909) and *My Neighbour* (1911). The ideas in them are now familiar enough to everyone and there was nothing original in them, as he would have been the first to declare, at the time. He was simply applying the more mature wisdom of older civilizations to these newly emerging conditions in Canada. What was original was that a native Canadian should be doing so. And the ideas which he propounded then were those at which he was to keep driving all his life. He would not have called himself a socialist in those days, I suppose; but it is significant that he was already saying that our inherited individual enterprise was not enough to deal with these new social problems but that they called for the intervention of organized community effort.

His fundamental faith from the start was in study and research, and in public education to spread the results of study and research. He wanted to bring the minds of his fellow Canadians up to date. He wanted to help them to tackle their twentieth-century problems with twentieth-century ideas. "I know a lot of my friends," he once said in a later political speech, "who won't drive a car that is of a model more than two years old. A great many of us have machinery in our heads that is of a model a hundred years old." Long before the C.C.F. was founded, and with equal persistence after it was founded, it was the same Woodsworth at work, filled with a passion for the spread of social understanding. This kind of intellectual pioneering is perhaps what we need most of all in Canada.

Mr. Woodsworth's career from the time of his return from Oxford falls into two clearly divided periods. The dividing line is the Winnipeg strike of 1919. Before that, as minister of the gospel and as social worker, he was to find himself unable to conform to some of the beliefs and practices of his society, and by the end of the summer of 1919 he was an outcast from all the respectable and right-thinking people among whom he had grown up. After that, from the election of 1921, he was to devote his life to building up a political movement which would give expression to the social and economic ideas in which he believed.

His religious studies had made him a modernist in theology. And very soon in his ministry in Winnipeg he found himself in intellectual difficulties about the doctrines of his church. He had already decided to resign as early as 1902 but was dissuaded. In 1907 he handed in his resignation along with a lengthy and forthright statement of his reasons. He could not accept the interpretation put by his church upon baptism and the Lord's Supper; he did not believe in the doctrine of the atonement; he had difficulties about the religious experience of conversion, and about many other things in the Methodist statement of faith. "Such are the doctrines of Methodism. Without discussing particular doctrines, let me briefly state my position thus: Many of the doctrines, of course, I believe, but there are some that rest upon historical evidence which for me is not conclusive. Some are founded on psychological conceptions and metaphysical theories quite foreign to modern thought, and are for me meaningless. Some deal with matters upon which, it seems to me, it is impossible to dogmatize. Upon some I must suspend judgment. Some I cannot accept in the form in which they are stated. Some I cannot accept at all. Yet I am required to 'sincerely and fully believe the doctrines of Methodism' and to 'endeavour fully and faithfully to preach them'! . . . Some may say that it is necessary only that I believe the essential underlying truths. But who is to determine what are the essential underlying truths? Words have well-recognized meanings. We cannot play fast and loose with them. . . . In this matter of personal experience lies the root of the difficulty. My experience has not been what among Methodists is considered normal. . . . My experience has determined my theology, and my theology my attitude toward the Discipline. And all three, according to our standards, are un-Methodistical."

It is of course possible for honest and intelligent men to differ as to how far historic statements of doctrine are to be taken in the literal or how far in the symbolic sense. At any rate, a committee of the Methodist Conference reported: "Having had a full and frank conversation with Brother James S. Woodsworth *re* the cause of his resignation, we find that there is nothing in his doctrinal beliefs and adhesion to our discipline to warrant his separation from the ministry of the Methodist Church, and therefore recommend that his resignation be not accepted and his character be now passed."

Eleven years later, in June 1918, Mr. Woodsworth again offered his resignation. In the meantime the war had come, he had publicly stated his opposition to conscription, and had lost his position in Winnipeg. This time he wrote in his letter of resignation: "As years went by, certain disquieting conclusions gradually took form. I began to see that the organized Church had become a great institution with institutional aims and ambitions. . . . Further, the Church, as many other institutions, was becoming increasingly commercialized. This meant the control of the policies of the Church by men of wealth, and in many cases the temptation for the minister to become a financial agent rather than a moral and spiritual leader. It meant, also, that anything like a radical programme of social reform became in practice almost impossible. . . . In the meantime another factor makes my position increasingly difficult. The war has now gone on for four years. . . . According to my understanding of economics and sociology, the war is the inevitable outcome of the existing social organization, with its undemocratic forms of government and competitive system of industry. . . . This brings me to the Christian point of view. For me, the teachings and spirit of Jesus are absolutely irreconcilable with the advocacy of war. Christianity may be an impossible idealism, but so long as I hold it, ever so unworthily, I must refuse, as far as may be, to participate in war. . . . The vast majority of the ministers and other church leaders seem to see things in an altogether different way. The churches have been turned into very effective recruiting agencies. . . . There is little dependence on spiritual forces. The so-called Prussian morality that might makes right and that the end justifies the means is preached in its application if not in theory. . . . Apparently the church feels that I do not belong and reluctantly I have been forced to the same conclusion."

This time the resignation was accepted promptly. Perhaps the Methodist church, in this contrast between its remarkable flexibility in dealing with the theological heretic and its very stern orthodoxy towards the political heretic during the hysteria of war, does not show up too well. But these transactions are not recalled here for the purpose of criticizing the church. It will be more fruitful for us to remind ourselves that it is possible for radical political parties as well as for evangelical churches to become over-institutionalized, to accept too whole-heartedly the values of the society in which they live, to become too intent on success according to the standards of that society. May the C.C.F. continue to produce its Woodsworths in the future as the Methodist church has done in the past!

While Mr. Woodsworth's resignation from the church was not accepted in 1907, he decided to abandon the regular work of a church pastor; and in that year he became head of All People's Mission, a settlement of the Methodist church in the north end of Winnipeg. Here he spent six busy years in social work. In 1913 a group of friends found the money to set up the Canadian Welfare League and to put him in charge. And in 1916 the governments of the three prairie provinces joined to establish the Bureau of Social

Research with J. S. Woodsworth as director. During these years he became, as Olive Ziegler puts it very truly in her biography, a "consulting sociologist" not merely for Winnipeg and its neighbourhood but for the whole of Canada. His successive offices became centres to which men of all classes resorted for advice and information. It was in these years that he published the two books already mentioned for the use of study groups in the church. He was also constantly on the move, investigating conditions all over the West and writing memoranda and reports upon them. He became a national figure as a lecturer, and was heard with approval in all parts of Canada. And in addition to his many other activities it is noteworthy that he was chosen as the representative of the Winnipeg Ministerial Association upon the Trades and Labour Council of the city. In these activities he found a field of work in which theological difficulties did not intrude; and everywhere he went his message was the same — the need to study and understand the emerging social problems of the new era in Canada. He made himself the interpreter of the working classes to the more comfortable and successful groups of our Canadian community.

All this work was brought to a sudden end in the winter of 1916-17 when he felt it his duty to publish his objections to conscription. His governmental employers at once closed down the Bureau of Social Research. He found himself out of a job and was bitterly denounced by many who had been his associates in his social work.

He moved out to the Pacific coast and took up a small mission charge at a place called Gibson's Landing some twenty miles from Vancouver. Here, cut off from all his former activities, he found temporary rest. But shortly he became interested in the local cooperative store, an enterprise which met with the stern disapproval of a gentleman who was a leading member of his church, and he had to leave. He was now one of the unemployed indeed. He moved into Vancouver and became a casual labourer, a longshoreman. This was the hardest period of all his life, but there is no need to dwell on what he went through. After the severe testing of these two or three years, as all who met him later in life can testify, nothing ever daunted him or embittered him. Here is an extract from an article he wrote at the time. The article is headed: "Come on in — the Water's Fine!"

"My Winnipeg friends who knew me in connection with church work or social service activities would probably hardly recognize a longshoreman in grey flannel shirt, overalls and slicker, who lines up with a gang alongside a ship. . . . Yet it is the same J.S.W. who, though declared to be down and out, is in reality feeling fairly fit and looking forward to the fight. . . . Yes, I hesitated to make the plunge. Where a man has spent all his time up to middle life along one line it is not easy to make a complete break and, as it were, start life all over again. But circumstances have a curious way of pushing one right up to the brink. Then, unless a man is a downright coward, it is a case of 'Here Goes!' . . . And the water was cold — no doubt about that! Longshoring is hard and monotonous and irregular and, taking it the year round, not much better paid than other unskilled labour. Being a town-bred boy and having gone through school and college into professional life, I had never done manual work. Piling heavy rice sacks or stowing flour or loading salmon or trucking up a steep slippery gangplank is no child's play. . . . But, once in, one has to make the best of it. No one sinks without a struggle, and in the struggle the blood goes coursing through one's veins till the whole body is atingle. . . . There is a certain exhilaration in having broken through artificial distinctions — in meeting men as men irrespective of nationality or creed or opinions — in being one of them. . . . Perhaps it is in part because 'he that is down need fear no fall' — that the workers 'have nothing to lose but their chains' — but there is a certain sturdiness and fearlessness about the workers that is not commonly found among the so-called higher classes. . . . At present the odds seem against us. But though muscles often ache and the back is tired and much is uncongenial, there is more than compensation in being as yet no man's slave. And what if, after all, as we believe, we are right! So, after the first shock, I have got my breath and shout back my message of good cheer: 'Come on in — the water's fine!' "

This was his apprenticeship for his later work as a labour leader in Parliament. He became a member of the longshoremen's union. He helped to organize the Federated Labor Party of British Columbia, wrote for the labour paper, became a regular speaker at labour meetings. In the summer of 1919 he was sent on a speaking tour of western Canada in the interests of the labour movement, and at Winnipeg he found himself in the middle of the famous Winnipeg strike.

The strike had begun as a dispute about collective bargaining in a few machine shops. By the time Mr. Woodsworth arrived this dispute had spread into a general sympathetic strike of the Winnipeg labour forces and had been going on for some weeks. It had become a trial of strength between the workers and the owning classes of Winnipeg. The latter persistently charged that the workers had ulterior motives, that they were aiming at a social revolution and the setting up of a Soviet government. But for a long time there were no outbreaks of violence. The provincial government failed to take any effective action. The so-called Citizens Committee, formed to put down the "revolution", devoted itself to a campaign of hysteria; and eventually trouble did break out between special police and processions of workers and their sympathizers. The Dominion government intervened to force a crisis, or at least that was how its action looked to the workers. (The chief representative of federal authority was the Hon. Arthur Meighen, Minister of the Interior. In 1942 it was to be the cause of special pleasure to many C.C.F.ers whose memories went back to the days of the Winnipeg strike that the C.C.F. served as the instrument in the famous South York by-election for retiring Mr. Meighen to private life.) Leaders of the workers were arrested and charged with seditious conspiracy. Against most of them the charges were successfully maintained after long trials in Winnipeg; and the strike was broken. It remains a landmark in our Canadian social and political history. For the first time we had clearly aligned against each other the two major classes into which modern industrialism has divided our society; and the manner in which the privileged class reacted to the events of that June in Winnipeg left no doubt as to which of the two groups was the more class-conscious or the more determined to fight by fair means or foul for its position.

Mr. Woodsworth immediately on his arrival in Winnipeg became active in addressing the mass meetings which the strikers were holding. It is worth recalling that the first of these meetings at which he spoke had as its opening speaker the well-beloved padre of the First Division, Canon Scott of Quebec. Mr. Woodsworth also helped in the publication of the workers' strike bulletin which they got out every day to present their side of the case. His set of the *Western Labor News* he later presented to the Library of the University of Toronto. As one reads it today one is struck by the mildness and coolness of its language and the reasonableness of its demands. Can we really believe that leaders who used such language were aiming at wrecking the comfortable homes of Winnipeg and bolshevizing the whole country? But the editor, F. J. Dixon, was arrested along with the other strike leaders; and after

Mr. Woodsworth had filled in for him for a week, he was arrested too. The charges against Dixon failed, and in due course the authorities quietly dropped their case against Woodsworth.

If you want to appreciate the atmosphere of panic in which the authorities in Winnipeg were working, it is worth while to read the items in the indictment by the Crown against J. S. Woodsworth. There were six counts, three of which consisted of articles appearing in the labour bulletin from the pen of Mr. Dixon. The three crimes of composition for which Mr. Woodsworth himself had been responsible were: (1) An article entitled "Is There a Way Out?", written shortly after his arrival in Winnipeg, pleading for an understanding of the underlying issues by both sides, suggesting a Royal Commission to investigate the whole situation, and ending "Let us reiterate that there are very reasonable men in both camps." (2) Two quotations from Isaiah (10:1-2 and 65:21-22). (3) An article entitled "The British Way", with long quotations from a manifesto of the British Labour party demanding a new social order. Well, it is no longer seditious to write about a new social order in Canada.

The Winnipeg strike will long remain a subject of dispute in our modern Canadian history. It was the first definite trial of strength between opposed social forces in our new industrial civilization. It showed how strongly entrenched are the established ruling groups in our society; how bitterly and unscrupulously they will fight for their privileged position; how prone is the government, which supposedly represents all the people, to take the side of the powerful; and how difficult it is for the other side to get its case before public opinion at all. As for Mr. Woodsworth, it left him a complete outcast from the respectable part of society. But, as things were to turn out, his identifying of himself with the labour cause was to give him a seat in Parliament for the next twenty years and to make him the natural spokesman of all Canadians who were seeking a more democratic social order after the war which had been fought to make the world safe for democracy.

In the federal election of 1921 J. S. Woodsworth was elected as member for Winnipeg North Centre, and he continued to hold this seat until his death. This later part of his career is more familiar to all of us, and there is no need to trace its events in any chronological order. There are several points, however, which are worth emphasizing.

The new phenomenon of the 1921 Parliament was the contingent of some 65 "Progressive" members. In this and the succeeding

parliaments of the 1920s and 1930s Mr. Woodsworth regularly had
one or two labour colleagues from the West, and they formed a
little labour party of their own. (On one occasion Bill Irvine explained about the labour party: "The member for Winnipeg North
Centre is the leader of the party and I am the party.") They co-
operated throughout these years with this larger and looser body of
Progressives. But the Progressives were never quite able to make
up their minds whether they were a new political party, or whether
they were an independent left wing of the Liberal party, or just
what they were politically. And after the first upheaval of post-war
unrest was over, they gradually disintegrated. Mr. King carried on
a patient courtship which, like most of his statesmanship, was somewhat slow in producing results but very effective in the long run.
Most of the Progressives, because they didn't quite know where
they stood, because they were well-meaning but unmeaning, disappeared into the Liberal party or were left at home in later elections by their electorates. Some of them, especially in Manitoba,
became known as Liberal-Progressives. And now we have "Progressive Conservatives" and "Labour Progressives" as well. That
fine word "Progressive", which seemed to hold such promise in
1921, must be said in our day to have acquired a certain smell.

In 1924 a few of the Progressives, who were determined to remain
independent and not to succumb to the embraces of parties run
from St. James St. or King St., broke away from the main Progressive body and formed an independent group which the newspapermen nicknamed the Ginger Group. Most of them were U.F.A.
members from Alberta who insisted on their function as spokesmen
of a distinct occupational group, the farmers, and who, like the
labour members, were denounced by right-thinking people for in-
troducing class distinctions into politics. Mr. Woodsworth worked
with them, and so did Agnes Macphail from Ontario. They were
the nucleus from which sprang the C.C.F. in 1932. Ten years'
experience in Parliament had shown them that it was perfectly
possible for farmer and labour representatives to agree on every
main issue that came up, and had confirmed the beliefs with which
they entered public life that what was needed in Canada was not
mere tinkering with tariffs or railway rates but a far-reaching
change in the whole economic and social system. By 1932 they were
ready to commit themselves to the launching of a party which was
definitely socialist in its programme. Their socialism came not from
any abstract philosophizing of their own or from imported ready-

made European philosophies, but from their practical experience in dealing with national Canadian problems in the post-war years. And the Regina manifesto, in the language and in the substance of its programme, was an expression of this fact.

The 1920s and 1930s, so far as Mr. Woodsworth's parliamentary work was concerned, must often have seemed to be years of rather fruitless agitation. Only this small minority of independent members survived to sit and vote with him. The resolutions which he presented in the House were always voted down by big majorities and usually were discussed very inadequately by those majorities. But we can see now that it was he who first advocated most of the social policies which with general consent we are just beginning to adopt today. And he did in the earlier years achieve one concrete result. In 1927 Old Age Pensions were adopted because of his pressure upon the leaders of the two old parties.

The first resolution which he drafted after his election in 1921 was one for unemployment insurance, which he was told by the Clerk of the House he could not move because only members of the government can make motions involving the expenditure of money by His Majesty's government. Steadily he kept pressing the question of the B.N.A. Act and of the obstacles which it presents to any advanced social-reform policy. And just as steadily the Liberal government kept making the B.N.A. Act an excuse for doing nothing. It was only at last in 1935 that Mr. Woodsworth succeeded in getting a special committee appointed to examine our constitutional difficulties, and the report of that committee is one step in the sequence of events that led to the Rowell-Sirois Commission. On foreign policy and international relations also it was likely to be Mr. Woodsworth, in any given session, who raised questions and forced some discussion in a very apathetic Commons. It was he who became the chosen spokesman for working-class groups when they had some grievance which they wished to get before Parliament and the public. It was he who more than any other private member, after the depression came, kept calling the attention of the government to the plight of the poor and the unemployed. And, in addition, he spent all the months between parliamentary sessions in missionary tours across the country speaking to all kinds of audiences in all kinds of assembly halls.

This work won for J. S. Woodsworth an acknowledged position as the chief private member of Parliament. His influence in the House and in the lobbies was far greater than any recorded votes would indicate. More important, when the C.C.F. was founded in 1932, he was its inevitable leader. He was known all across the country. He and his farmer colleagues had learnt the technique of organized team-work in Parliament and had found that they agreed on all major issues. He was chosen leader of the new movement because of his acknowledged mastery of those issues. In Parliament and in the country at large he had built up a following who had come to accept his analysis of the problems facing Canada and who trusted without reserve his essential honesty of purpose.

The C.C.F. grew slowly but surely. In the years when it seemed hardly to grow at all Mr. Woodsworth worked tirelessly at his missionary task of bringing social and economic realities before the Canadian people. He did not go in for emotional rabble-rousing, he did not indulge in personal invective or in party manœuvring. Under his leadership his party won the reputation of sticking to the issues that were really important. And today, now that he has gone, no one needs to be told what that has meant in the growth of popular support for the C.C.F.

In September, 1939, came the second world war. Mr. Woodsworth refused to compromise with his life-long convictions, though he knew that he could not carry his party with him. He stood up in Parliament by himself and opposed our participation in the war. Never was his hold on the respect of Parliament, of opponents as well as of followers, so clearly shown as in the hearing which was given to this last great speech of his.

Then, shortly after, came the breakdown in his health, his enforced retirement from public activities, and finally, on the 21st of March, 1942, his death. "After this it was noised abroad that Mr. Valiant-for-truth was taken with a Summons. . . . When he understood it, he called for his Friends, and told them of it. Then said he, I am going to my Father's, and tho with great Difficulty I am got hither, yet now I do not repent me of all the Trouble I have been at to arrive where I am. My Sword, I give to him that shall succeed me in my Pilgrimage, and my Courage and Skill, to him that can get it. . . . So he passed over, and all the Trumpets sounded for him on the other side."

We are trying now to raise an Ontario memorial to him. Let us remember that the best way to perpetuate his memory is to cultivate those qualities for which he was distinguished — his moral courage, his wide social sympathies, his passion for truth, his intellectual pioneering. The C.C.F. will remain his greatest work, and a special responsibility rests upon its leaders and its members to hold firm to the values which he cherished. Politics by itself is apt to become an accursed profession — as it was once called by one of its most eminent English practitioners — for it involves so much competitive striving for personal and party success; and politicians are under a constant temptation to become so concentrated upon victory over the enemy — or even, alas, at times over their own friends — that the purpose of victory is forgotten. The C.C.F. is still what Mr. Woodsworth left it, a movement devoted to social and economic change in the interests of the great mass of the plain common people. Let us resolve to keep it a movement and to save it from sinking into being merely a party intent on collecting votes. And one of the best ways to do that is to foster through this Woodsworth Foundation a vigorous programme of imaginative social study and research, so that Woodsworth House may become a source of the same kind of inspiration as radiated from J. S. Woodsworth's successive offices of church minister, social worker and member of Parliament.

(Since this address was given there have been two good biographies published of J. S. Woodsworth: Grace MacInnis — *J. S. Woodsworth, a Man to Remember* (1953); and Kenneth McNaught — *A Prophet in Politics: a Biography of J. S. Woodsworth* (1959).)

6. The Party System in Canada

(A paper read at the annual meeting of the Canadian Political Science Association, 1932, and printed in its *Proceedings* for 1932.)

Party is a body of men united for securing by their joint endeavours the possession of national office by means of some particular campaign fund in which they are all agreed to share. . . . I propose to draw attention to some of the features of our national two-party organization and to discuss some aspects of those more recent postwar developments which offer a challenge to the established system.

In 1867 we took over, or rather continued, the British names for our two parties along with the rest of the paraphernalia of the British constitution. The essence of our party history since then has consisted in the fact that in the process of growth the two parties became more and more American in their composition, machinery of organization, methods, and personnel. Canada, like the United States, was a gigantic loosely knit nation extending across half a continent, with a tradition of national unity still to be built up, and with a wide variety of sectional interests engaged in a perpetual struggle with one another which, in the nature of things, could only be partially and temporarily reconciled. Each party contained representatives of the main sectional and racial groups into which geography and history had divided the country. Inevitably the main task of the party politician was to keep peace among these rival interests within his own party; his statesmanship was measured by the number and variety of different interests which he could keep marching together under the party banner. And Canadian statesmanship reached its highest pinnacle of achievement when in the same cabinet under one prime minister there sat side by side the head of the Orange Order and the spokesman of French Catholic Ultramontanism. Had Mr. King in 1921 been able to inveigle Mr. Crerar and the Progressives into his fold, thus presiding over a cabinet containing the embattled prairie farmers along with Ontario and Quebec manufacturers, he too would have attained to the *ne plus ultra* and gone down in history as a statesman of the calibre of Sir John Macdonald.

This composite character of parties has meant that party leaders could seldom speak with a clear voice upon any issue. Canadian parties, in proportion as they became national in scope, drifted further and further from their English namesakes, and their English names became more and more meaningless. They ceased to represent a conflict between two clear-cut philosophies of life or between two social classes. The real deep-lying differences of opinion in our public affairs have tended to be within each party rather than between the two parties. Each party has had to satisfy the fierce determination of English-speaking Protestants that the North-West should not become a second preserve of the French Catholic hierarchy and, at the same time, has had to be careful not to alienate Quebec. Hence all the confusion over issues like the Riel execution and the Manitoba school question. Each party has had to give satisfactory guarantees of tariff protection to the industrial interests of the eastern cities who provide most of its campaign funds and, at the same time, has had to soft-pedal protection or devise some cry to counterbalance it when appealing to its agricultural following. Each party has had to give voice to the growing nationalism of the country and simultaneously pay its respects to the sentiment of imperial unity. The necessary result of all this complex process of balancing, of concessions and compensations, has been to enthrone insincerity in our national politics. Nor is the real nature of the system altered one whit by impressive references to our British capacity for compromise in practical affairs.

It should be noted in passing that the essential function of Laurier in Canadian political history was to complete the process by which both parties became national in this particular North American sense. Under him the Liberal party as well as the Conservative party became a party which made its appeal to all sections of the Dominion and therefore ceased to stand for anything in particular. Before Laurier the party had been cursed with principles and had been unable to attain to office except accidentally. The Liberals in Quebec had been strongly anti-clerical; in Ontario they were Grits, whose primary appeal was to the pioneer farmer of the western Ontario peninsula. Both the Rouge and the Grit sections of the party had a deep-rooted suspicion of the big business interests whose capital was in Montreal. Alexander Mackenzie, the first Liberal Prime Minister of the Dominion, had his home in the pioneer section of western Ontario and he was never happy with financiers and railroad promoters. Goldwin Smith remarked of him that if his strong point as prime minister consisted in his having been a stone mason his weak point consisted in being one still; but this was only the snobbish Oxford Englishman's way of expressing the fact that Mackenzie was a true representative of the pioneer agrarian democracy and that the Liberal party under him was an expression of these simple democratic instincts.

It was not until Laurier took charge that the Liberal party acquired sophistication and felt really at ease with railway promoters, land companies and industrialists. Laurier put an end to the anti-clerical Rouge tradition. Fielding put an end to the stiff-necked Cobdenism of Cartwright. And in Sifton, who was apparently the main driving force of his administration, Laurier had a disciple of Alexander Hamilton who believed with all his heart in the gospel of creating prosperity by tying to the government all the private profit-seeking interests who could most effectively exploit the material resources of the country.[1] The Laurier-Fielding-Sifton party had thus emancipated itself from its narrow English liberalism; it was now North American; it was truly national in its appeal. It had become all things to all men, and could compete on equal terms with the so-called Conservative party which Macdonald had created. . . .

One or two features of our Canadian party-system need to be specially emphasized. To the working of our federal constitution our parties have supplied the most essentially federal elements. Each national party is a loose federation of provincial machines depending for its success upon the efficiency with which the provincial machines are working at the moment. . . . Moreover, the coping-stone of the constitutional structure, the party cabinet in Ottawa, is, as was predicted by Christopher Dunkin in 1865 and as has been pointed out so often by commentators ever since, essentially federal in its structure. The prime minister necessarily chooses representatives from each province whose main function is not to

---

[1] J. W. Dafoe in his official biography of Sifton, *Clifford Sifton in Relation to His Times,* heads each chapter by a quotation from some book or speech. Chapter IV, "Early Experiences as Minister", is headed by a quotation from Bismarck; and Chapter V, "Policies of Development", by a quotation from F. S. Oliver's book on Alexander Hamilton. Which would seem to throw some unintended light on the liberalism of Clifford Sifton.

administer their departments but to see that the party fences in their province are kept in order.

At one point this loose federation of provincial party machines, having in common only the desire to obtain office, becomes so loose that it is almost true to speak of the national party as merely an alliance of sectional groups rather than a federation. The party system has never really bridged the deep gap between French and English in this country. Quebec's representatives have always sat in party caucuses more as ambassadors from an independent power than as associates in a partnership. They have usually been able to get what they wanted, partly because of the solidarity of the group they represent and partly because of the completely realistic manner in which their group has been accustomed to shift its alliance from one party to the other according to cold calculations of its own interests. Quebec politicians have never been either Liberal or Conservative; they have always been simply and whole-heartedly French. In this respect, no doubt, they have differed from the politicians of other groups and sections chiefly in the clearness with which they have envisaged their own interest and the frankness with which they have pursued it.

In the face then of this inherent and persistent sectionalism of Canadian politics, should we not ask ourselves to what extent the supposed unifying force of the two-party system really operates, or whether such unity as we have gradually achieved in Canada may not be chiefly due to quite other economic and social forces?

But the most important result which follows from this composite nature of our national parties has yet to be mentioned. A party which depends for success (*i.e.*, for office) upon the different and often contradictory appeals which it must make to different sectional interests will inevitably in course of time become mainly dependent upon and responsive to those interest-groups which are themselves best organized and most strategically located for applying effective pressure upon the party leaders. In Canada there are two such groups who have always held a dominating position in our politics because of their superior internal organization — the French Catholic Church in Quebec and the interlocking financial-industrial-commercial interests which we usually refer to nowadays as big business. The Quebec church owes its power to the effectiveness with which it can control and direct the mass voting of its parishioners. Big business depends primarily upon campaign contributions, also upon constant official and unofficial lobbying, and upon all the complex economic and social relationships between business and political leaders.

No political party can safely neglect other groups in the community altogether; but the other groups do not take the same intense and untiring interest in politics which is manifested by these two groups, and they are not organized so as to make their pressure felt so directly. Certain other interests, like that of the mere consumers, are not organized at all. Others, like that of the prairie farmers, cannot, however well organized, operate so quietly behind the scenes as can big business. The impression which prevails among the more naive of eastern newspaper readers, that the prairie farmer is always either squealing for help or holding a pistol at the government's head, is due to the fact that the farmer has no other way of making his influence felt except that of organizing with his fellow-farmers in public and carrying on public agitation. And just because his activity must be public it is the less effective, because when the farmer gets something, other groups, according to the well-understood rules of the system, have to get something also in compensation. Whereas a business corporation can make a quiet campaign contribution to the party organizer which in some mysterious fashion induces the party leader to favour the policy that the corporation wants, even though the leader himself is innocently unaware that the contribution has been or is about to be made.

The net effect of all this — and it is so well known to every intelligent Canadian that there is no need to labour the point to or attempt a comprehensive survey of all the methods by which big business influences government — is that for all practical purposes our two parties are normally and regularly the servants of big business. Other interests can influence party policy but they can do so only spasmodically. And the real function of the two-party system since the Laurier era has been to provide a screen behind which the controlling business interests pull the strings to manipulate the Punch and Judy who engage in mock combat before the public. Both parties, in other words, are Hamiltonian, though the so-called Liberal party pays lip service to what in the United States would be called Jeffersonian principles. Both parties take for granted that their first duty in office is to assist the triumphant progress of big business in the exploitation of the country's resources.

The fundamental defect of the two-party system, then, as it has worked out in practice, is that it does not provide an effective means by which economic interests other than those of organized business can exercise a reasonable influence in the determination of national policy. The representatives of these other interests are overwhelmed in each party caucus by the weight of members whose political life depends upon business support. The balance of influence might be otherwise if the party financed itself by public subscriptions from the mass of its membership. The situation would be different if one of the parties, the Liberal, were really based on the principles it professes and offered a real alternative to the control by financiers and industrialists which is exercised with careless lack of concealment over the Conservative party.

Sooner or later there was bound to be a revolt by some of the groups who felt that their interests were unduly sacrificed in this two-party system. The revolt came in Canada with the farmer and labour movements which swept over the prairie and Ontario after the war. Today, eleven years after these upheavals, it is easy to see that the new movements have not fulfilled the hopes of their adherents. Labour, because of internal quarrels in the trade union world, because the bulk of eastern workers had been too thoroughly indoctrinated with the political philosophy of their employers, and because of the great difficulties of mere distance between Canadian urban centres, has not as yet succeeded in launching a really national political movement. The farmers spent the decade after 1921 in learning by a painful process of trial and error what form of organization was best suited to their needs; and most of them who had started the experiment with enthusiasm dropped it in disillusionment sometime in the next ten years. Only the United Farmers of Alberta organization has remained firm through all vicissitudes; and it is open to argument perhaps whether its success has been due, as it maintains, to its strict occupational basis of membership or to the fact that, in its control of a provincial government, it could provide the patronage and the jobs which are necessary to satisfy the appetites of the less idealistic members of any political movement.

At any rate the U.F.A. survived and the Progressives who conceived of themselves as left-wing Liberals or as forerunners of some vague new democratic mass movement all disappeared.

In an age like ours and on a continent like ours, when the plutocratic elements of the community are becoming more and more closely organized, a mere unorganized mass democracy holding up the now somewhat tattered banners of early nineteenth-century liberalism will be increasingly ineffective. The only answer to organization is counter-organization. This is the one main reason why all who do not welcome a business man's civilization should rejoice in the emergence of these new class organizations like the U.F.A. and the Independent Labour party, whatever may be the theoretical textbook objections to class warfare in politics.

Today everyone is discussing the possibilities of a new left-wing movement in Canadian politics. Unless such a movement has a solid core of stubborn class groups like the present U.F.A. and Labour groups it will disintegrate when the emotional atmosphere changes just as the 1921 movement disintegrated. The union of all the forward-looking elements in the community of which Mr. King becomes the apostle once every four years will never get anywhere until it is in charge of some forward-looking leaders who are looking forward to something more than immediate office.

Nor need we worry greatly over the horrible spectre of the group system as practised in France and continental Europe. There is no proof which is convincing to any but the smuggest of British patriots that countries with a variety of groups are worse governed than those with two parties. Nor is there any immediate likelihood of our party-system dissolving into a chaos of groups. It is the part of practical statesmen to meet difficulties as we come to them; and the danger of a group-system in Canada, if it is a danger, is still far in the future.

The problem which is urgent is the excessive rigidity of our actual two-party system, which is due to the growth in power of the party machine. This is a difficulty which faces all English-speaking democracies as well as Canada. The centralization of authority in the hands of the managers who run the party machine is a universal phenomenon; and there is no apparent way of preventing it. But it means inevitably that the party comes to express only that range of ideas which are approved by the machine; independence within the party becomes less and less possible. . . .

But behind all these particular questions of political organization there looms up today a much more fundamental problem. Two and a half years of world depression have made us all conscious that our civilization must face the task of political control of its economic activities or perish. Everywhere in all countries the phrase "A Planned Economy" is on men's lips. Our absurd North American party system has worked well enough hitherto because it had no very important tasks to perform. We all took for granted that the real work of developing the country was being done elsewhere than in Parliament; it was being done by private profit-seeking business concerns, and the functions of politics was merely to distribute in a haphazard, happy-go-lucky way the privileges and special opportunities sought by business. This care-free, planless era has gone forever. If democracy cannot organize its economic life, the necessary task of organization will be taken over by other forms of government. Russia and Italy provide us with alternative methods, and neither of them admits of the parliamentary institutions to which we are accustomed. The challenge of our times is whether parliamentarism as a method of organizing the political and economic life of a people can survive. In the face of that challenge the simple trust of our orthodox leaders in the kind of two-party system we have in Canada becomes more and more pathetic.

7. The Conception
of a National Interest

(A paper read at the annual meeting of the Canadian Political Science
Association, 1935, and printed in the *Canadian Journal of Economics and
Political Science,* August, 1935.)

"We form a new and distinct political organization for promoting
by a joint endeavour, the national interest upon a particular principle on which we are agreed." So ran the "Address of the Canadian National Association to the People of Canada"[1] in January,
1874. The Canada First movement of the early 1870s represents
the first intrusion of intellectuals as such into the discussion of
Canadian public problems. Its story has been surrounded with a
romantic halo by our Canadian bourgeois political historians,
prone as they are to fall an easy prey to the rhetoric of nationalism
wherever they run across it. But the moral which really emerges
from a study of the young idealists of Canada First is the difficulty
of defining "the national interest" as something which comprehends
and transcends those particular group interests whose competition
with one another has ever since Confederation formed the subject
matter of our day-to-day federal politics.

W. A. Foster and his friends thrust themselves into public affairs
because they were filled with a vision of the potentialities of the new
nation which had been born in 1867 and they wanted Canadian
national policies to be based upon clear conceptions of the national
interest. They thought by an appeal to national sentiment to lift
the making of policy out of the rut of sordid sectional bargaining in
which it was carried on. They were impatient with the sectionalism
and the provincialism of their elder contemporaries. They were
contemptuous of the political technique which was successfully
being standardized by John A. Macdonald, the technique of keeping things going by a process of purely opportunistic bargaining
and manipulation among the sectional units of the new Dominion,

---

[1] Printed in *Canada First: A Memorial of the late William A. Foster*
(Toronto, 1890).

of holding the members of the Federation together through bribes first to one section and then to another. They were the first to point out that it was this process which constituted the true essence of Canadian party politics, and that the terms Liberal and Conservative were meaningless as applied to actual Canadian parties. They wanted to emancipate their country from politics of this kind, to inspire in its citizens a national sentiment in the spirit of Edward Blake's Aurora speech.[2] And in place of the old parties that had no higher aim than to act as brokers among competing sectional interests, they wished to substitute new parties that would answer to the famous definition of Burke which they quoted in their manifesto.

But when they descended from these lofty generalities to the task of formulating a concrete policy which would genuinely be the expression of a national interest, the prophets of Canada First found themselves involved in the same perplexities as have worried most other Canadian public men. Their eleven-point platform showed distinct evidences of the same efforts at fence-straddling and the same ambiguities about controversial questions for which they had denounced Tories and Grits. Was it, for example, to the national interest of the new Dominion to aim at independent status, or should she seek self-realization in imperial federation? This was a question much discussed in the 1870s. "We no more advocate independence than we advocate the Day of Judgment," W. A. Foster had declared in one of his speeches; but Plank 1 of their platform ran: "Consolidation of the Empire and in the meantime a voice in the treaties affecting Canada." Did they lean towards the farmer or the industrialist? Plank 6 declared for "Encouragement of immigration and free homesteads", but Plank 7 was drafted with the skill of the old political hand: "Duties for revenue so adjusted as to give every possible encouragement to native industry." The other planks of their platform concerned themselves with minor technical reforms such as vote by ballot, and the whole platform concluded with that old standby of politicians and business men alike: "Pure and economic administration of public affairs."

The most revealing insight into the Canada First movement comes, however, from a perusal of the pages of the *Nation*, the

---

[2] *"A National Sentiment"* (Ottawa, 1874).

weekly journal which they established to expound their ideas and policies and which continued publication for some two years. The *Nation* began its career just at the time when George Brown, on behalf of the Mackenzie government, was trying to negotiate a new Reciprocity Treaty with the United States. Reciprocity was a policy in which all Canadians had believed or professed to believe. Here, one might say, was a "national interest" if ever there was one. But the year 1874 marks a turning point in the development of our national fiscal policy. The Americans would not discuss a reciprocity agreement unless it included a wide range of manufactured articles as well as the natural products of farm, forest, and mine of the 1854 Treaty. Eventually Brown got a draft treaty accepted by the State Department which contained such a list; it came to nothing because the American Senate would not consider it. But it raised the issue of the conflict of industrial and agricultural interests in Canada. When its terms were published there was an immediate outcry from the organized industrialists. Local boards of trade in the main urban centres passed resolutions by large majorities against it, and the Dominion Board of Trade meeting at Saint John also condemned it. Already the sacred phrase, "a National Policy", as applied to industrial protection was in the air. Two years later, in 1876, Macdonald was to adopt it as the main slogan of the Conservative party. It is interesting to follow the course of the *Nation* and the Canada First men on this issue. Their platform, as we have seen, had already shown signs of incipient protectionism. But the editorials about Brown's Washington mission begin with expressions of general approval of the principle of reciprocity, reservations being added as to the necessity of shielding Canadian industry from undue external dangers. (One must remember that the depression of 1873 was in full swing.) As the weeks go by the reservations come more and more to the forefront, until the writers end by denouncing Brown as whole-heartedly as any protectionist could wish.

This was what the vague idealism about a national sentiment came to when put to the test of practice. The young men of Canada First were mostly residents of Toronto; it was easy for them to identify the special interests of Toronto with the general interests of the nation as a whole. Their movement, after all, represented only the rhetoric of nationalism; they had not thought their way through the conditions which limit and determine any definition of the national interest. In the final analysis the Canada First movement was only a sectional movement clothing itself in the impressive garments of nationalism. When it came to identify the national interest with protection for infant industries, it had no further contribution to make to the discussion which could not equally well be made by the regular exponents of the philosophy of industrialism, the Conservative party. So it disappeared. But perhaps its short history is worth recalling today as a warning prelude to our contemporary discussions about the relationship of the general interest of the nation as a whole to the particular interests of its parts.

One of the marked effects of the depression upon Canadian intellectuals — an effect which can be abundantly illustrated from the programmes of the meetings of the Canadian Political Science Association in the past few years — has been an outburst of scholasticism on the subject of our federal institutions. The proverbial innocent visitor from another planet, if he happened to attend the meeting this year, would conclude, after glancing over the titles of the papers presented, that what we are suffering from in Canada at present is a crisis of federalism; whereas the truth is that, like every other country in the world, we are suffering from a crisis of capitalism and that the crisis has tended to take much the same form in all countries regardless of whether their political institutions are federally organized or not. No doubt the Communist historian of the next century will point to this curious eagerness of Canadian political scientists to focus their attention upon their federal political institutions instead of upon their capitalist economic institutions as merely another variation in the escape technique adopted by timid intellectuals in a revolutionary period.

At any rate, we have now a crop of ingenious rationalizers of the group interests which are located in the more depressed areas of our national community. They are erecting elaborate intellectual structures posited upon certain general principles as to the nature of federalism, and are demanding in consequence certain changes in the actual working of our federal institutions. Canadian Calhouns, if not as yet any Canadian Jeff Davises, have been springing up in East and West — not to mention Quebec where they have always flourished in profusion. This particular intellectual activity is, of course, a reaction, stimulated by hard times, against the long domination of our national economy by Hamiltonian ideas in their crudest interpretation. Such a reaction is in itself thoroughly healthy. But discussions about federalism, as about other political and legal concepts, quickly become involved in abstruse intellectual subtleties. We need to remind ourselves frequently of the obvious, that what is at issue in Canada today is the question, first, of how our communal income is to be restored to a level which will make possible the standard of living to which we had become accustomed, and, second, whether this be possible or not, how that income is to be divided among the ten million inhabitants of the country. In this major problem our federal political institutions provide only a minor complication.

This tendency to concentrate attention upon the political forms in which a society is organized instead of upon the economic forces which lie behind them is a characteristic of the modern bourgeois liberal mind. During the last fifteen years we have been having a costly object lesson in the bad results to which it leads in the realm of international relations. Liberal thinkers and statesmen go from refinement to refinement in working out the correct relationship of the abstract national state with the abstract international League of Nations, blissfully neglecting the concrete economic purposes which are institutionalized both in the national state and in the League. They talk eternally about the obstacles to progress caused by national sovereignty but do nothing about the imperious drive for profits carried on by the dominant economic groups which control the sovereign national state. We must beware of allowing our discussions about federalism within Canada, about the relationship of central and provincial governmental authorities, to drift into a similar liberal futility.

Dominion and provinces are not entities existing *per se*. The root conflicts which divide our ten million people are not between national and provincial governments, or between central provinces and outlying provinces. They are conflicts between various economic interest groups all of whom strive with varying success to use the political machinery of federal and provincial governments to assist them in achieving their purposes, *i.e.*, in staking out for themselves vested claims to a special share of the collective income. And in this competition of group interests each competitor does his best to identify his own special interest with that broader comprehensive national interest to which all profess adherence but which no one since Confederation has ever successfully defined. We must try to see these interest struggles within Canada in a pattern which is genuinely relevant to the facts. The starting point of all fruitful discussion about our present communal problems must be a clear understanding of the significance of what happened in 1867. Our elder Whig historians, legists, and political scientists have been allowed to dwell too long upon the setting up of a federal structure with elements curiously mixed from British and American sources, upon the working out of "the logic of responsible government", etc. Our younger neo-Whigs, the disciples of Turner, are too fond of dwelling upon the essentially sectional nature of the Canadian nation. What we are told on all these topics is no doubt true enough as far as it goes, but as a contribution to the understanding of our present difficulties it is superficial and is becoming out of date.

The essential work of the Fathers of Confederation was to weld the scattered British possessions in North America into a unity within which Canadian capitalism could expand and consolidate its power, to provide for the capitalist *entrepreneurs* of Montreal and Toronto a half-continent in which they could realize their dreams and ambitions. The dynamic drive which brought Confederation about had its centre in Montreal among the railway and banking magnates who were dreaming of new fields to conquer. It was for this purpose, and not merely to illustrate the abstract beauties of brotherly love, that Macdonald and Cartier built up their Anglo-French *entente;* it was for this purpose that Galt and Head and Monck drafted their paper schemes of British-American union and carried on their obscure negotiations behind the scenes. Federalism was only an accident imposed by the circumstances of the time; union was the essential achievement. In brief, what Macdonald and his associates accomplished in the 1860s in the northern half of this continent was an exact parallel to what Lincoln and Co. were accomplishing at the same time in the southern half. The two sets of statesmen worked with materials which were superficially very different; the incidentals of their statesmanship seem to have nothing in common; but the fundamental objectives were the same. It was Lincoln's function to eliminate the southern planter aristocracy, the only effective rival to northern industrial capitalism; to preserve the Union intact as a continental field of operations for the subsequent triumphant advance of American industrialism; in short, to establish the political framework within which the present economic empire of New York could be built up. Macdonald and Co. had not to save a union but to create one. But the ultimate end of their activities, of which they themselves were quite sufficiently conscious, was to capture and pre-empt for Montreal the opportunity of building up another similar economic empire extending across half a continent.

Since the 1860s these two economic empires have gone through a rapid expansion. The frontiers of settlement and exploitation have been steadily pushed back to the ultimate territorial limits of each empire. More important, there has gone on simultaneously a steady process of economic integration, of concentration of control at the centre. And this process of concentration has been accompanied inevitably by a distribution of income in which an increasingly larger share has been apportioned to the small group who sit with their hands upon the levers of power in the great metropolitan centres. This point as to the increasing concentration of economic power which characterizes all modern national capitalist systems does not need to be laboured here. It is the theme of innumerable books and studies in the United States and elsewhere; and the recent investigations of the Price Spreads Commission have thrown considerable light upon some aspects of it in Canada. Moreover — and here again I merely repeat an accepted commonplace which does not need to be developed or illustrated — this increasing concentration of economic power has been accompanied by a similar concentration of political power. The federal form of our institutions masks this process to some extent; but it is now fairly well recognized by all except a few incurable liberal romantics that political institutions on the whole only operate so as to express the economic balance of power within any given society. The individual citizen and his fellows who are without economic power gradually become the forgotten men of politics. And the more narrowly economic power tends to be monopolized in the hands of a small group, the more widely will the forgotten men of politics be distributed throughout the other classes of the community.

It is true that class divisions in Canada, as in the United States, are still only in process of emerging out of the sectional geographic divisions which resulted from our spreading over an empty continent. Because we are just passing out of this pioneer stage in the exploitation of our natural resources, our society is still more fluid than that of Europe, our population is more mobile, opportunities for individual advancement are more abundant; and so the evolution of North American capitalism has not yet produced the comparatively clear-cut class stratification which characterizes older economies. The two Turner principles of interpretation — the significance of the frontier and the significance of sections in American history — are still valid and still yield fruitful results in increasing our understanding of the past of this continent. But the frontier has now almost disappeared, and the ever-increasing concentration of capitalist control is levelling down the vertical divisions between sections. Eventually capitalism in America produces the same social pattern as in Europe.

If this, then, has been the fundamental trend of our social evolution since 1867, it was inevitable that during this period national interest should be interpreted primarily in terms of the interests of this industrial-financial group which was steadily emerging into a position of economic dominance. Significantly enough, the only policy in our history which ever reached the dignity of being called the National Policy was that of the protective tariff imposed in 1879. But at the same time this position of dominance was only gradually achieved after a long series of conflicts, bargains, and adjustments with other interest groups in the community. And broadly speaking, all these struggles tend to fall into the pattern of one main underlying struggle between industrial and agrarian interests. The conflict of interests is accompanied by a conflict of ideas; and the two generations since Confederation have resulted not merely in the victory of industrial and finance capitalism but in the imposition of its ideology upon our society as a whole. Man does not live by bread alone. He also requires slogans, catchwords, rationalizations of his activities. This complex interplay of interests and ideas goes on incessantly, of course, in all living societies.

When we realize this, we understand at once what has been the function of our party system in this process of formulating the general national interest; and we emancipate our minds from those mystic abstractions called Liberalism and Conservatism. It was the function of party leaders to act as brokers in an intricate process of bargaining and compromise, of manipulation and management, among competing interest groups, and to endeavour to reach some workable agreement among them, some *modus vivendi* which would hold the nation together. But if the *modus vivendi* was to be really workable, it must be presented to the public accompanied by a body of interpretative ideas, and the ideas must be infused with emotional uplift. Mr. Walter Lippmann in his book on *Public Opinion* (New York, 1922) has explained with great insight and subtlety how this process works; and he has pointed out that the bigger and more complex the society is, the more necessary it is for the unifying interpretative ideas to be empty of too much positive content. The most ingenious philosopher in his study could not have invented any concepts which would more perfectly fill all these requirements than the concepts of Liberalism and Conservatism with which our statesmen have worked since the 1850s.

The *modus vivendi*, such as it was, which was achieved under the guidance of Macdonald and Laurier, was the more easily reached because Canadian capitalism was going through a phase of marvellous and intoxicating expansion. In the rapid exploitation of the virgin natural resources of half a continent it did not much matter if some groups fared less well than others. There was plenty to go round, and those who were less successful at the moment were always buoyed up by hopes of the future. The increasing subservience of the national government to the acquisitive appetites of big-business-men-on-the-make seemed to be justified by results. Every Canadian, after all, was a business-man-on-the-make, big or little. Every Canadian was speculating on a future which promised to be automatically bigger and better. As long as there was, or promised to be, abundance, the question of an equitable distribution of the collective income did not arise in any pressing form. Thus while inequality was steadily rooting itself more deeply in our society, Canadians could still interpret their institutions as affording substantially equal opportunities to everyone with energy and ambition.

Intellectuals have always an important part to play in any community in helping to build up or tear down the communal ideology. What contribution has been made by Canadian intellectuals from the days of Canada First to the 1920s to the development of our national ideology, to the formulation of what came to be the prevailing conception of the national interest? This is a subject which contemporary students have hardly begun as yet to investigate. But a brief provisional report can be made with some confidence. Our economists have played the humble self-imposed rôle of minor technicians, never questioning the major purposes of the capitalist system in which they found themselves, never venturing any opinions about the general planning of the machine or the powering of its engines, pottering about with their little statistical measuring instruments, doing occasional odd repair jobs on Royal commissions, such as putting new brake linings into the financial mechanism, happy in their unambitious way as the intellectual garage-mechanics of Canadian capitalism. Our historians have played a rather flashier rôle. Not for them the greasy grimy jobs of testing and repairing in the workshop. They have been out among the white-collar boys in the sales-office in front, helping to sell the system to the public with a slick line of talk about responsible government and national autonomy.

But the synthesis which was undertaken by the Fathers of Confederation and carried on by their successors is now breaking down. The expansionist phase of our capitalist development has come to an end, and with a million and a half on relief our system is failing to deliver the goods. Along with this failure in practice goes a gradual disintegration of ideology. The traditional loyalties which provided the necessary psychological unifying force begin to dissolve as one group interest after another becomes conscious of its grievances and organizes a movement of protest. The social solidarity which seemed to have been achieved by two generations of experience as a nation begins to appear for what it was — only a temporary *modus vivendi* among competing interest groups. And the minor adjustments, which in the hands of a Macdonald or a Laurier looked like national statesmanship, no longer avail to soothe the growing discontent. An irrepressible conflict looms up which can no longer be banished or delayed by the old formulae. All the values of the old system are in question. . . .

What we need in Canada just now, and what only our intellectuals can give us, is "a trial philosophy of national interest" such as Mr. Charles A. Beard has recently been expounding in the United States in his two books, *The Idea of National Interest* (New York, 1934) and *The Open Door at Home* (New York, 1935). An examination of our natural and human resources and the way in which they are organized at present would provide the material on the basis of which we might proceed to formulate objectives such as might reasonably be aimed at by the Canadian people. In such objectives the elements of abundance, security, and equality would dominate, unless one has entirely misread the significance of our national history. The task would then remain to draft plans in the spirit, as Beard puts it, of "engineering rationality" for the realization of abundance, security, and equality. It would quickly become evident that the main obstacle to such plans was the monopolistic control of the instruments of wealth production in the hands of a few men seeking private profits. The work of the statesman would then be to mobilize those groups whose interests are thwarted by the dominant position of this small controlling group and to consolidate their force behind a new formulation of the national interest.

Would this amount in the end only to the old process of identifying the national interest with the particular interest of some special group or groups? Perhaps so. Would the victory of such a policy eliminate the conflicts of interest among different groups in our society? Of course not. But the new synthesis would release new energies, it would widen the range of opportunities for great masses of the people. It would not eliminate human selfishness. Men would still seek their own interests, but there would be more opportunity to take broad views and long views of what those interests are. At any rate, the alternatives to attempting some such programme are a continuance of the present chaos or the imposition of a solution of our troubles by demagoguery or by force. Plato's philosophers, one recalls, reluctantly intervened in human affairs to save themselves from the fate of being ruled by worse men. It is dangerous, we are told, for the social scientist to concern himself with objectives. Of course it is dangerous. But in a dangerous age there is no escape, even for social scientists, from living dangerously.

8. Keep Canada
out of War

(This article was published in *Maclean's* magazine, 15 May, 1937. It was
one of a series from various contributors discussing the Canadian defence
problem.)

It is now familiar knowledge that some time about 1933 or 1934
the world passed from the post-war into the pre-war era. The great
European powers are feverishly preparing for another war with one
another. They have not yet reached the stage at which the actions
of each government are regulated by the inexorable demands of
the military timetable of its general staff, but they are getting per-
ilously close to it. There is nothing much that a small and distant
country like Canada can do to stop this terrible drift towards war
in Europe. Our chief concern from now on must be whether we
are to go into the war or stay out of it.

There is, indeed, one thing that we can do to make a world war
less inevitable, and since 1935 our government has been doing it.
In international trade, Canada is not a small power but one of the
most important nations of the world. All economists agree that the
best way to relieve those pressures which threaten to produce the
explosion of a war is to enlarge the volume of international trade,
so that by a freer exchange of goods and services the standard of
living of all peoples may be raised and prosperity may be more
widely shared. Canada should do whatever she can in this way to
ease the economic and psychological strains that are slowly driving
the peoples of Europe mad. On the trade front we can give a lead
and show an example to the world.

Strangely enough, if you look around the contemporary scene,
you will notice that those who are most vehement in demanding
that we arm ourselves against unspecified enemies are also the very
people who have most obstinately opposed all steps towards freer
trade. There must be a moral somewhere in this.

To exchange goods and services freely with all peoples is the one
effective contribution which we in Canada can make towards world
peace. It is too late now to pretend to believe that, by promising

183

our military support to the League of Nations or to Great Britain, we help to assure peace in Europe. All that we help to assure by such action is the burying of 60,000 more Canadians somewhere across the ocean. It may be that another such mass burial service will also assure world peace, or democracy, or freedom — *after* the next war. But our experience during and since the last war should have made us sceptical about such claims. And we should be especially suspicious of all those elderly statesmen and publicists who so nobly dedicated one generation of Canadian youth to these high causes in 1914, and who can now think of no more fitting way of sanctifying that sacrifice than to dedicate another generation to a similar sacrifice.

As a force for maintaining collective security or for eliminating the threat of war from the world, the League of Nations no longer counts. Failing a lead by some great European power, primarily by Great Britain, there is nothing that we in Canada can do to gal- vanize it into life again; and there is not the remotest chance of such a lead in Europe being given. This hard fact is now recognized by everybody except a few inveterate idealogues in our League of Nations Society.

The choice, therefore, which we have to make as we face the European situation is whether we shall try to keep ourselves free from the contagion of war by sticking to our own affairs here in our North American home, or whether we shall plunge into the next European war on whichever side the present British Government may decide to support. There is no third choice. Ingenious diplo- mats may manœuvre so as to line up the League with its moral prestige on their side of the trenches. Skilful propagandists may try to persuade us that the cause of liberty and democracy is inextric- ably bound up with the victory of their side. And we may flatter ourselves that we can discern the issues clearly. But our historians will later disillusion us about all these things. All that we can decide at the moment is either that we stay out of the war or that we go into it blindly on the side of Britain and stay in it till the bitter end.

I believe, with the late John S. Ewart, that we in Canada should emulate Ulysses and his companions, and sail past the European sirens our ears stuffed with the tax-bills of the last war.

It will be said, however, that, in the present unsettled condition of the world, Canada herself lies in an exposed position, that we are in danger of attack from some international brigand, and that our only ultimate security lies in the power of the British

Empire. And if we accept protection from the Empire, we ought to contribute to its defence. We should not sponge upon Great Britain or, alternatively, upon the United States. Let us examine this proposition.

We may note, first of all, that the identity of these international brigands who are about to leap upon us is never specified. The various Little Orphan Annies who are trying to make our flesh creep with tales of how the foreign goblins will get our Pre-Cambrian shield if we don't watch out, never condescend to give us concrete details.

The fact is that Canada's chief protection lies in her geographical position. As the Russians used to depend upon their famous Generals January and February, so we are guarded by Generals Atlantic and Pacific. No one has produced the slightest evidence that it is possible for an armed force of any size to land upon and take possession of Canadian territory. Enemy fleets cannot operate thousands of miles from their base. Bombing airplanes have not merely to cross the ocean with their bombs, but to get back to their base again. I have yet to hear of any competent military authority, either within or outside of our Department of Defence, who thinks that an effective invasion of our territory from overseas is practicable, or that we need to guard against any danger greater than that of sporadic hit-and-run raids. We should put our coastal areas in proper defensive condition against such eventualities, by provision of mines, submarines, air bases, etc. We should take steps to protect shipping near our shores. We can do all this without any enormous expense.

But this is something quite different from what our government is starting out to do this year; namely, to construct the skeleton framework of a great national armed force, a framework which can be filled in and expanded by mass enlistment or conscription on the outbreak of war, and which is primarily designed not for local defence at all but for a series of expeditionary contingents overseas. I have yet to hear of a single journalist or military man in Ottawa who doesn't (in private) laugh at the Government's pretence that its present defence expenditures are meant for defence here in Canada.

If we equip ourselves with a defence force which is designed to meet such dangers as can reasonably be calculated by our military experts, it is highly unlikely that any invading force coming by sea or air from across the ocean can do much damage to us.

Moreover, there is no potential enemy across the Atlantic or Pacific who is in a position to try the experiment of an invasion of Canada. When we pierce through all the vague alarmist talk about the portentous dangers that threaten us, it becomes clear that there are only two powers who could possibly contemplate an expedition against us. They are Germany and Japan. (The Italian baritone, whose voice is already becoming a little cracked, can't even subdue the half-armed Spaniards at the other end of his Mediterranean lake.)

There may be some excitable persons in Canada who get nightmares dreaming about a gratuitous unprovoked attack by a German or a Japanese army which will travel thousands of miles and suddenly out of a clear sky pounce upon us. We should enlarge our mental hospitals to accommodate any citizens with such over-stimulated imaginations. No situation is conceivable in Europe or in the Far East in which either of these two Fascist powers would have its hands free to embark on a serious expedition across the ocean to attack us. In Europe the balance of forces on the Rhine, the Danube, the Vistula, across the Alps, and across the English Channel, compels Hitler and his advisers to keep their attention concentrated there. Even today, as everyone knows who has been following the Spanish situation, Hitler's Reichswehr staff is gravely alarmed at his recklessness in sending troops and equipment so far afield as Spain, when they may be needed any moment much nearer home. People who imagine that in a European war Germany would detach some of her forces to invade a country 3,000 miles across the Atlantic are more insane than any German Nazi has ever been alleged to be. And after the European war is over both sides will be too exhausted for adventures in America. Similar considerations hold good for Japan. She has staked her future in China, and with Russia watching her, next door, she is not going to dissipate her forces and make new enemies for herself by trying to seize British Columbia.

There is one special danger in the future for which we should prepare on our Pacific front. If Japan and the United States ever go to war, our British Columbia coast will lie on the great circle line which will be the natural air route by which their air squadrons would try to get at one another. If we want to stay out of such a war, we must establish such a control of our coast as will discourage either belligerent from the temptation to violate our neutrality. But this is not an immediate danger. With the best will in the world to do so, the Japs and Americans cannot yet go to war because they are so far apart that neither power can injure the other in any vital spot. So we have considerable time until engineers and scientists have advanced our twentieth-century civilization to the point at which a trans-pacific war is practicable.

Let us then equip ourselves to meet such dangers as competent military experts may tell us are real, and let us refuse to excite ourselves over the nightmares either of the honestly mistaken alarmists or of the politician-salesmen of armament firms. We can provide for our local defence here in North America without needing to sponge either on Britain or on the United States. This is all that our national self-respect demands. With fires breaking out in various parts of the world, we must take out some insurance. But this is purely a business proposition, and the amount of our insurance can be proportionate to our risks.

It will be said, however, that Canada depends for her livelihood upon foreign trade, and that it is not merely our geographic territory that we have to protect. There is truth in this, but let us keep our sense of proportion. For the fiscal year 1936, 56.8 per cent of our imports came from the United States and 42.5 per cent of our exports went to the United States. North and South America as a whole accounted for 63.2 per cent of our imports and 46.4 per cent of our exports. All this part of our trade is carried on overland or along American coasts, and is not likely to be affected by wars on the far side of the oceans.

Of the other part, the transoceanic trade, only a small fraction is carried in Canadian vessels or by Canadian crews. In submarine- and airplane-infested waters this trade cannot be protected completely. But the British and French navies protected it in the last war and they will do their best to protect it in the next one — not because they wish to do us a favour which puts us in their debt, but because they need our goods. In the same way, they will protect the trade of the Argentine, of Denmark and the Scandinavian countries, of the United States, of any country that will trade with them. We ourselves cannot possibly protect this trade except by such an expenditure as would cost more than the trade is worth. And before we decide to try to protect it by joining Britain in her next European war, we should ask ourselves seriously just what the full cost in men and money of such action is likely to be, and how far the profits of that part of our external trade — less than half of the total trade — justify such a cost.

There still survives in Canada a dwindling body of belated colonials who treat any frank discussion of our relations with Great Britain as high treason, and who regard it as our duty to spring to arms whenever the summons comes from Westminster. It is useless to argue with such people. But there are not many of them left, and there are no more of them being born. They have an undue share of the more dignified posts in church and state, and this makes them seem a more important section of our community than they are. The rest of the community, and especially the younger members of it, are now for the most part able to discuss the question of our British relations from a purely Canadian point of view.

The military advantage of the British connection is supposed to be that it guarantees our security. I have tried to show that, whatever may be the case of other parts of the British Empire, we in Canada are not in a position of any great insecurity, whether we are in or out of the Empire.

Whatever the advantages of the connection, if the British Commonwealth is to be treated as an offensive and defensive union, it involves for us also certain heavy costs. In the first place, if we tie ourselves to British leadership, we are committing ourselves to go to war in Europe whenever the present Chamberlain-Hoare-Baldwin Government stumbles into a war. Are we quite sure that our Canadian frontier also is on the Rhine? Are we prepared to profess a blind faith in the rightness of the present British Government's foreign policy? Let us not deceive ourselves by fine phrases. We have no means of controlling the policy of the present British Government; it simply presents us with a *fait accompli*. Armaments may honestly be intended for the preservation of peace; but their ultimate use, and the use to which they have always been put in the past history of Europe, is for the fighting of war.

It is ultimately to the fighting of a war that we commit ourselves when we line up behind the present British Government. And this is an unlimited commitment. For, as the ancient Greek historian long ago pointed out, the course of war cannot be calculated. We cannot go into it on any limited basis. All past wars have been expected by the belligerents to be short ones, but most of them have turned out to be long and exhaustive.

We shall also remember something else.

The British navy does not exist for our defence. If Canada went out of the Commonwealth tomorrow, the British navy would not be diminished by a single destroyer. It was built and it functions for the defence of Great Britain and her dependent Empire, of which we are not a part. Nor need we worry about the alleged shameful contrast between the heavy burden borne by the British taxpayer and the slight cost of defence which falls on the Canadian citizen.

That heavy burden of the British taxpayer is due to the fact that he enjoys the profits from an extended Empire and that he (or his government for him) thinks that it is worth while to spend money and men in the defence of that Empire. His present government has shown repeatedly that it is not prepared to fight for democracy or for the principles of the League. It would run no risks for international morality in Manchuria or Ethiopia. But it will fight for its Empire. And that Empire is not our Empire. We get no profits from it; the benefits accruing to us since 1932 from the preferences given by the British dependencies are negligible. We have no investments in it; Canadian external investments are almost entirely in the United States and in Central and South America. Our sons get no well-paid jobs in the Imperial service in Africa or Asia. The Gibraltar-Suez-Aden-Bombay-Singapore life-line is not our life-line.

When, therefore, our native Colonel Blimps or peregrinating Imperialists from across the ocean orate to us about our partnership with the mother country in defence, it is fitting for us to ask: Defence of what? The solidarity of the Commonwealth must be based upon something that will appeal to our reason more forcibly than the defence of British investments in Africa and Asia.

We do share certain ideals and traditions with the people of Great Britain, and these are the most precious part of our civilization. But surely we require something more plausible than the record of the present British Government since 1931 to make us believe that it is for these ideals that we shall be asked to bury more Canadians in Europe. If the price of cherishing these ideals is to be that Canada is bound to support with arms the kind of policy which has recently been pursued by the British Government, it may occur to a good many Canadians that perhaps we can best nourish those institutions — free speech and assembly, the rule of law, government by discussion, toleration of minorities — by confining ourselves strictly to our own affairs here in North America. And pointing out considerations of this kind is not being anti-English, it is merely being pro-Canadian.

There remains the most important of all the considerations which

Canadians should bear in mind when they discuss the problems of our external policy. And that is the disastrous effect upon our national unity of plunging into another overseas war.

On July 1 of this year, 1937, we shall celebrate the seventieth anniversary of our Canadian Confederation. As we take stock of our assets and liabilities, we must all regretfully admit that the experiment of building up a united Canadian community here in the northern half of North America has not been too successful. We are all more acutely aware today than we have ever been before how deep and wide are the cleavages that divide different sections of our people. Our national unity is threatened by bitter disputes between races and religions, between geographical sections of the country, between occupational groups, between employers and workers, between rich and poor. Provincial particularism is rampant from the Atlantic to the Pacific. (It is only the citizens of Ontario who labour under the curious delusion that when they give vent to their parochial Ontario prejudices they are expressing a national point of view.) And all of these differences, which have been accentuated by seven lean years of depression, seem to be in no wise softened by the return of better times.

We should recognize now, as we think over our two generations of experience as a nation, that a real solidarity of interest and sentiment can only be achieved slowly in a society composed of such diverse elements as our Dominion. We need time, and above all, we need quiet and peace. If fortune grants us time and peace, we may hope that gradually a healthier tone of tolerance and conciliation and kindliness will be established in the intercourse of our eleven million Canadians with one another.

But nothing is more certain than that our entry into another war, except one which is forced upon us by an actual invasion of our territory, will destroy overnight all such unity as we have hitherto achieved. Relations between French and English in our country are still embittered by the memories of the last war; and in another war there will be no unanimity even among the English-speaking Canadians. Another war will put such a strain upon our national structure as it may not be able to withstand. It will substitute an atmosphere of hate and hysteria for one of reasonableness and goodwill. By the imposition of an artificial unity enforced through the machinery of a totalitarian state, it will delay and perhaps make impossible the growth of any genuine unity based on conciliation and consent.

Most fatal of all results, war will accentuate all the existing social and class divisions within our society. For in an economy which depends upon the motive of private profit, there are no effective means by which government can "conscript wealth" or "take the profit out of war". To encourage hopes of such a Utopia is merely to ensure that the ultimate popular disillusionment will be all the more bitter. When it is discovered how the profits and the sacrifices of war are actually being apportioned amongst our people, the consequences are going to be extremely ugly. And they will not be rendered any less ugly when the realization spreads that, in many cases, the men who were loudest in preaching this next war for democracy were also the men who were most determined in their opposition to all those movements for collective bargaining and for social security in which the poorer members of our democracy are most directly interested.

Most Canadians believe that the experiment of building up a united democratic national community in Canada has been worth while hitherto, and is worth continuing. They should think seriously about what will happen to that experiment if we deliberately plunge our country into the civil discord which participation in an overseas war will provoke.

9. The Canadian Party System in Transition

(A paper read at the annual meeting of the Canadian Political Science Association, 1943 and printed in the *Canadian Journal of Economics and Political Science,* August, 1943.)

The Canadian Political Science Association, half-way through the second year of the Century of the Common Man, naturally devotes some of its attention to the prospects of democracy in our own country. It is fitting that we should inquire into what has been happening to our party system, for we have had as long an experience as most modern countries in the working of popular political parties as part of the machinery of democracy, and our experience should be of some significance to other peoples as well as to ourselves. How little systematic study has been done on this subject, however, is brought home to a Canadian after he has lived for a time in the United States and has had to try to answer Americans when they ask for books on the principles, organization, and history of Canadian parties, such as they produce so abundantly on their own parties. It might not be a bad idea, therefore, to begin this paper with some reference to recent American discussions of their party system. One can usually derive from a study of American experience the most useful categories of thought in which to arrange our own Canadian experience. And American books on democracy in general and on political parties as one of the techniques of democracy have been pouring from their presses in great profusion in recent years.

Now the essential picture of their party system on which all the American authorities agree is that of two national parties, each trying to collect votes from all the major interest groups in the country; each holding its supporters together by patronage and by appeals to traditional ideology, in slogans, symbols, myths, which may have little relevance to the continuous process of bargaining, compromise, and adjustment carried on by its leaders amongst the various competing interest groups; and each doing its best to remove the threat of such third parties as may arise among groups whose claims have not been satisfactorily adjusted, by taking over whatever seems expedient of the third-party programmes. It is through the two national parties that the "broker" function of the modern democratic state is mainly performed. A democracy is simply a society in which all interest groups have an equal chance to present their claims for benefits from the gains of civilization and to get them adjusted. It follows from this analysis that the pressure-group organizations which conduct the bargaining with the party organizations are as essential to the working of democratic politics as the parties themselves. And the well-brought-up American undergraduate in political science today is not only acquainted with the history of the Democratic and Republican parties, but with the activities of the National Association of Manufacturers, the Chambers of Commerce, and all the organizations speaking for business; the A.F. of L., the C.I.O., and other labour organizations; the American Farm Bureau Federation, the Grange, the National Farmers Union, and other agrarian associations; the American Legion, the Anti-Saloon League, the League of Women Voters, and all the other groups who conduct propaganda and keep lobbyists at Washington or the state capitals to attend to their special interests.

In Canada this double set-up of parties and pressure groups through which the politics of democracy is carried on is not so fully developed as in the United States. Or, at any rate, it has not been so fully studied and documented. But I presume that most academic students of politics in this country would accept the same kind of analysis of our party system as Americans make of theirs. They would agree, that is to say, that the national political parties of Canada and the United States, have differed from those of most other countries, including other English-speaking countries, in their lack of any clear-cut philosophy or programme, a condition which arises from the fact of their being composed of a fairly representative cross-section of all the interest groups of a continent-wide nation. Though the history of both countries has seen a long struggle between rural agrarian and urban industrial interests, agrarian protest movements against the domination of politics by industry and finance have never produced a successful agrarian party. Modern industrialization did not lead, as it did everywhere else, to the rise of an industrial workers' party. Through all social and economic changes the established classical North American two-party system persisted. Age could not wither it nor custom stale its infinite variety.

I propose at this point to turn to a recent American discussion of this subject of the politics of democracy.[1] Its author is Professor Pendleton Herring of Harvard University, and it appeared in 1940. It is a brilliant defence of this classical North American two-party system, as good a defence as will ever be written, urbane, moderate, sensible, acute. It makes the same sort of sophisticated appeal to the educated élite which Walter Bagehot made to a similar class of readers in the 1860s when he wrote his exposition of the English Constitution as the best technique for carrying on popular government in the kind of society which existed in mid-Victorian England. Professor Herring is indeed a conservative very much like Bagehot, sceptical and realistic, and very much given to emphasizing the efficient part of the constitution as contrasted with the dignified.

His thesis is that the existing party system is the best way of conducting politics in our contemporary North American democracy. Most writers about American parties manage to convey in ironical overtones or in sidelong wistful glances at English and European politics their own preference for parties which would be more definitely the expression of opposed alternative tendencies in philosophy and programme. But Professor Herring has no use for an alignment of conservative *versus* liberal, right *versus* left. In a society which is so diverse as that of the United States and which lacks the leadership of a traditional cohesive governing class such as England enjoys, he thinks that the function of producing workable compromises among the claims of competing interest groups is best performed by parties of the American type. He doubts if American unity is strong enough to stand the strain of open organized conflict between such parties as the British Conservative and Labour parties. He has little sympathy with demands for a new party of the left which would make democracy more real by giving expression to the interests and ideals of the common man; this sort of language, he explains, is merely the rationalization instinctively adopted by rising interest groups who desire a change in the *status quo*, and it has been familiar in American history since the day of Jefferson's Democratic Republicans who "cherished the people". Concepts such as "the people" and "public opinion" are democratic myths, not tools of descriptive analysis to be used by political scientists. "In practice our major parties are primarily concerned

---

[1] Pendleton Herring, *The Politics of Democracy: American Parties in Action* (New York, 1940).

not with framing issues and drawing up distinctive programmes but
in trying to discover some way of bringing together in a harmonious
relationship as large a proportion of the voters as possible. . . ."[2]
"The object of representative government is not to represent men
in all their divergencies but rather to establish freely their common
grounds. . . . The accomplishment of party government lies in its
demonstrated ability for reducing warring interests and conflicting
classes to co-operative terms. . . ."[3] "If our parties," he wrote in
answer to a criticism of his book by Max Lerner, "come to stand
for strongly divergent points of view and demand the strongest
loyalty of their followers . . . the cleavages within society will be
deepened and that area of common agreement wherein men may
safely agree to disagree will be narrowed."[4]

Even in Britain, he points out, the differences between parties are
not as clear-cut as we may imagine. In the nineteenth century the
Conservatives passed as much factory and health legislation as the
Liberals, and in our own day they have done as much to extend the
social insurances and services such as public housing as has Labour.
In fact his common-sense remarks on the Laski myth of two opposed
political armies confronting one another in modern society with
irreconcilable philosophies and programmes — socialism *versus*
capitalism — may be recommended to those Canadian editors who
have been trying to make the shivers run up and down our backs by
ghost stories about how the doctrinaire socialist goblins will get us
if we don't watch out.

The root criticism of Professor Herring's type of analysis is that
his book would inevitably defeat its own purpose if it were read by
many plain ordinary citizens. He admits himself at the end that
some readers may find too much agnosticism in what he has written.
Once let the knowledge spread that party leaders are only brokers
bargaining among competing interest groups, and the loyalty of
the masses to the party slogans and symbols which hold them to-

---

[2] *Ibid.*, p. 102.

[3] *Ibid.*, p. 131. A few pages later he quotes with approval a statement of
Professor W. E. Hocking: "The politician is the man who deliberately faces
both the certainty that men must live together, and the endless uncertainty
on what terms they can live together, and who takes upon himself the task
of proposing the terms, and so transforming an unsuccessful group into a
successful group."

[4] Mr. Lerner reviewed the book in the *Nation*, September 22, 1940. Professor Herring replied to the review in a letter, October 26, 1940.

gether will disintegrate. The party only manages to function as a broker because it can count on the steady support of great numbers of voters who believe in it for the ideals and the principles they suppose it to embody. One of the fundamental troubles in our modern democracies is the feeling of disillusionment and futility which has become so widespread in people's attitude towards politics, and the faith in democratic parties is an essential part of the faith by which our democratic society is maintained. If parties are to deserve that faith, there must be some more direct connection between their actual practices and their professed ideals. And this is why the English type of parties with coherent philosophies and programmes is preferable to the American in our present critical times.

Only university professors can stand the shock of the new Machiavellianism now so popular in academic circles, which discovers that the basis of popular government is merely a collection of myths, symbols, folklore, ideology about "liberty, fraternity, equality", "sovereignty of the people", "the general will", "public opinion", etc. and that human society consists of an élite who understand these esoteric truths and the masses whose fate it is to be manipulated by the skilful use of these democratic or of other anti-democratic myths. This conception that the masses exist to be manipulated is the basis of all anti-democratic thinking. Professor Herring declares himself a democrat in the sense that he holds that belief by the masses in the democratic myths rather than in the totalitarian myths makes for a more flexible and experimental society and so in the long run for a happier and more stable society. But this is hardly what a belief in democracy meant when educated people still really did believe in democracy.

However, Professor Herring's book is a remarkably acute and realistic analysis. It may be recommended to all hot gospellers, either of the left or the right, who imagine that in the large-scale complex society of the United States or Canada we are ever likely to have parties in power putting into practice rigid dogmatic principles of action and making no compromise with expediency. The danger will always be with us that by the time a party has reached that degree of maturity which has brought it close to power it will have come to stand for nothing in particular, that the North American environment will have absorbed it. . . .

Well, this is a long-winded, round-about, professorial way of approaching the subject of Canadian political parties in our contemporary crisis of democracy, the topic which was assigned to me. So now let me approach it more directly.

My main thesis will be that what has been happening in Canada for the last twenty-odd years is a transition from an old two-party system to a new and more effective one. Obviously, since the end of the last war, the classical North American party system, as expounded by all the American commentators, has broken down in our part of North America. In the generation before 1914 the Canadian parties of Macdonald and Laurier had become almost perfect examples of this type. They functioned in a society in which there was general agreement that the chief duty of government was to produce material prosperity by supporting business enterprise. Both parties proclaimed essentially the same policy of material expansion through this partnership of government and capitalistic business, and there had been no challenge to their monopoly of the political stage. Canada had not even seen such a challenge as the muckraking era provided in the United States. As it happens, the best book that has ever been written about Canadian politics, André Siegfried's *The Race Question in Canada*, which was published in 1907 at the height of the Laurier era, contains an analysis of Canadian parties along the exact line now made familiar in the standard American books on American politics. Siegfried was especially struck by the frank appeals of politicians on material grounds, and by the care of leading statesmen to avoid issues which might really divide the public into sincerely and passionately opposed political parties. "They exert themselves to prevent the formation of homogeneous parties divided according to creed or race or class. The purity of political life suffers from this, but perhaps the very existence of the Federation is the price. The existing parties are thus entirely harmless."[5]

But the war of 1914, as we now all know, brought to an end the Arcadian North American serenity which made possible the working of this free and easy North American party system. The war put a strain upon our national structure from which we did not recover during the long armistice. In particular we never returned to the normalcy of the old party system. Third parties broke up the monopoly of the two old parties, and since 1918 no party in our federal general elections has won the support of a majority of the

---

[5] André Siegfried, *The Race Question in Canada* (London, 1907), p. 143.

voters except once, in 1940, when the Liberals got 55 per cent of the votes cast.

The new situation produced by the last war has been so clearly explained in the report of the Rowell-Sirois Commission that I cannot do better than quote from it here. "In Canada as in other countries the War had revolutionary effects. . . . A society which prided itself on equality of opportunity found itself being divided into classes. The inequality of burdens and benefits arising out of the War promoted stratification. . . . The opposition of farmer and labour elements to conscription was symptomatic of deeper discontent. . . . The federal political parties had been based upon the common acceptance, with varying interpretations and emphasis, of certain general policies. The alliance of powerful groups of agriculture and labour in the progressive movement was based on the view that the old line parties had become organizations to further class interests prejudicial to the general public interest. It involved reliance upon class political organizations as a means of redressing the balance in their favour. The denial that the national policies of the two old parties furthered common national interests was a new political doctrine."[6]

In fact the two old parties had worked reasonably well as long as they had to deal with economic issues, in a society which had no deep or rigid class divisions; they had never been continuously successful in adjusting the conflicts of race and religion. Now after the war there was a deeper and more bitter race cleavage than that generation had ever known, and added to it were new class and occupational differences which the old parties had little experience in handling. Since the war everything that has happened has tended to concentrate economic power, and hence political power, into the hands of a small group. However much trouble the old vertical divisions between geographical sections may have continued to cause, the new horizontal division between classes has tended to become more and more the dominant fact in our society as in every modern industrialized society. In dealing with these new conflicts among group interests the old parties were too much under the control of one class group to function as honest brokers any more.

The result of this failure of the old parties to provide a national

---

[6] *Report of The Royal Commission on Dominion-Provincial Relations* (3 vols., Ottawa, 1940), Book I, pp. 89-109.

leadership that would seem attractive to a substantial majority of the people in the way that the leadership of Macdonald and Laurier had seemed to be was, of course, to give third party movements in Canada an opportunity such as they had never had before. It is a paradox of the two-party system that it works best when there are more than two parties, for the challenge of new parties preserves flexibility in the old ones. But the function of the minor parties in North American politics had always been to formulate issues before the major parties were ready to take them up, to agitate and educate, to present new points of view, and to leave the great responsibility of adjusting conflicts and working out a national policy to the major parties. . . .

Obviously there are too many variables in the present Canadian situation for any predictions to be made with confidence. And academic political scientists have no tools for measuring these processes of change which are as reliable as the guesses of good newspapermen. But it may be said that an election in the existing confusion which failed to give a majority of seats to any one party would make a coalition of Liberals and Conservatives almost inevitable. And this would sooner or later lead to a new two-party alignment in which the division would be more clearly between right and left than it has ever been in our lifetime, much more in fact like the English alignment of parties than like the American. The issue would then be as to the extent of government control over the economy and of public enterprise in making the economy function at a high level of employment; and an extension of government functions would be supported or opposed because such extension promised to result in a distribution of the national income more favourable to certain groups who have done comparatively badly in the past and less favourable to others who have done very well in the past. This issue would be presented on one side as that between the people and the economic royalists, and on the other as that between freedom and regimentation. It would not be a clear-cut issue between capitalism and socialism, partly because in our complex society all sorts of other issues would cut across it, but mainly because capitalism and socialism are now only abstract ideas laid up in a Platonic heaven to be argued over by newspaper editors and university undergraduates. Practical politics is concerned with the question of who gets what, when, where, and how.

A new alignment of this kind would differentiate us from the United States where Democrats and Republicans are as completely in charge of politics as ever. And it is worth noting that the reason for the survival of the old party system south of the border is that it adjusted itself sufficiently to meet the new responsibilities imposed on politics by the depression. In Canada we had no New Deal, no A.A.A. or other measures designed to give agriculture a "parity" with urban industry, no Wagner Act for the trade unions, no great public housing schemes, no C.C.C. camps for unemployed youth, no T.V.A. to reconstruct a vast blighted area, no Federal Writers or Federal Artists Projects, no new parkways about our big cities and no new recreation camps among our lakes and forests, and — last but not least — no fireside chats. In the United States there came together under the leadership of one of the old parties a North American model of the popular front which succeeded in making the necessary adjustments in party policy to keep the old system sufficiently flexible and adaptable to new needs and demands. But while no new party arose in the United States, there did develop there a new phenomenon in the alignment of the voters, a division more clearly on class lines. In the 1936 and 1940 elections organized workers and farmers, the little men in general, were more solidly lined up in the support of one of the parties than had happened for a long time in American history.

In Canada there is another complicating factor which differentiates us from the United States. This is the relationship between the two major racial groups. Canadian national parties from this point of view have never been much more than loose coalitions of English-speaking and French-speaking groups. On the way in which these coalitions have worked in the past and will presumably continue to work in the future there are two observations to be made. One is that French Quebec has always tended, like nationalist Ireland from O'Connell to Parnell, to be a one-party democracy. A minority nationality seeking both local self-government and cultural autonomy seldom feels that it can afford the luxury of party division within its ranks. From the time of Papineau Quebec politics have been marked by the domination of one major party which achieves a disciplined cohesive support behind its leadership for which there is no parallel in English-speaking Canada. Today there seems little likelihood of any of the English-speaking political groups, old or new, making much headway in Quebec; but sooner or later the majority French group which emerges from the present confusion in the French province will reach the position where it considers a working agreement with one of the English groups.

What this coalition may call itself is immaterial. In the past similar coalitions have been called in turn Conservative and Liberal. They have always been coalitions of equals, with each partner running its own local affairs.

In the second place, this bi-racial coalition has always been kept together through trials and troubles by the close co-operation of a pair of leaders, one English and one French, who have found each other intellectually and temperamentally congenial and whose personal partnership has held their followers in line. Without this kind of leadership the coalition is unstable. This was the way in which things worked under Baldwin and LaFontaine, Macdonald and Cartier, King and Lapointe. Macdonald did not find Chapleau quite a satisfactory successor to Cartier; and one of Laurier's weaknesses after 1896 was that he never found an English-Canadian partner to whom he could give his complete trust. Perhaps he would not have had to look for one had Blake remained in Canadian politics, for Laurier and Blake had common tastes and common opinions about most of the issues and individuals of their time; in particular they agreed philosophically and temperamentally on the issue which has made it most difficult for the two races to work together in the last fifty years, that of British imperialism.

At the present moment a good deal of the confusion of our politics is due to the fact that we are waiting both for the new party groups and the new leaders under whom there will be resumed this peculiar Canadian technique of a bi-racial coalition. If the long era of the Liberal form of this coalition is coming to an end — perhaps it is not; if the separatism so dear to some Laurentian hot-heads is in the long run impossible, and the imposition of an English-dominated government, equally dear to some hot-heads in Toronto, is equally impossible; then one of the main responsibilities of our party system after the war will be to work out the terms on which the two races can co-operate for another generation through some new coalition party. It would be highly dangerous to speculate here on the intriguing subject of which of the various groups in English and in French Canada are the parties of destiny and who will be the joint leaders of the new coalition. . . .

After this war we shall need a positive national policy in which a bold and imaginative leadership by the national government will create, or seem to create, opportunities for all groups rather than imposing restrictions and irritating controls. Under such leadership differences of interest can be adjusted at a high level of national income rather than at a low declining level; and the process of adjustment will result in national harmony rather than in the national disintegration which we experienced during the 1920s and 1930s. The process of adjustment, that is, will have to be accompanied by policies which make for full employment and for social security.

So I bring this long rambling discourse to a close with the conclusion of a student who is older and wiser than I am, Professor Carl Becker, the most acute and judicious of American historians. Writing about the political future in the United States, he has said: "Whatever it turns out to be, it will have been created by the traditional American procedure — by fighting for good bargains by means of ballots and economic pressure, by unlimited indulgence in the blare and blarney and pandemonium of free propaganda all compact of truth and falsehood, by imputing bad faith to opponents and invoking the American way of life on behalf of every special interest. . . . This is the normal American way of life, and whatever comes of it, supposing it to be something less than disaster, we will still call it democracy."[7]

---

[7] Carl Becker, "Democratic Virtues" (*Yale Review*, Summer, 1939; quoted by Herring, *The Politics of Democracy*, p. 419).

10. Random Remarks on Socialism and Freedom

(*Canadian Forum,* August, 1947.)

This is the season of midsummer calm. . . . It is, therefore, a good season for a calm discussion of the subject of socialism and freedom.

Most of the local attacks on the C.C.F. in this connection have been so outrageous in their misrepresentations that the C.C.F. leaders have apparently decided to ignore them. It is doubtful whether this is good policy. It is not enough to keep on repeating that the C.C.F. is a democratic movement controlled by its rank-and-file members. In 1932 the leaders who launched the C.C.F. during the depression conceived of socialism as an emancipating movement which promised to free ordinary men and women from the most oppressive tyranny of all — the economic regimentation and degradation that are caused by poverty, unemployment, and insecurity. But since then the world has had a terrible demonstration of what organized state power can do when in the hands of fanatics who care for power alone. And it is foolish for socialists to pretend that there are no dangers in the extension of state activity which their programme involves.

Socialist panegyrics about the mystic beauties of Planning are apt to be just as silly, and sometimes just as dishonest, as the hymns to Free Enterprise which are intoned by their opponents. And when socialists keep on harping about controls as the essence of their policy, they lend plausibility to the charges that they are really frustrated bureaucrats with an itch to manage other people's business for them. As a matter of fact, there does not exist anywhere in the world, not even in Russia, an example of pure planning in the abstract which covers the whole of a community's life from start to finish. What we have is a complex of particular partial plans mixed in with a great deal of improvisation and *ad hoc* experiment. "Planning" in the universal sense is just as unreal and ideal a concept as "Free Enterprise", which also has never existed save in economic textbooks and newspaper editorials. The real subject of controversy is how much central planning shall be mixed with how much private enterprise.

The theoretical demonstrations of the Hayeks and Lippmanns that planning must *a priori* be totalitarian are mere exercises in verbal definition, very much like the old scholastic discussions of how many angels could stand upon the point of a needle. They have been answered by other theoretical disquisitions. But the real answer as to whether socialism is compatible with liberty will come from experience in Labour Britain and New Zealand and such places. And there is not the slightest evidence that liberal socialists need to be much worried as yet.

Still, socialists should ease up on their persistent talk about controls. What the world needs chiefly at present is enterprise and imagination, initiative and vision. The defenders of capitalism are quite right in maintaining that these qualities were given full scope in the capitalism of the past and that this was the reason for the great material progress of recent generations. We still need enterprise; and it is up to socialists to demonstrate, when they become responsible for policy, that public enterprise is just as possible as private enterprise. The mere taking over of the economy under state control is no guarantee in itself that public enterprise will be forthcoming.

Also, socialists who come out of the liberal tradition of the nineteenth-century English-speaking communities need constantly to remind themselves of those two good old liberal proverbs: eternal vigilance is the price of freedom; all power tends to corrupt, and absolute power corrupts absolutely. In any society there will always be a need for checks and balances upon power, wherever located in that society. Socialists should do more thinking than they are fond of doing upon the problem of how these checks and balances may be institutionalized in a socialist society.

There are two simple tests that contemporary socialists might impose upon themselves if they want to find out how far they really believe in liberty. One is an easy private test which should be made compulsory among Canadian C.C.F.ers. Most of us at some time or other in our past found Bellamy's *Looking Backward* a very attractive book. We should re-read it now to see how it strikes us. Bellamy's ideal society was one of the most authoritarian ever imagined. He speaks constantly of an "industrial army"; he mentions that of course there is no right to strike against the government which runs all the economic activities of the community. His hero is entranced on Sunday morning when he hears a propaganda sermon issuing from the radio (which Bellamy has already imagined in the 1880s) praising the existing form of society as against the old unregenerate society; but it never occurs to him to ask whether critics and heretics have access to the state radio. The masses of the people, *i.e.* the industrial army, have no power to choose their leaders and controllers. People who still find Bellamy's society attractive, after re-reading his book with the experience of Russia and Germany in their minds, should reinvestigate their own liberalism. They have been dazzled by his picture of a perfectly harmonious society fully equipped with the gadgets which we North Americans think to be the visible proof of civilization. Liberal socialists should be mature enough to understand that a society, however organized, which is not full of controversy and friction, is not likely to be a free society. Bellamy achieved harmony exactly as Hitler and Stalin did, by eliminating dissenters (he is not very clear about this) and by preconditioning the minds of the masses so that they would want exactly what their governors supplied for them.

The second test is one which non-socialists are applying to socialists in western countries every day. It is their attitude to "Soviet Democracy". Western socialists who are still worshipping or indulging in subtle hair-splitting, as they prostrate themselves before the fairy-story of a society of workers and peasants ever marching on to ever new democratic victories, are justly objects of suspicion to their fellow citizens. All those who in this year 1947 still refuse to see the police-state with its political N.K.V.D. and its concentration camps, its single totalitarian party and its régime of terror and mass-deception, are convicting themselves. And when they hold up American capitalism as something equally to be deplored with this sort of thing, they make the verdict upon themselves inevitable. The real division in the world today is not between socialism and capitalism, it is between freedom and totalitarianism.

This still leaves us with the problem of how excessive state power is to be checked and balanced in a socialist society. Three great and necessary checks will be trade unions, churches, and political parties — free trade unions, free churches and free political parties. What will be the conditions of freedom for these three institutions is a question that needs much more examination. Trade unions, for example, will inevitably change their function to some extent when the employer is not a hostile capitalist but the democratic state which represents all the people. English trade unionism is finding difficulty, *e.g.* in the coal mines, in adjusting itself to this change now. But it is to be hoped that trade unionism doesn't become, as it has mainly become in Russia, simply another state agency for manipulating the workers, encouraging them to Stakhanovism, etc. How will wages be fixed, how will industrial disputes be settled, how will labour be distributed among different industries — there are questions to which trade unionists who vote for socialist parties might give more attention.

Similarly as to political parties. It is extraordinary how enticing to the ordinary socialist is the vision of a single-party state which inaugurates socialism once for all. The ultimate test of freedom is the right of minorities to criticize and agitate in the hope of becoming majorities. This means a plurality of political parties.

Political parties are concerned with making opinion, and it is in the "opinion industries" that the difficulties confronting freedom are most intricate and subtle. How do we ensure that education does not degenerate into indoctrination? How do we safeguard the freedom of teachers in a state educational system? These are two questions that will become more acute in a socialist régime.

Also as to news in the papers and upon the radio. How shall we ensure that it shall be objective and shall present the citizen with a fair balance between competing points of view? How is the publishing of books to be carried on? Hitherto it has been assumed that all these questions are solved satisfactorily enough by the free competition of private enterprisers, that freedom emerges from this kind of competition. The terrible power in making opinion that is possessed by a ruthless state authority under modern conditions has been vividly illustrated for us in Nazi Germany and Communist Russia. What are the proper checks upon power of this kind in a socialist community?

Our own experience goes to show that the most effective safeguard of freedom in these fields is the professionalization of teachers, journalists, radio broadcasters, and other workers in the opinion industries. A properly organized profession with high professional standards can stand out against undue pressure both from political authority and from great private corporations. But what a joke to talk about professional standards in the journalism and the radio-broadcasting of our day! And most teachers are not as yet very comfortable in their professional independence.

At any rate the secret of freedom in any society consists in checks and balances. Let us have more study and discussion of what these checks and balances are to be.

PART III
The Calm of the 1950s

1. Notes on the Massey Report

(This review of the report of the Massey Commission on National Development in the Arts, Letters and Sciences appeared in the *Canadian Forum*, August, 1951. For some further discussion on this subject of our Canadian culture and its relationships with American culture, see my paper on Hilda Neatby's book, *So Little for the Mind*, in the *Transactions* of the Royal Society of Canada, 1954; my article in the *Saturday Review* of 24 October, 1959, entitled "A Country in Search of an Image"; and my article in *Queen's Quarterly*, Autumn, 1959, entitled "Canadian and American Ties with Europe".)

The chief danger is that the Massey Report will become merely another historical document — like the Rowell-Sirois Report of ten years ago. Both are the products primarily of our university intellectuals. The commissioners themselves, the special investigators who worked for them, and the groups who drafted the briefs that were presented to them, have been nearly all men and women trained in Canadian universities. Future generations of historians, sociologists and political scientists will pay tribute to their thorough work in searching out and assembling the relevant facts, to their imaginative grasp of their subject, and to their masterly presentation of a programme of action. Both reports show what new insights into different aspects of our national problems may be reached through well-directed team work by men and women of trained intelligence. But the Rowell-Sirois Report still remains a programme only, and it is now almost forgotten by the politicians who are responsible for action. The Massey Report may suffer the same fate. It is already being brushed aside by the "practical" men as the work of long-haired highbrows. There is no other country in the world where intellectuals suffer from such low repute as in Canada. . . .

When Royal commissioners or lesser people write about Canada it is always revealing to find out whom they take to represent the people of Canada. Read a journal such as the *Financial Post*, and you soon discover that it assumes as self-evident the proposition that the Canadian Manufacturers' Association or the local chambers of commerce express the opinions of the people of Canada. Read the editorial page of the Toronto *Globe*, and it gradually dawns on you that Mr. George McCullagh intuitively senses what the people of Canada are thinking, and that there is no need to look farther than his intuitions. The members of the Massey Commission seem to have assumed that the "voluntary bodies" who appeared before them spoke collectively for the people of Canada. But the people of Canada never actually appear in any active rôle except when they vote at general elections, and even then the functioning agent is that sixty or seventy percent of the adult population who can be induced to mark ballot-papers. The voluntary bodies who appeared at the Massey Commission hearings did not include the most powerful of voluntary bodies in this country, the business corporations; and, in fact, they represented only the minority of persons who are actively interested in the arts, letters and sciences. The overwhelming majority of the people of Canada, or even of the radio listeners, were not there at all because they were not interested enough. Unfortunately this minority who were interested in the subject, and who had very valuable things to say, are a minority who have little financial power and who are not organized so as to make their voting power felt.

The report is very well written. It is a pleasure to read a document written by individuals who evidently recognize a good sentence when they see it in a brief and know enough to quote it, and who also know how to write good sentences themselves. One is in doubt whether to be impressed more by their picture of the poverty-stricken condition of all the activities concerned with the arts and letters in Canada, or by the vigour with which these poverty-stricken groups presented their case. But one has an uneasy premonition that the real attitude of the government to their grievances is shown by the price of the volume in which the report is published. A federal government which took this subject seriously would have subsidized the publication sufficiently to make it possible for the lower-income class of reader to buy it. When Pitt was pressed to prosecute William Godwin for his work on Political Justice, he replied that there was no danger of subversion from a work which cost three guineas the set. So our business men may rest easy.

I enjoyed the polite restraint with which the commissioners set out the shortcomings of the various national cultural institutions in Ottawa. Much more explosive language might have been used, and has habitually been used for the past generation in university circles. But as a university professor in the field of the humanities, I was, of course, chiefly impressed by their chapters on the universities and the humanities. There is nothing here which is very new, even in Canada, but it is said with force and eloquence. Extracts from these chapters should have been far more widely reprinted in our daily press than they have been. (As usual, the *Winnipeg Free Press* seems to be the only daily which is giving the report good publicity.) The natural sciences have been steadily fostered in the universities at the expense of the humanities, though we are now conscious that it is not from the sciences but from the humanities that must come the wisdom for the solution of the deepest social and philosophical problems of our age. How often have I heard these things said or read them in official utterances at the University of Toronto!

The commissioners have a very pertinent remark on Canadian university libraries: "If the size of a university library is not an unfair index of the attention devoted to the liberal arts, and particularly to research in this field, the relevant facts are illuminating. If a list of North American universities were to be arranged in accordance with the number of volumes in their academic libraries, the best equipped Canadian universities would be distressingly far down in the roster." When I joined the University of Toronto staff in 1927, one of the first things I remember hearing was a plea from the librarian for more room and better equipment in the university library. It is now 1951, and nothing has been done in the interval to improve the facilities of the library. Yet I doubt if historical research could turn up a single speech on general university policy by anyone in authority at the university during that period in which the speaker did not refer in glowing terms to the vital importance of the humanities and did not affirm his determination to keep the university from sinking into a mere utilitarian scientific technological centre. And this illustrates the real trouble with the humanities in Canada. It is not that the Canadian public is apathetic — the masses everywhere are apathetic — but that those in authority, who profess to be interested, seldom feel any responsibility for fitting their actions to their words.

. . . There is one theme in the report about which some searching questions should be asked. The commissioners seek a national Canadian culture which shall be independent of American influences. Several times they speak of these influences as "alien". This use of the word "alien" seems to me to reveal a fallacy that runs through much of Canadian nationalistic discussion. For we cannot escape the fact that we live on the same continent as the

Americans, and that the longer we live here the more we are going to be affected by the same continental influences which affect them. It is too late now for a Canadian cultural nationalism to develop in the kind of medieval isolation in which English or French nationalism was nurtured. The so-called "alien" American influences are not alien at all; they are just the natural forces that operate on a continental scale in the conditions of our twentieth-century civilization.

The fact is that, if we produced Canadian movies for our own mass consumption, they would be as sentimental and vulgar and escapist as are the Hollywood variety; and they would be sentimental, vulgar and escapist in the American way, not in the English or French or Italian way. Our newspapers, which are an independent local product, do not differ essentially from the American ones. The kind of news which the Canadian Press circulates on its own origination is exactly like that originated by A.P. or U.P. Like the American ones, our papers become progressively worse as the size of the city increases, up to a certain point. Somewhere between the size of Chicago and the size of New York another force comes into operation, producing a different kind of newspaper. We haven't any daily as bad as the *Chicago Tribune*, because we haven't any city as big as Chicago; but also we haven't anything as good as the *New York Times*. . . . It is mass-consumption and the North American continental environment which produce the undesirable aspects of "mass-communications", not some sinister influences in the United States.

If we could get off by ourselves on a continental island, far away from the wicked Americans, all we should achieve would be to become a people like the Australians. (And even then the American goblin would get us in the end, as he is getting the Australians.) Let us be thankful, then, that we live next door to the Americans. But if we allow ourselves to be obsessed by the danger of American cultural annexation, so that the thought preys on us day and night, we shall only become a slightly bigger Ulster. The idea that by taking thought, and with the help of some government subventions, we can become another England — which, one suspects, is Mr. Massey's ultimate idea — is purely fantastic. No sane Canadian wants us to become a nation of Australians or Ulsterites. So, if we will only be natural, and stop going about in this eternal defensive fear of being ourselves, we shall discover that we are very like the Americans, both in our good qualities and in our bad qualities.

Young Canadians who are really alive make this discovery now without going through any great spiritual crisis.

The root cultural problem in our modern mass-democracies is this relationship between the mass culture, which is in danger of being further debased with every new invention in mass-communications, and the culture of the few. The United States is facing this problem at a rather more advanced stage than we have yet reached; and the more intimately we study American experience the more we shall profit. What we need, we, the minority of Canadians who care for the culture of the few, is closer contact with the *finest* expressions of the American mind. The fear that what will result from such contact will be our own absorption is pure defeatism. We need closer touch with the best American universities (*not* Teachers College) and research institutions, closer touch with American experimental music and poetry and theatre and painting, closer personal touch with the men who are leaders in these activities. The Americans are now mature enough to have come through this adolescent phase of believing that the best way to become mature is to cut yourself off from older people who are more mature than you are. It is about time that we grew out of it also. I think the Massey commissioners should use their leisure now to study the Americans much more closely than they seem to have done hitherto.

2. Canada and
the Canadian Question 1954

(This article was written for an issue of the *Queen's Quarterly*, Winter 1953-4, which was celebrating sixty years of publication.)

When *Queen's Quarterly* began publication in 1893 the communal confidence of Canadians in their experiment of building up a new nation in the northern half of North America was at about the lowest point which it has ever reached. "We have come to a period in the history of this young country when premature dissolution seems to be at hand," wrote Wilfrid Laurier in a private letter to Edward Blake in December, 1891. "What will be the outcome? How long can the present fabric last? Can it last at all? All these are questions which surge in my mind and to which dismal answers suggest themselves." As one studies those dark days one gets the impression that there were many other Canadians besides Laurier who were tempted in private to lose faith in the future of their country. Few of them went as far as Goldwin Smith in his *Canada and the Canadian Question* published in 1891. But Smith's book was a distillation of defeatist tendencies that were strong at the time; and all modern discussions of the Canadian question still revolve around the points which he raised.

The long depression which had begun in 1873 had lifted for a short time in the early 1880s but had then settled down again upon the Canadian economy. Population was hardly growing at all, so great was the exodus of young people to the United States. The two great nation-building policies of the Conservative government of Macdonald, tariff protection and the building of the transcontinental railway, had not brought the promised expansion and prosperity. "The Conservative policy," wrote Blake in his West Durham letter, "has left us with a small population, a scanty immigration, and a North-West empty still; with enormous additions to our public debt and yearly charge, an extravagant system of expenditure, and an unjust and oppressive tariff. . . . Worse; far worse! It has left us with lowered standards of public virtue, and a death-like apathy in public opinion; with racial, religious and

Provincial animosities rather inflamed than soothed; with a subservient parliament, an autocratic executive, debauched constituencies and corrupted and corrupting classes."

Superimposed upon the frustrations of economic depression was the bitterness between English and French Canadians produced by the North-West rebellion of 1885 and the execution of Riel. Thoughtful men were appalled by the outburst of passion over Riel. And the fires of racial and religious animosity were kept alive by Mercier's Jesuit Estates Act in Quebec. In Toronto the *Mail* was editorializing about smashing Confederation into fragments. As the new *Queen's Quarterly* began, all this excitement was being stirred up again by the Manitoba Schools question. Confederation, which had been adopted as a way of settling racial and religious conflicts, seemed only to have inaugurated a long imperialist struggle between Ontario and Quebec for the possession of the West.

It was in the midst of this period of economic, moral and spiritual depression that Goldwin Smith published his volume on Canada and the Canadian Question, the most completely pessimistic book that has ever been written about our country. Smith's thesis was: that the experiment of Confederation had by this time proved a failure; that Canada was only a geographical expression consisting of four northerly extensions of the American fertile belt, each of which was more closely connected with the corresponding part of the United States than with the other sections of Canada; that too much of the Canadian government structure represented a blind imitation of British forms without consideration of their unfitness for a different kind of society in North America, and that in particular Canadian political parties, however British their names, were mere factions without principles; that French Canada lay like a non-conductor between Ontario and the Maritimes, a permanent obstacle to national consolidation; that its society, dominated by a reactionary Catholic clericalism, could never assimilate with the liberal democratic society of English Canada; that the building of the C.P.R. had been over-ambitious and imposed too heavy a burden on the young country; that the prairie North-West would be another disruptionist force and would revolt against the colonial status imposed upon it by the protectionist East; that enthusiastic visions of a great federated British Empire were an unsubstantial mirage; and that British North America, "rich by nature, poor by policy", could realize its promise only by a continental union, commercial and political, with the United States.

Each one of Smith's points was hard to answer if taken by itself. We have, in fact, been engaged ever since in working out answers to his indictment. No demonstration of the extent of our national success today, some sixty years later, could be more striking than a simple list of quotations from *Canada and the Canadian Question*. But this would also demonstrate the historian's favourite thesis that time never finally solves any of the deeper problems of a society; it merely carries them forward into a new phase. We are still debating our economic future, the nature of the union of French and English in a Canadian community, the essential meaning of our relations with Britain and the United States. . . .

1. *"Modus Vivendi* without Cordiality"

Goldwin Smith had little favourable to say about French Canada. Its clericalism, its archaism, its separatism repelled him. "Its character has been perpetuated by isolation like the form of an antediluvian animal preserved in Siberian ice." British statesmanship had made an irreparable mistake in the Quebec and Constitutional Acts when it provided facilities for the preservation of French nationality. Catholicism under the domination of an ultramontane clergy he regarded as a sinister force which denied every value of nineteenth-century civilization and with which no compromise could be made. "Science and democracy do not go to Canossa." He wrote always as if Leo XIII had never succeeded Pius IX, and he assumed a monolithic solidarity in Catholic thinking which did not exist.

As to the separatism of Quebec, he failed to pay sufficient attention to the economic processes by which transportation, manufacturing and finance were making one fabric of the economies of Quebec and the rest of Canada, processes which have been going on for sixty more years since he wrote. And the spread of French settlement southwards into New Brunswick and westwards into Ontario and the Prairies gave Quebec another tie with English Canada. She took over the function of the protector of exposed French minorities in the other provinces, and has been exercising it ever more vigorously. If Smith could have foreseen this he would have been more outraged than ever. But these two forces, economic and spiritual, have made our Canadian union indissoluble, even if frequently uncomfortable.

Smith was well aware of one factor in English-French relations which he denounced all his life, though we can now see that it has provided the chief means by which two racial groups have achieved in the political field such unity as does exist. This was the bi-racial composite political party. Macdonald's coalition of English and French in the Liberal-Conservative party seemed to him only an unholy alliance of political racketeers who held the country together by paying out bribes first to one section and then to another. Yet this bi-racial party has been our one creative Canadian invention in political science. It began with the Reform coalition of Baldwin and LaFontaine, and it has been carried on successfully now for a full century by Macdonald, Laurier and King. When Laurier's party broke up in the crisis over conscription, with the French Liberals all taking one side and most of the English Liberals taking the other, few persons could have foreseen that the party would have been so quickly and triumphantly reconstructed under Mackenzie King. Mr. King's superiority as a national leader over all his rivals during a long career was shown most conclusively by his clear grasp of the principle that in a country like ours the only party capable of government is one that can draw substantial support from both French and English. The new parties that have sprung up since 1918 have all failed completely when put to this test. The Conservatives since Macdonald have never got the principle quite clearly into their heads; and when Mr. Drew came along he showed his political illiteracy by wooing the extremists in Quebec rather than the moderates. So the existing Liberal régime seems likely to be prolonged indefinitely.

Intellectuals in Canada from Goldwin Smith to the present have never been fond of this Canadian version of the North American political party. They are disgusted, as he was, with the compromises which it involves, the sordid deals, the bargaining for power and place, the sinking of principle in expediency. Laurier was denounced by the French-Canadian intellectual, Bourassa, for compromising about French rights ("When Sir Wilfrid Laurier reaches the gates of paradise the first thing he will do will be to propose a compromise between God and Satan"), and by the English-Canadian intellectual, Willison, for yielding to the dictates of the

French Catholic hierarchy. In our own day King has been sneered at by most of the intellectuals because of his long success in this balance-of-power politics. But as a technique for keeping French and English uneasily together it remains our great constructive Canadian invention. Apparently only one party at a time can rise to become genuinely national in this particular Canadian sense. But the system has now been working so long that we can say with confidence that it is a permanent device for maintaining national unity.

There is one other problem in the practice of democracy, however, in which French and English are far from any mutual understanding. Does democracy mean majority rule or does it mean minority rights? English Canadians have always assumed the first meaning. French Canadians have always thought of themselves as a special kind of minority, a people who are already in the deepest sense a nation, with a special way of life of their own, living within the wider artificial national structure of 1867, and therefore possessing special minority rights. There are certain questions, in their view, about which the majority has no moral right to impose its will on the dissentient minority; and these questions must be settled by concurrent majorities from each communal group. They have never produced a French-Canadian Calhoun to define this doctrine of concurrent majorities, though Bourassa came very close to it; but we are all acutely conscious of the persistence with which they have fought for the principle on the issue of conscription. English Canadians have never shown any sign of understanding what the French were talking about. Democracy, as the philosopher is bound to conclude, means both majority rule and minority rights, and it is the function of statesmanship to manage things so that these two principles do not come into conflict in questions that may stir up mass passions. But it is a sign of the intellectual weakness of our Canadian political life that there are no classic Canadian debates or books to be quoted on this ultimate insoluble question of the nature of democracy.

This failure to try to understand what is going on in the other group's mind is, of course, what explains why our French-English union has been so superficial beyond the field of politics. We have failed to do what every healthy vital nationality always does, to produce national symbols and myths. We have no national flag and no national anthem which all of us can sing. We have no great historical figures like Washington and Lincoln in the United States, about whom our national imagination has brooded so as to produce characteristic legends and symbolical myths. The French Canadians themselves have plenty of these symbols and myths of their own, but these are their private possession not shared by us English Canadians. And we have never attracted each other's sympathetic understanding.

Still it must be that daily contacts in Parliament, the courts, business and labour, scholarship and science, and in all the activities of social life are steadily and unconsciously building up some solid structure, as coral insects build up a coral island from generation to generation. We did, after all, avoid a cleavage over conscription in World War II like that which split the nation in 1917. Mr. St. Laurent seems genuinely popular all across English Canada, as Laurier was before him. And one might accumulate evidence of this kind.

Yet it is also true that French-Canadian nationalism is much more self-conscious, organized and articulate than it was in Goldwin Smith's day. An unregenerate English Canadian may feel that the Bourassa gospel of a special French-Canadian mission to preserve some part of this continent from Anglo-Saxon materialism is as unreal as most such fanatical nationalist gospels always are, and that English Canadians who see a higher spiritual quality in French Catholicism than in our Protestant Puritanism are letting their romantic tendencies run away with them. But still the phenomenon of intransigent French-Canadian nationalism remains. Duplessis succeeds to Bourassa as well as St. Laurent to Laurier.

So one concludes on this matter of relations between the two main communal groups in Canada that we still haven't got much beyond André Siegfried's "*Modus vivendi* without cordiality".

2. "Old Boys' Association"

It was a Dutch journalist a few years ago who compared the modern British Commonwealth to the alumni association of a school whose members meet together periodically on ceremonial occasions to engage in certain rituals, to listen to a speech from the headmaster and to enjoy themselves by free indulgence in nostalgic sentiments. Goldwin Smith would have been delighted with this twentieth-century simile; for an Old Boys' Association was pretty much what he maintained that the Empire had already become in the 1890s.

The Canadian Question which he discussed was the issue whether Canada should (1) remain a dependent colony; or (2) achieve independence; or (3) join Britain in an Imperial Federation; or (4) unite economically and politically with the States. Choice No. 1, he correctly pointed out, was already impossible. Choice No. 2 was natural, but he himself had lost faith in the capacity of his fellow-Canadians to make a success of an independent nationality. Choice No. 3 he demolished by destructive analysis; and everything he said about the inacceptability of a close federal union between Britain and the Dominions has been justified by later experience. Choice No. 4 was, of course, his own preference; but he did not intend this to mean a complete break with Britain. For in the ultimate future he foresaw "a moral federation of the English-speaking peoples". He would not find our situation in the 1950s altogether displeasing.

It would be tedious to trace out here all the steps by which we reached our present position of independence without separation. Laurier defeated all attempts to set up any form of centralized government or control in the Empire, and his achievements in preparing the way for the completely decentralized Commonwealth have been duly celebrated by his biographers. That this was the only kind of association which Dominion nationalism would find tolerable is now obvious. But Laurier's nationalism had a strong strain of North American pacifist isolationism in it, which most Canadian liberals and all French Canadians found congenial. There is no need today to pretend that this outlook on the world was sufficient. From our present point of view Borden's claim that "Canada cannot be a hermit nation" seems to show a much truer understanding of world politics. However, we did not accept as more than a temporary expedient the Borden-Smuts Commonwealth in which the British nations worked out a single common foreign policy by continuous consultation in the Imperial War Cabinet. There was no Imperial Peace Cabinet after 1919; and the Borden-Smuts Commonwealth was replaced by the King-Hertzog Commonwealth in which each British country pursued its own individual policy and refused to bind itself to future Commonwealth or League of Nations commitments. By the end of the 1930s Mr. King was forced to admit that this was not a completely satisfactory solution in a world of clashing ideologies and competing power politics. But it was the solution which divided us in Canada the least; and, because he had avoided previous commitments, Mr. King was able to carry a united country into war in 1939 when once the issue in Europe had been made clear.

The important point to grasp now is that Mr. King's delaying tactics have produced a result in the 1950s which he may have foreseen dimly in the 1930s but which most of his fellow-Canadians did not foresee at all. He had always understood clearly — and this is one of the proofs of his greatness as a Canadian statesman — that no form of Canadian-British association which excluded the United States would be finally satisfactory. And when the Canadian people were at last ready, after 1945, to undertake definite commitments, it was not in any exclusively Britannic alliance that we joined, but in the United Nations and the North Atlantic Treaty Organization. Except for the Colombo Plan, our specific obligations to action are such as tie us to other countries as well as to our fellow-British communities. The British Commonwealth is left in a position something like that of the smile on the face of the Cheshire Cat.

Canada takes part in repelling aggression in Korea along with a considerable list of other United Nation powers, and indubitably under American leadership and management. We keep up forces on the continent of Europe as partners in NATO, in which again the United States is the indispensable senior partner. We are united with the United States in a special exclusive regional North American defence alliance. Australia and New Zealand are joined with the United States in a Pacific security pact from which they have politely but firmly excluded Great Britain. Economically, Canada is part of the dollar area; and every British effort to make the sterling bloc successful only emphasizes the point that we have distinct interests which are not identical with what British leaders conceive to be their interests.

The hard fact is that the secret of the long success of the British Empire was the economic and military power of Great Britain; and that this power has so declined in the middle of the twentieth century that Britain can no longer give the leadership which was hers in the nineteenth century. The British are now, in their connection with us, just poor relations. Gushing sentiment about the supposed experience and know-how of British diplomacy — which is not exactly a self-evident fact in Europe or Asia or Africa at this moment — cannot serve as an escape from the realities of power. The British Commonwealth, whatever the framework of co-operation, cannot provide by itself for its own security in the present world. It depends on the power of the United States. Since the Americans also depend on the power that we can supply in an association with them, we are all bound together till death us do part. Our chief concern for the next generation will be not to escape from this new association but to accustom the Americans to the older Commonwealth methods of procedure, in which smaller powers argue freely with bigger ones and cannot be committed without their own consent.

Perhaps what we chiefly need in Canada just now is a Canadian Bagehot to educate us to see our external relations as a complicated structure with certain older more "dignified" parts and certain newer more "efficient" parts. Our British associations are passing over to the dignified part of our external policy, and our American associations have become the efficient part.

3. The Revolution of 1940

The oldest and most tenacious tradition in our communal memory centres around our determination not to become Americans. This is also the one tradition in which English Canadians and French Canadians have been whole-heartedly united. Our forefathers made the great refusal in 1776 when they declined to join the revolting American colonies. They made it again in 1812 when they repelled American invasions. They made it again in 1837 when they rejected a revolution motivated by ideals of Jacksonian democracy, and opted for a staid moderate respectable British Whiggism which they called "Responsible Government". They made it once more in 1867 when the separate British colonies joined to set up a new nationality in order to preempt the northern half of the continent from American expansion. They built the Pacific railway and established the protective tariff as anti-American defences. In 1891 and 1911 they rejected Reciprocity. "A British subject I was born, a British subject I will die." "No truck or trade with the Yankees." In fact it would be hard to overestimate the amount of energy we have devoted to this cause. One can never tell what will be the next occasion on which we'll gird up our loins and save ourselves once again from the United States. One can only predict with confidence that the occasion will come.

But in 1940, just ten years after the last of these exciting occasions (when Mr. Bennett led us to salvation by another high tariff), a revolution took place in world power politics. We are never going to live again in the same world in which we of the older generation grew up. For our world was a world in which the leading power, the power that dominated our imaginations, was Great Britain. But in 1940 Hitler overran western Europe and almost overran Britain. The immediate reaction here in Canada was our *permanent* defence alliance with the United States, a commitment of a sort such as we had never been willing to make with Britain. For a hundred years, ever since Lord Durham's Report in 1839, we had gradually been growing independent of Britain; but we were like one of those pathetic ineffectual young men who never succeed in getting clear of their mothers' apron-strings. Now we are going to have to spend the next hundred years in trying to maintain our independence from the United States. And it's going to be a much tougher century. But our younger generation will gradually come to take for granted this central position of the United States in our destiny; while at the same time the Americans, growing up to their responsibilities of world leadership, will gradually come to recognize the necessity of not taking us for granted. And so the poison in our present Canadian-American relationship, which is due to the fact that Americans are "benevolently ignorant" about us whereas we are "malevolently informed" about them, will work itself out. (I owe the phraseology to an editorial in the *Saturday Review* of June 7, 1952, by Merrill Denison. The title of his editorial is "4000 Miles of Irritation".)

Once we become accustomed to this new world we may look forward to the day when our Department of External Affairs will occasionally discover some issue on which the United States is right and Britain is wrong. It will be as toughly Canadian as our Departments of Trade and Commerce and of Finance; *i.e.*, it will be able to be tough with British statesmen as well as with American.

By that time, also, we shall all be looking at trade questions with fresh eyes. Most of us are still living in imagination in the nineteenth century when free-trade Britain was the world's great market, always stable and dependable. We have all suffered too much from the vagaries of American tariff-makers to be able to take long views about the American market. And so we are all worrying too much about the domination of our foreign trade by our American neighbour. But the fact is (and this also dates from 1940) that it is the British market today which is inherently unstable, because the British economy is in so precarious a condition. On the other hand, the steadily rising standard of living in the United States is making her more and more dependent upon imports for future expansion. The Paley Report with its projections of American demand in 1975 for a long series of essential commodities, most of which are produced in Canada, should be more familiar in this country. This long-term trend may be slowed up temporarily by the aberrations of tariff-makers in Congress, but it cannot be fundamentally altered.

Another thing is happening which it would pay us to watch. Of course, protectionism is far from dead in the United States, but it is now clearly on the defensive. The Paley Report is only one example of this fact. The coming Randall Report will probably be another. American big business is becoming more and more low-tariff in sentiment. It would not be too fantastic to picture the United States as standing today just about where Britain stood at the beginning of the 1840s when the free trade movement started to sweep over the country. Detroit, the centre of the most advanced technology, is evidently casting herself for the rôle of Manchester. Whether Detroit can produce a Cobden and a Bright remains to be seen. And it is admittedly difficult, considering his first year of weakness and futility, to see President Eisenhower as another Peel. But all the underlying conditions are ripening for a great change in American economic policy. "It appears to me that a moral and even a religious spirit may be infused into that topic," wrote Cobden to Bright in 1838 when they were starting on their campaign. The Americans also are good at religious crusades.

The other great cause of our worries in Canada, when we consider our relations with our great neighbour, is the invasion of American mass culture. American movies, American radio and television, American popular magazines and cheap books, American advertising, American slang and American chewing gum, American divorce and American juvenile delinquency, all threaten to overwhelm our Canadian way of life. At least that is how we put it. But we are not defining the problem in quite the correct way. We tend to see it as a problem of Americanization when it is really the problem of mass democracy. All these phenomena which we cite as examples of Americanization (which the French have nicknamed coca-colonization) are just typical expressions of a society in which the masses have at last arrived and are demonstrating their lack of interest in the more severe intellectual and moral standards of an older aristocratic civilization. The United States has been going through this revolution of mass democracy ever since President Jackson arrived in the White House in 1829. But we all have to go through it in our turn; and turning our backs on the United States will not save us. We have no native inherent sense of higher standards which might preserve our Canadian purity if we could shut out the American invasion. Look at our native Canadian examples of mass culture, from professional hockey to the Social Credit movement, and let us not kid ourselves.

We are bound to do a great deal of cultural importing from our neighbours. And because the Americans have had a longer experience with the dangers of mass democracy than any other people, they are likely to find the desirable correctives sooner. So, instead of deploring the corrupting influences of our proximity to Hollywood and Times Square and Madison Avenue, we should be looking for other cultural imports besides the products of these centres. We should be inquiring about some of the good things we might import in addition to the bad things that we are certain to import (or to manufacture here in Canadian branch factories). We might, for example, investigate the good programmes of music and talks which go out from F.M. stations in New York and Boston, and then ask why our F.M. facilities on the C.B.C. continue to be wasted through long afternoons of soap opera and long arid Saturday nights of hockey. Our universities might investigate what the better American universities have been doing in "general education" and in institutes on foreign policy or American Civilization. Our libraries might make more display of the ever-growing number of high-class American university quarterlies. How many Canadians know, for example, that the Number One football factory, Notre Dame, also publishes one of the best quarterlies in the country, the *Review of Politics*? Our newspapers might subscribe to more of the better American columnists. And our professional Christians would certainly profit by reading more of the good American religious journals. The thing which is most impressive to anyone who really tries to make himself acquainted with American civilization is the extraordinary variety of American cultural expression, and the extraordinary variety of self-criticism within the American community.

Well, we have come a long way since the period of some sixty years ago when Goldwin Smith wrote his *Canada and the Canadian Question* and *Queen's Quarterly* issued its first number. Where are we going in the next sixty years? There was a time in the early

1900s when Canadians were announcing that the twentieth century belonged to Canada. This naive optimism is as impossible to us today as is the acute pessimism of the early 1890s. To that extent at least we have matured. But in the greater world society of which we became a responsible member when we plunged into the war of 1914 we have not played any part so far which was not determined by our triangular relationship with Great Britain and the United States. In the meantime the British century in which we grew up has come to an end. How we solve the Canadian question in the 1950s and thereafter depends on how we face up to the realities of the American century which lies before us.

3. Canadian Liberal Democracy in 1955

(This was an address delivered at Queen's University on 10 January, 1955. It was one of the lectures given that year under the Chancellor Dunning Trust, the other one being given by Mr. George Ferguson of the Montreal *Star* on the press in Canada. The two lectures were published by Queen's University in a volume with the title *Press and Party in Canada* (Ryerson Press, 1955).)

I have to thank you, Mr. Principal, and I have to thank Queen's University for the honour you have done me in inviting me to be one of the lecturers this year under the Chancellor Dunning Trust. It is a very high honour to be chosen to talk on the theme of freedom, of the free individual in a free society, to a Queen's audience. For in Canada Queen's is our great liberal university. All universities should be centres of liberalism, liberalism with a small "l". But my own University of Toronto, surrounded as it is by the City of Toronto, has never quite managed to make itself a congenial home for the liberal spirit.

More than a hundred years ago Toronto, the city, was turning Anglo-Irish gentry like the Baldwins and the Blakes into liberals, by way of reaction against their environment, and driving William Lyon Mackenzie into revolution. "In Toronto," said Mrs. Jameson in 1837, "we have conventionalism in its most oppressive and ridiculous forms ... In this place they live under the principle of fear — they are all afraid of each other, afraid to be themselves: and where there is much fear, there is little love and less truth." And ever since then it has been generally true that such liberalism as has shown itself in that great metropolitan community has survived in spite of, rather than because of, its environment. In Toronto the new mayor of 1955 starts off his duties by trying to protect the university male undergraduates from the demoralizing influence of art exhibitions in Hart House which contain drawings of nude females.

So it is with a certain sense of exhilaration that one comes to visit Queen's, the university of G. M. Grant, of Adam Shortt, of O. D. Skelton — to mention only some of the giants of the past — the

227

university of the *Queen's Quarterly*. Incidentally, I have sometimes wondered why someone at Queen's hasn't undertaken to publish a selection of the more or less journalistic writings of Grant, Shortt, Skelton and other Queen's men, their comments on Canadian public affairs from the 1880s to the 1930s, as published in the *Queen's Quarterly* and other Canadian journals and newspapers. It would provide a fine liberal political anthology, an interpretation of Canadian political history much more penetrating and enlightening than most of our modern professional history writing. It would be more cheerful than the *Bystander* comments which that grim English liberal, Goldwin Smith, poured forth for forty years from his intellectual prison in Toronto; and it would be almost as well written.

I propose this morning to make some more or less journalistic comments of my own on the state of our contemporary liberal democracy in Canada. There are various topics which one might discuss under this heading but which I shall avoid. Having now reached the age at which men prefer to repeat themselves and to thresh old straw over again, whatever the effect on their audience, I am going to confine my remarks chiefly to the working of our Canadian democratic politics.

However, when a Canadian speaker, lecturing to a Canadian audience, proposes to deal with liberal democracy in the middle of the twentieth century, he must mark out rather carefully some important reservations of territory into which he is not going to trespass. As everyone knows, our western world in the mid-twentieth century is going through a profound crisis of liberalism. The triumph of the liberal democratic way of life which seemed so sure in the generation before 1914 is now anything but sure. Today our western free society, instead of spreading its liberal institutions and ideas over the rest of the world, is again on the defensive; and the attackers this time are the most dynamic, confident and ruthless opponents that the West has ever met.

More dangerous than this attack from outside is the attack upon western liberal democracy from within. We have lost a large part of that faith in the rationality of man upon which liberalism essentially depends. At the same time we have lost our belief in progress, in the indefinite perfectibility of man and his institutions. Liberalism is in essence a Utopian faith with a confidence in the possibilities of human nature. But our modern psychologists have uncovered deep subconscious instinctive drives in us which pervert our reason; our theologians have achieved a renaissance of Original Sin; and we have had to witness in the last generation outbursts of the demonic elements in human nature whose existence we had forgotten. We have learnt to our cost the terrible potentialities of man's inhumanity to man. We have had borne in upon us how fragile is our civilization. Our life seems to be one continuous process of preparing for, fighting, or recovering from war. Religious thinkers, moreover, tell us that this sickness of our civilization is directly due to its liberalism, to western man's belief that he could solve his problems by reliance upon himself alone, without having recourse to supernatural help.

Apart from this omnipresent violence which defeats all our better aspirations, we have another problem. Even in those countries of the West where liberal democracy has proved most stable and where it has not disintegrated, we seem to be faced by the frustrations of a social order which has got beyond the capacity of the individual citizen to control or to understand. He stands alone, afraid, in a world he never made, surrounded by great power organizations; big business and big labour, big opinion industries — the press, the movies, radio, television, advertising enterprise, all of which have learned the techniques of manipulating and moulding and exploiting him — big churches, big political parties, and, looming over all, the big state; which, in proportion as it has become more democratic, *i.e.* formally more under his control, has also become more unlimited in the demands which it makes of him.

But as soon as one has tried to sum up in this way our twentieth-century crisis of liberalism, one becomes aware that one is really talking about the world outside of Canada. We Canadians have been mainly spectators at this tragic process of the disintegration of nineteenth-century liberal democratic values. We have taken part in the wars of our time, but we have experienced little of the moral perplexity or the spiritual agony, not to mention the material destruction, which our contemporaries have gone through. Whether we are too placid, or too insensitive, or too lethargic, or too superficial, we are incapable of either the messianic exaltation or the existentialist agonizing of some of our contemporaries. Our limitations, in fact, make us a people incapable of tragedy. No poet could write of any experience through which we have gone that a terrible beauty is born of it. And while the world has been going to pieces all around us, how can we understand what the poet means when he exclaims that

Things fall apart; the centre cannot hold,
Mere anarchy is loosed upon the world.

The best lack all conviction, while the worst
are full of passionate intensity.

And what rough beast, its hour come round at last,
Slouches towards Bethlehem to be born?

Yet it was as long ago as 1919 that the Irish poet wrote these lines.

Canada, in fact, is still living mentally and spiritually in the nineteenth century. Our problems of liberalism and democracy are mostly nineteenth-century problems. It was almost one hundred years ago, in 1859, that John Stuart Mill published his essay *On Liberty*. When 1959 comes round and the centenary of Mill's Liberty is celebrated, I suppose that in most countries commentators will remark that our age is familiar with dangers to liberty such as Mill never dreamt of, that we have probed depths of human depravity such as he could not have imagined. Mill thought that coercive organizations of power were no longer a danger to modern society. What worried him was the mediocrity, not the potential depravity of mass man — "collective mediocrity" as he called it. He was afraid that in democratic society there would not be room for the distinctive uncommon individuals, the individuals of superior intellectual and moral qualities, from whom, he believed, came the leadership that made progress possible.

When one sets Mill's apprehensions over against what has actually happened, one has to say that his fears of the death of individuality in his own England have not been justified. Democratic England continues to throw up men of genius from all classes in all activities of life; and the dead uniformity of mediocrity has not settled upon English existence, except perhaps at English dinner tables. Every Englishman still continues to go to heaven in his own way as he did when Voltaire first drew attention to this phenomenon.

Nor in the United States has the democratic uniformity come about which was feared by Tocqueville, who was Mill's teacher in these matters. American intellectuals have unduly slandered their fellow-citizens. The mere fact that such a hullabaloo has to be raised by those one-hundred percenters who want to impose upon everybody what they call the American way of life shows how difficult it is to enforce uniformity upon the American people. A really conformist community would not publish so many books and articles each year denouncing its own sinister tendency to conformity. The lengths to which McCarthyism was allowed to go are not more significant than the rapidity with which this latest anti-intellectual demagogue has outworn his welcome. In fact, if one looks at our American neighbours realistically, one realizes that, far from their being a conformist population, there is likely at any given moment to be a higher percentage of American citizens raising less corn and more hell than you will find in any other country.

No, when 1959 comes round and the English-speaking world commemorates the essay *On Liberty*, it will not be in Britain or the United States that critics will most easily find cases to illustrate what was worrying Mill and Tocqueville. The typical community in which collective mediocrity and democratic uniformity reign supreme and unquestioned will be our own English-speaking Canada. We Canadians are immune to most of the ills that have produced the deeper and darker aspects of the twentieth-century crisis of liberal democracy. As I have said, we are a people incapable of tragedy. Our democratic failings are the simpler, more superficial and more genial ones of the nineteenth century. We are the political animals about whom Mill and Tocqueville should have made their generalizations.

Well, such being the nature of our Canadian community, I shall devote the rest of my remarks not to these great themes connected with the crisis of twentieth-century liberalism — about which I could do little more than quote from books written by Englishmen, Americans and Frenchmen — but to the more modest and humdrum topic of the functioning of some of our democratic political institutions in Canada.

When one looks back over the generation that has elapsed since the end of World War I, what are the main things that have happened in the working of Canadian government? We are all conscious of one outstanding development, the series of upheavals in our Canadian party system, and to that I shall return in a moment. We are not so conscious as we might be of another change which has transformed the whole atmosphere of Ottawa. I mean the emergence of a great body of expert administrators in the federal civil service. The Laurier and Borden reforms emancipated the civil service from patronage and political pressure through the introduction of the system of appointment by graduated competi-tive examinations. This has brought about a professionalization of our public services which is surely the greatest advance in the functioning of Canadian democratic government in our generation. The net result is that our federal government is now equipped with an expert civil service which can reasonably be compared for its high standards with that paragon of public organizations, the British Civil Service. Our Canadian universities can be proud of this development, for it has been our graduates who have staffed the upper ranks, the policy-making ranks, of the service. Inci-dentally, this has been a development with which certain famous Queen's names are specially connected — Shortt, Skelton, Clark. What I wish chiefly to emphasize here is that the secret of the success of this important instrument of democratic government in our country is professionalization, the establishment in the civil service of standards similar to those which prevail in the learned professions.

But while we have here one of the great advances in the art of democratic government in the twentieth century, there is a danger that some of the most important advantages which we might derive from this highly professionalized service will be lost to us because of too wide a gap growing up between those who govern us and us who are governed. We have committed ourselves in Canada to complete democracy, mass democracy with all adult citizens parti-cipating as voters in a society in which there is no select governing class based on status or inheritance or wealth. Our equalitarian democratic experiment will not work unless the masses of the citi-zens can be stirred to some continuous interest in the problems of government and can be given some intelligent understanding of the complex considerations upon which are based the policies of the government and its expert advisers in the civil service.

Now, the two chief instruments in democratic communities for mediating between the government at the centre and the citizen body at the circumference have always been the press and the party system. The new instrument of radio and television is still far from being able to take the place of the press. And it seems to me fairly evident that neither press nor party is performing its function very satisfactorily at present in our Canadian political society.

I had intended at this point to deliver myself of some rather sweeping criticisms of our Canadian newspaper press. But there is no time. My chief point was to be that this question of the functioning of our Canadian dailies needs to be discussed, not in the frame of reference of freedom of the press, but in that of the professionalization of journalism. As a mere lay observer I cannot see that our Canadian press in my lifetime has gone through anything like that advance in professionalization which has transformed our federal civil service.

At any rate, Canadian journalists are rather too easily satisfied with low standards of performance. They assume that it is not necessary to compare Canadian newspapers with the *New York Times* or the London *Times* or the *Manchester Guardian*, just as the Canadian Authors' Association assumes that it is not necessary to measure Canadian poetry by the best American and English standards. Both assumptions are survivals from the parochial colonial stage of our history and it is time that we grew out of them. Surely we are approaching the stage, at least here in central Canada, with our two metropolitan cities of Toronto and Montreal, when we might expect at least morning papers that were more directly aimed at the more intelligent and educated groups in the community. Most of our evening papers we can, of course, abandon to the mass-entertainment industry, along with Hollywood movies and Madison Avenue television. But our political democracy is in danger unless we can rely on some part of our press setting itself seriously to the task of reporting the unseen environment to us every morning so that we can make reasonably intelligent judgments about it.

This desirable end can be achieved only by further advances in the professionalization of journalism. I do not know how such further professionalization of journalism is to be brought about. As a university man I suppose I should look forward to schools of journalism in our main universities. But as an old-fashioned Arts professor I have as little hope of getting better journalists from schools of journalism as I have of getting better teachers from colleges of education.

Let me turn to the subject of our party system.

Party is the great, all-important instrument which mediates between the government and the governed. Its function is to organize public opinion, so that government shall be carried on in accordance with the opinion of the citizens and also that the citizens shall be kept informed what the issues of government are. Political parties first grew up in England; and in that country they have adapted themselves with marvellous success to the economic changes that transformed a mainly agricultural community into the highly industrialized, mainly urban community of today, and to the political changes from a narrow oligarchy to the twentieth-century mass democracy. Through all these changes Britain has kept a two-party system; which has the great advantage that it presents the voters with a fairly clear-cut choice between alternative men and policies at election time, and secures a stable, solid majority basis for the government from one election to the next.

In Canada we reproduced the British two-party system as well as we could, and it served our purposes satisfactorily down to the end of World War I. Our two parties called themselves by the British names, Conservative and Liberal. But, in effect, they alternated in office after 1867 in accordance with the success of one or the other in convincing the people that it was the nation-building party. Macdonald's Conservatives built up a support in all sections of the Dominion through their great expansionist, nation-building policies of railway-building, tariff-protection and immigration, and through their ability to keep French and English working together in one party. When their momentum was exhausted by the 1890s, Laurier and his Liberals took their place with almost identically the same nation-building policies. Laurier also made the Liberal party a successful bi-racial party just as Macdonald's Conservative party had been in its great days. By the early twentieth century each party was a fairly representative cross-section of the Canadian people. Their British names suggested a division between a Right party and a Left party, but their practical politics resembled much more the intricate group-diplomacy of the composite non-ideological Republican and Democratic parties in the United States. By 1914 no one could have told what Canadian Conservatives were trying to conserve, what Canadian Liberals were trying to liberate. In fact, hardly anybody bothered to ask. Those were happy days.

After World War I this simple, carefree, two-party structure broke up, and it has never been restored. Only a small minority of Canadians are now old enough to remember what a two-party system was like.

At the beginning of the 1920s the western prairie farmers staged a revolt against the control over party organization and policy exercised by eastern big business. Their so-called Progressive movement had been defeated by the end of that decade, and in the 1930 election the old-time, two-party régime of Conservatives and

Liberals seemed to have been restored. The French-Canadian nationalist revolt, which had culminated in the conscription crisis of 1917, had also by this time died down, and the French were back in the Liberal party.

But the depression of the 1930s shook up the Canadian collective mind even more violently than the war had shaken it. In 1932 a new Socialist party, the C.C.F., took over where the Progressives had left off. We can see now that the essential thing about the C.C.F. was not its socialism, which is by this time about as hard to define as the Liberalism of the Liberals or the Conservatism of the Conservatives; it was its attempt to establish a British pattern in Canadian politics, a division between a Right and a Left, with a genuinely radical party democratically financed on the Left in opposition to big business on the Right. So far this attempt has failed.

In 1935, in Alberta, a still newer phenomenon emerged, the Social Credit movement, which turned that province almost into a one-party state and set new standards for Canada in demagogic plebiscitary democracy. And the depression of the 1930s also brought French-Canadian Laurentian nationalism to life again, in the new incarnation of the Union Nationale.

Out of all this confusion of the 1920s and 1930s and out of the strains and stresses of World War II there has emerged a political situation in Canada which no one could have foreseen and about the full implications of which none of us are very certain. Of these various competing party groups only one has succeeded in maintaining itself as a national party in the full sense of the term — the Liberals. All our experience goes to show that this country cannot be governed, so long as it remains free and democratic, except by some kind of party or coalition which attracts support from all the major interest groups in the country — ethnic, religious, linguistic, geographical and economic. Only the Liberals have met the specifications for a party capable of government in this sense, and they have now been in office continuously since 1935.

Whether you approve of him or not, it is almost impossible to overestimate the importance of the statesmanship of the late Mr. Mackenzie King, which was what chiefly brought about this result. He undermined the Progressives and the C.C.F. by treating them kindly, as impatient Liberals, and by stealing enough of the planks in their platforms from time to time to keep farmers and working-men and little people in general from flocking in crowds to the new movements. He was the only man in his day who could hold French and English together inside one party. He was the greatest master who has yet appeared in our country in this peculiar North American political art of group diplomacy.

But it is now clear that Mr. King was too successful for the good of Canadian democratic politics in general. He destroyed the possibility of an effective opposition at Ottawa. Today the Opposition consists of three splinter groups, each of which would rather see the Liberals in office for the time being than either of the other two opposition groups, and none of which seems by itself capable of growing from the status of a splinter group into that of a national party. The result is that it is no longer possible to have general elections in Canada in which the voter is presented with a real choice between possible alternative governments, because there is no party except the Liberals that is capable of forming a government. And what this means was shown in our last general election, that of 1953, the dullest, dreariest and drowsiest within living memory. Our democratic ritual of consulting the people at elections has become dangerously unreal, and evokes a dangerously widespread apathy.

This element of unreality comes out most clearly if we compare the Canadian election of 1953 with the American presidential election of 1952. The Americans still get fun out of their politics, which is a sign that their politics is in a pretty healthy condition. We Canadians feel a prim genteel disapproval of the boisterous, vulgar circus aspect of American party politics, but thousands of us attended the circus in 1952 by listening to the two American party conventions in Chicago on the radio or watching them on television, and we had fun too. Perhaps it is a national Canadian characteristic that we take our pleasures sadly, but surely that doesn't necessitate anything so sad or so drab as a Canadian general election campaign. We are sad because we are conscious that we are just going through the motions, not making any real choice. In the American campaign it was obvious that at each party convention there was a real fight over candidates and policies, and that a genuine democratic choice finally emerged from the fight. And this was followed by a real and exciting fight in the election campaign from August to November. Many good patriotic Canadians must have envied their American neighbours this opportunity to make a real choice, even if the choice turned out to be for the

Republicans — for practically all Canadians, of course, vote Democratic in American elections.

This blanketing of our Canadian federal politics by one national party, with the resulting impossibility of an effective opposition at Ottawa, has had a further effect. By some instinctive, subconscious mental process the Canadian people have apparently decided that, since freedom depends upon a balance of power, they will balance the monopolistic power of the Liberal government at Ottawa by setting up the effective countervailing power, not in Ottawa but in the provincial capitals. Her Majesty's loyal Canadian Opposition now really consists of the Social Credit governments in Alberta and British Columbia, the C.C.F. government in Saskatchewan, the Conservative governments in Ontario and New Brunswick, and the Union Nationale government in Quebec. These are all governments who get elected in their own provinces in order to save their people from the malign influence of Ottawa. Furthermore, there must now be thousands and thousands of Canadian citizens who vote Liberal in federal elections and anti-Liberal in provincial elections. What substantial or intelligible meaning is left in the words Liberal, Conservative, Socialist, Social Credit, in such circumstances? Of all conceivable party systems under which free government can be carried on in a democratic community, I should say that our present Canadian system is about the worst.

All this might have been prevented had any of the movements of the Left succeeded in building up a new party capable of fighting the Liberals on equal terms and shoving them rightward out of their monopoly position in the centre. But Mr. King, with his shrewd and subtle policy of No Enemies on the Left, prevented that. Things would be different also if the Conservatives had ever succeeded in making a firm comeback as a genuine national party of the Right.

But the Conservatives are now almost reduced into being an Ontario party. Their effort to woo Quebec through Mr. Duplessis shows a fantastic misreading of the lessons of Canadian history, lessons which point to the necessity of winning the Quebec moderates, not the Quebec separatist nationalists, if a successful bi-racial federal party is to be built up. Last year, 1954, was the hundredth anniversary of the birth of the Liberal-Conservative party of Macdonald and Cartier; yet, if the anniversary was celebrated in any way by the present Conservative party, the celebration failed to attract public notice. Think of a Conservative party which is so insensitive to history and tradition that it doesn't even take care to cultivate its own history! And how strange it is that all over the western world conservatism in politics should be going through a renaissance, with Conservatives in office in Britain and the United States, and yet that this new conservative spirit should be so voiceless in Canada.

Most distressing of all, in this point of view, is the failure of any Conservative philosophy to show itself in Canada now in the 1950s. Where are our Canadian "Wall Street Journals" and "Fortunes", trying to instil intelligence and imagination into a business man's conservatism? Where are our Canadian Russell Kirks and Peter Vierecks? Incidentally, Peter Viereck, besides being a conservative historian teaching in an American college, is a poet. I just can't imagine a poet among our Canadian Conservatives.

Now, obviously this permanent hold on national office by the Liberal party is fundamentally unhealthy. What can be done about it? Surely the time has come to give serious consideration to one possible change in our political machinery, the introduction of some system of proportional representation. For when we examine what actually happens in our elections, one startling fact emerges. The Liberal party, which has such an overwhelming majority of the seats in the House of Commons, never wins anything like this proportion of support from the voters. In 1953, when they captured 170 seats out of a total of 265, they got only about 48 percent of the votes. And a similar picture can be traced through nearly every general election right back to 1921 when Mr. King first came into office. This fantastic disproportion between the distribution of the votes among contending parties and the distribution of the seats at Ottawa is due to our single-member constituency system and our practice of accepting as elected in each constituency the candidate who gets a plurality of the votes rather than a majority. Surely, if we take the idea of government based on public opinion at all seriously, we should do something to make the balance of power at Ottawa approximate more closely to the balance of opinion in the country.

Of course, the present system is defended by all orthodox political scientists in Canada, *i.e.* by all political scientists in Canada, as having the great virtue that it makes for a strong stable government in office, a government with a secure majority. And it would be foolish to deny the force of this argument. But it is possible to have too much of a good thing; our governments at Ottawa are too strong and too stable. Our academic authorities also all hold up their hands in horror at the idea of Proportional Representation; since P.R., according to the standard textbooks, makes for a multi-group system rather than a two-party system. Look at what happens in France, they say, and among the benighted continental Europeans generally. And by contrast look at the admirable two-party system in Britain.

I think that an examination of British and French history would show that the two-party and multi-party systems are not due to electoral machinery but to much deeper causes in the structure of English and French society. At any rate, we have in Canada a society of greater diversity than that of Britain. It may be that the British division into two cohesive disciplined parties is not a natural expression of our social conditions, though it is probably necessary if our British cabinet system of government is to work well. I think a fair case could be made for the thesis that we should either have two loose parties in Canada like those of the United States — a system that works well under their American division of powers between executive and legislature but is not adapted to our cabinet system — or a multi-group system as in France and continental Europe. And, as a matter of fact, we have not had a two-party system since before most living Canadian citizens began to vote. Surely the whole structure of our electoral machinery needs re-examination.

There is another reform in the working of our parties which is badly needed to help break up this deeply entrenched Liberal domination of the Ottawa Parliament. Under modern conditions, with every question of policy needing long expert study and analysis, the government in office has, in the nature of things, an over-whelming advantage over its opposition critics. It has at its disposal all the accumulated knowledge and experience of its Civil Service officials. It can call for information from them at any time on any subject. Cabinet ministers only make speeches after being briefed by their expert advisers. It is high time for our Opposition parties to stop whining about this domination of Parliament by the government and to set themselves to do something more effective about it, rather than just sitting in their seats waiting for some juicy scandal to break — like that of the horses on the army pay-roll. If the opposition parties want to achieve a position of some intellectual equality with the government, they must equip themselves with brain-trusts, with expert secretariats, staffed by some of the brightest of young university graduates, and they must do much more than they have yet done to draw on the intellectual help which they could easily get from university departments of economics and political science and sociology and history.

But all our parties need well-organized brain-trusts and secretariats of a new higher quality for a much wider purpose than this — for the purpose of carrying on the political education of the voters. How is a party today in the 1950s going to build up an intelligent body of public support for the policies which it thinks important if it continues to depend on obsolete nineteenth-century techniques — on public meetings which the public will not attend, on newspaper reports of political speeches which are squeezed in among the much more attractive columns devoted to sport and crime and sex and advertising and the comics? Our Canadian parties are, in fact, still living in the horse-and-buggy age. Outside of the proceedings in Parliament, they mostly go to sleep between elections. They have learnt little from all the modern techniques of mass propaganda, and they don't take the task of political education seriously at all. They should study how things are done in Britain — read the mass of material that pours out regularly there from the two party headquarters, read the books that are written every year by Conservative and Labour politicians, publicists and professors, attend the summer schools and study groups and lecture series that are going on somewhere all the time, listen to the party broadcasts and other political discussions over the B.B.C. In Canada, so far as I know, only the C.C.F. in Saskatchewan during the 1930s and 1940s, when it was building up its position amongst the wheat farmers, has tried to do or succeeded in doing anything comparable to this in the way of public education.

Lacking such organization and such mental stimulus, our Canadian party politics is at this moment sunk in a profound and death-like apathy. This cannot be cured by the usual spasmodic synthetic hysteria which is worked up at quadrennial election campaigns. And the potential danger of the situation is obvious. If there is no political education available to the masses of the voters, if current politics offers nothing to stir their interest, everything is prepared for the arrival one of these days of the messianic demagogue. Some day, when men are stirred to unrest by depression, he will arrive, exploiting to the full the techniques of modern advertising, playing on fears and hatreds and cupidities, substituting slogans for programmes, intensifying his appeal by a religious brand of messianism, inviting the public to entrust themselves to the charismatic leader, substituting plebiscitary democracy for parliamentary government. We have had a foretaste of what such a movement could amount to in the success of Social Credit in Alberta and British Columbia. Our English-Canadian protestant community, with its proliferation of little fundamentalist sects, seems almost predestined to throw up such a movement on the national scale one of these days. In the two western provinces these little sects are already beginning to function as the Social Credit party at prayer. Ontario, where politics for a long time has been almost completely devoid of intellectual content, has the potentialities for making Alberta and British Columbia look tame and colourless. All that we need at this moment, indeed, is an Ontario Aberhart. Perhaps he has already graduated from one of our teacher-training or theological institutions.

Well, this is a sad conclusion into which to decline after talking so long. But, at least, a bigger and better Aberhart is something more cheerful to look forward to than a Canadian Hitler or Malenkov. We can escape this fate only by revitalizing our Canadian liberalism, both the liberalism with a small "l" whose natural home is in our universities, and the Liberalism with a capital "L" which regards Ottawa as its home because it has had such a long lease there.

A few months ago I came across some sentences in the *Political Quarterly*, the organ of the Labour party intellectuals in England. The sentences were part of an editorial criticizing the Labour party for its lack of new creative ideas, now that it had fulfilled its mandate of 1945; and they seem to me relevant here in Canada — as applied to Liberalism with a capital "L".

> As the years pass, those in power and at the head of a party, particularly if they have led the party to success, tend to grind over and over again the same old political tune upon the old party organ. Their speeches, which used to sound like trumpet calls, now sound like an old gramophone record with the needle stuck in a groove. Only a vigorous left wing, with a clear, honest left-wing policy, can prevent this political hardening of the arteries, which is always threatening to destroy the party.
>
> (*Political Quarterly*, July, 1954.)

It strikes me that these sentences could be applied without change to the Canadian Liberal party. The Liberals are now intellectually bankrupt. They have wrung out the last drop of sentiment and of ideas which can be extracted from Mr. Mackenzie King's *Industry and Humanity* of 1918. Their intellectual bankruptcy has not become a public scandal only because the other parties are equally bankrupt. A party with 170 seats in the House of Commons, however, is not likely to feel the need of revitalization.

So I turn to our universities. A revitalizing of liberalism with a small "l" can come only from our universities. I think it will have to be preceded by some much deeper soul-searching than Canadian academic liberals have yet found congenial, into the causes of the crisis that confronts liberalism throughout the western world. We in Canada cannot much longer remain aloof from the deeper intellectual currents of the twentieth century. It is high time for our younger academic liberals to start something.

4. The Winnipeg Declaration of the C.C.F.

(This appeared in the Toronto *Globe and Mail*, 21 August, 1956, on the occasion of the new declaration of policy made by the C.C.F. at its Winnipeg convention in the summer of 1956. The article was written on the invitation of the editor of the *Globe and Mail* who, naturally enough, made some critical editorial comments on it when he printed it on his editorial page.)

When the Co-operative Commonwealth Federation drew up its new Declaration of Principles at Winnipeg a few weeks ago, this was a major item of news in the papers. Which shows that, in spite of their professions, the newspaper editors are not yet quite sure that the C.C.F. is only a minor party with a regional appeal on the prairies. What keeps it in the headlines is their fear that it may yet become a major party.

The best way we have discovered in the English-speaking world for conducting democratic politics is through a two-party system, in which two major parties compete for office and power, while a variety of minor parties do what they can to cause trouble by raising new issues or ventilating neglected grievances. For the two-party system works best when there are more than two parties. The function of minor parties in past history, however, has not been to win office or power, but to keep the major parties on their toes, alert to minority interests, flexible in adjusting themselves to new demands of hitherto neglected interest-groups in the community. Minor parties, as a rule, have not had a long life. They cause intense irritation for a while; and then they disappear, as one or the other of the major parties adopts what is valuable in their platforms.

Unfortunately in Canada we have not had a two-party system since the election of 1921, *i.e.*, since before most present-day Canadian voters began to vote. We have had one major party, the Liberal, which can attract substantial support from all across the country, from urban and rural areas, from English and French Canadians, from Protestants, Catholics and Jews, from capitalists and workers. But the other party, the Conservative, has never recovered from 1917; it has lost almost all its appeal west of Lake

Superior, its wooing of Quebec has so far been repulsed, it can't win Federal elections even in Ontario.

So the problem of where the second major party in Canada is to come from still remains. And that is why the C.C.F. is still news after an existence of twenty-four years — a long time for a minor party. As a minor party it has had a very great influence in helping to bring about the modern social-welfare state in Canada — as all politicians will admit in private. But it is still presenting its challenge to become a major party.

Political parties, as their experience grows, are like churches and all other human associations: they modify their views without changing their identity. No one would dream of claiming that Liberals and Conservatives must remain monolithic unalterable entities frozen in the form given to them by Gladstone and Disraeli. In fact they have changed so much in my lifetime that the chief difficulty now about liberalism and conservatism is to find out what it is that Liberals are trying to liberate or Conservatives to conserve.

Liberals once believed in *laissez-faire*, in unregulated private enterprise, having a faith that an Invisible Hand would bring about the public good if only every individual were left free to seek his own private good in his own way. Everyone knows that this isn't what they believe today.

Conservatives as late as 1914 in England were fighting against social insurance and denying that the poor had any claims on society or on the state except the right to expect Christian charity. Conservative right-wing Republicans in the United States still don't like the welfare state. But English and Canadian Conservatives have made the transition to it during the past few decades.

Why not, then, admit that Socialists also can modify their views in the course of time without betraying their principles or deserting their traditions? Especially, since the change of emphasis from the Regina Manifesto of 1932 to the Winnipeg Declaration of 1956 is nothing like as great as the intellectual transformations through which Liberals and Conservatives have gone during the lifetime of men not yet in their seventies.

The point on which critical commentators have seized in the Winnipeg Declaration is that the C.C.F. no longer affirms, as in 1932, that it will not rest till it has eliminated capitalism from our economy. No doubt it was too emphatic in this peroration. "Never" is a concept to which politicians should never have recourse. But we should in fairness remember the conditions of the 1930s.

The C.C.F. was launched as a Socialist party in 1932 at the depth of the great world depression. At that time it was easy and natural to speak of capitalism and socialism as two entities which had nothing in common. The capitalism referred to in the Regina Manifesto was the capitalism of that time which had no solution for the problem of millions of unemployed and destitute men and women and their children. It was irresponsible in its social attitude, denying any duty to its employees, offering only incantations like those of Herbert Hoover and the bankers. In the United States it was saved in spite of itself by Franklin D. Roosevelt and his New Deal; and all over the western world economic recovery came only as the state stepped in to become the universal employer through munitions contracts.

Today the irresponsible power of the capitalist has been checked by state regulations and by the rise of a new countervailing power in the form of the great trade unions. Keynes has exploded the old sterile orthodoxies of the banks and the treasuries. Western capitalism is not only producing abundance again; much more important, it is admitting a social responsibility towards the workers in its plants in the form of guaranteed annual wages, fringe benefits, etc. The capitalism of the 1950s is something very different from the capitalism of the 1930s, even if it is still capitalism.

So the socialism of the 1950s is different from the socialism of the 1930s. Socialists have seen some terrifying demonstrations of what unlimited state power can mean. All sensible and honest Socialists now admit that there are dangerous potentialities of totalitarianism in their doctrine, just as there are dangerous potentialities of anarchy and chaos in the old doctrines of capitalism. The secret of freedom is the presence of checks and balances. So socialism in the West no longer talks of the complete socialization of the means of production, distribution and exchange. And big business, one hopes, would no longer tolerate the domination of the economy by the anti-social adventurers and speculators who were on top of the world in 1929 just before the crash.

Socialism in the 1930s tended to emphasize too much the economic means towards the better society that they were seeking. Their end was a society of brotherhood. And since the capitalist rulers of society seemed so completely without a sense of social responsibility, Socialists concluded that they must be replaced by state enterprise. Experience has demonstrated that state enterprise doesn't necessarily produce the society of fellowship. And most decent business men, while still anti-Socialist, admit the necessity of some state controls. So we are shaking down to a mixed economy, in which the main differences of opinion are as to how much state enterprise shall be mixed with how much private enterprise.

The essential basis of the Socialist faith is ethical, not economic. The Socialist dream is of a society which is a brotherhood, a fellowship. The word socialism comes from the Latin word "socius", which means an associate, a fellow, an ally. "Socialist" as a word came into the English language in 1828, when it was used in an obscure English journal published by some followers of Robert Owen to describe themselves. Owen's gospel was co-operative production by the workers in an industry, and he had no use for the political state. It was because, as the nineteenth century went on, there seemed no chance of bringing about this Co-operative Commonwealth without state action on a wide scale that socialism gradually came to emphasize state ownership as its panacea. But this was a means, not an end. Modern Socialists still remain faithful to their end, but they are rethinking their means.

This rethinking has gone furthest in the British Labour party. If you want to see what is implicit in the Winnipeg Declaration of the Canadian Socialist party, read the new Penguin volume, *Twentieth Century Socialism*. This is written by a group of the moderates in the Labour party who are close to Hugh Gaitskell; and it develops at length the argument which I have briefly sketched here about Socialist ends and means. It is also very frank in admitting that intelligent Socialists today are not completely certain about their means.

The C.C.F. started in the 1930s as a Fabian Socialist party, applying to Canadian conditions the general ideas of the moderates in British Labour. It is once again following the British example by bringing the ideas of the early 1930s up-to-date for the conditions of the late 1950s. I think it should have done this much sooner. I think it should add to its present declaration of principles, which is inevitably somewhat abstract, a list of priorities containing the concrete policies which it would carry out in a first period of office. General principles are too apt to become the politician's line of escape.

But the important thing is that the C.C.F. has admitted that it has learned from experience. This is what makes it a potential major party. Only minor parties remain dogmatic and fundamentalist, because they never really mean to seek office and power. Rather than tackle the responsibilities of power, they prefer to enjoy the bliss of contemplating their own intellectual and moral superiority.

Do Canadian Liberals and Conservatives never modify their ways of thinking, or do they get over the difficulties of adjusting themselves to changing experience by just not thinking at all? The C.C.F. is following the example of British Labour. A good Britisher like myself would feel much more cheerful about the prospects of Canadian politics in general if our Conservative leaders showed any awareness of the publications on Conservative philosophy and policies which issue from the Conservative Political Centre in London, and if our Liberal leaders showed any sign that they had ever heard of *The Economist* and *The Manchester Guardian*.

5. Political Stagnation in Canada, 1956

(This article appeared in *Maclean's* magazine, 13 October, 1956. It was published as one contribution to the section entitled "For the Sake of Argument", and *Maclean's* gave it the title "Let's Stop Leaving our Future to Old Men". These remarks of mine were first given in a talk, broadcast by C.B.C., at the Couchiching Institute in the summer of 1956.)

Enthusiasts would have it that we have entered upon our Elizabethan Age in Canadian history. There is a new exhilarating spirit of adventure, so I have been assured, a sense that we are setting out towards new horizons. Our seemingly limitless economic potentialities are intoxicating in themselves. We have also begun to make a name for ourselves in world affairs. And new springs of cultural activity are bubbling up everywhere. But there is no sign that I can see of a new era in our politics. Our political life remains mean, drab, petty, insignificant. Why should this be? Why the contrast between the general promise of Canadian life and the lack of promise of its politics? Why do we take for granted that Canadian politicians as a class should be dull and fatuous, and that nothing imaginative or creative is to be hoped from them? In the reign of Elizabeth I politicians were inspiring poetry.

One thing wrong with our present-day politics is the age of our politicians. Politically we have become an old man's country. Elder statesmen are expected to show a balanced judgment and a ripe wisdom, but they are not likely to have the dynamic energy that ushers in a new age. In fact, the old man in a hurry has become proverbial in history for having been usually in a hurry about the wrong things. It is the young man's imagination that is creative.

Let's go back to a period in our Canadian history when our politics was genuinely creative, to the month of October 1864, at the meeting of the Quebec Conference that drew up the framework of Confederation. In October 1864, the oldest of the leading Fathers of Confederation, George Etienne Cartier, was just over 50. John A. Macdonald was just under 50. George Brown was 46. D'Arcy McGee was only 39. Charles Tupper was 43, and Leonard

Tilley 46. Of the outstanding public men of that time there was one great figure who failed to rise to the opportunity of the moment. He was, of course, Joseph Howe; and what was wrong with Howe in October 1864 was clearly that he was too old for constructive politics; he had reached 60.

Go back a little farther to another creative period in our political history. In December 1837, when he broke into rebellion, William Lyon Mackenzie was 42. His fellow rebel in Lower Canada, Louis Joseph Papineau, was 41. Lord Durham, whose famous Report started a new era, was 47 and at the end of his career when the Report was published in 1839. Robert Baldwin, who had the interview with Durham in Toronto in 1838 that insinuated the idea of responsible government into Durham's mind, was at that moment only 34. After a long fight for his great idea, he retired from politics in 1851 at 47. His great French-Canadian colleague, Louis LaFontaine, retired with him in 1851 at 44. Think of it — two of our greatest statesmen retiring from politics, their work done, at the ages of 47 and 44!

Now look at the situation today. Mr. St. Laurent, the prime minister, is 74. His two senior colleagues are Mr. Howe, 70, and Mr. Gardiner, 72. The leader of the opposition, Mr. Drew, is 62. Mr. Coldwell of the C.C.F. is 67; Mr. Low, the Social Credit leader, is 56. In the two chief provinces, Mr. Frost of Ontario is 61, and M. Duplessis of Quebec is 66. And if you turn to the younger men, look at the Liberal front bench in Ottawa. Mr. Pearson is 59, Mr. Martin is 53, Mr. Harris is 52, Mr. Pickersgill is 51. These are the young hopefuls who are shortly, so one presumes, to take over the Liberal government and give us twenty or thirty years more of Liberalism with a capital "L". Yet they are all today older than was Cartier in 1864, though Cartier was the oldest of the leading Fathers of Confederation. All of these contemporaries whose names I have mentioned are men of exceptional ability. But where are the young men in our public life?

Another thing that we all agree to be wrong with Canadian politics at present is the phenomenon of over-powerful governments. Since the end of the war in 1945 only two provincial governments have been upset in elections, and the federal government has been in office since 1935. There they sit to the right of Mr. Speaker, with overwhelming majorities in the representative assembly, so secure in their hold of office that they become contemptuous of the puny helpless oppositions facing them, and grow careless, arrogant and cynical in the exercise of their power. But Her Majesty's Opposition is just as necessary for free, democratic parliamentary institutions as is Her Majesty's Government.

Now, if we examine the voting figures in the elections that placed these over-powerful governments in office, we find nearly always that the balance of seats in the House is fantastically divergent from the balance of votes among the electorate. This is due to the working of our electoral system of single-member constituencies in a multi-party grouping of candidates. The successful party seldom gets even a majority of the votes, but it may get 70 percent or more of the seats. Thus the Liberal party in recent federal elections got 46.5 percent of the votes across Canada in 1935, 54.8 in 1940, 41.4 in 1945, 50 in 1949, and 49.9 in 1953. But in the House of Commons it has been accustomed to ride roughshod over oppositions that can easily be outvoted, because at these successive elections it won 176, 181, 125, 193, 172 seats.

The picture is similar in the provinces. Last June, M. Duplessis was re-elected for the fourth consecutive time in what the newspapers described as a landslide; but, actually, even with the help of all those remarkable devices by which elections are won in Quebec, he got only some 52 percent of the votes. His majority in the Assembly, however, enables him to behave as if the opposition were as insignificant, practically, as an opposition in the Supreme Soviet at Moscow. In Saskatchewan last June, also, Mr. Douglas was re-elected for the fourth time. He has 36 out of 53 seats, but he only got some 45 percent of the votes. And so one might go on indefinitely.

It seems to me that, if we really think that Canadian governments are becoming too powerful in office, we should do something to change our electoral system, so as to give minorities a representation in the House more in proportion to the votes they receive in the country at large. Of course, our practical politicians, who enjoy the unearned security of unbeatable majorities in the House, will do nothing to make the working of our electoral system fairer to minorities. And those prim, prissy old maids, the professors of political science in our universities, will warn us that if we flirt with proportional representation we may be seduced into a fate worse than death. For P.R., so the experts assure us, makes for a multi-party system rather than a two-party system. But we have a multi-party system already; and it could hardly produce worse results than it does at present.

I am well aware that it is useless to argue with Canadians about electoral systems. The Canadian people don't really want parliamentary government as it is understood by historians and political scientists. They want to vote a government into office and leave it there to run the political machinery, while they themselves can get on with the serious business of making money. To us, as to our American neighbours, an election is a way of escaping from politics for four years.

Let me go on to say something about the peculiar working of our multi-party system. I assume without argument that a two-party system is a better way of conducting democratic politics than a multi-party or a group system. I believe also that a two-party system like that of Britain ,where the division is fairly clear-cut between a party of the Left and a party of the Right, is preferable to a two-party system like that of the United States, where each party contains all varieties of opinion from left to right, and where the method of political dialectic is for both parties to take both sides on every issue — except on the issue of which party is to be on the inside and which on the outside of every office.

Most of the confusion of our national politics today is due to the fact that we haven't had a two-party system, of either the British or the American variety, for longer than most Canadians can remember. Since the election of 1921 we have suffered from a multiplicity of parties whose action and reaction have not been dynamic or creative enough to produce a new two-party system, but which have now been with us too long for a return of the old two-party to be possible. We are wandering between two worlds, one dead, the other powerless to be born.

A few years ago a well-known American journalist, Mr. Joseph Harsch, while broadcasting about American politics to a British audience over the B.B.C., made a comparison between British and American parties that I think is suggestive for Canadian politics. He said:

> Your Conservative Party specializes in conservatism, your Labour Party in socialism. There may be an odd socialist in the Conservative Party, and vice versa; but by and large your British voter has a point of view which puts him automatically into one party or the other. . . . Your British parties, like your shops, specialize in one particular line of goods. The American political party is like a big American department store. It tries to appeal to customers of all classes, doctrines and social persuasions.

Now in Canada, broadly speaking, we had by 1914 two political parties that called themselves by English names, Liberal and Conservative; but they were really two American department-store parties, each offering something for shoppers of every range of taste and pocketbook. Just before 1914 each was advertising its own special brand of naval goods, but otherwise the customer stood to get pretty much the same things, whichever store he patronized. This system was burned out by the fires of conscription in 1917. We found ourselves after the 1917 election with the worst possible kind of a two-party system — two parties of which one was English-Canadian and one was French-Canadian. But by 1921 the English-Canadian combine had gone to pieces. And since then the strains of war and depression have produced divisions in our Canadian community with which the old department-store parties have not been able to cope successfully. The Progressive, C.C.F., Social Credit and French-Canadian nationalist movements were revolts against this old department-store type of politics. They accused the old department stores of selling high-quality goods at low prices to rich customers, and cheap shoddy goods at high prices to poor customers. But they all failed, in the sense that none of them was able to build up a new party with a wide enough appeal to make it capable of winning a majority of seats at Ottawa — i.e. capable of government.

To win such a majority a party must be able to make some effective appeal to English Canadians and French Canadians, to Protestants and Catholics, to city dwellers and urban dwellers, to easterners and westerners, to employers and workers. Only the Liberal party has measured up to this necessity and built up a really national following. In this sense only the Liberal party has deserved to be in office.

But the old two-party system of the *two* department-store parties never recovered. The Conservative department store failed to stock itself with goods that appealed to French-Canadian customers or to the mail-order customers out on the prairies. It gradually declined into an old-fashioned Victorian country store, with oil lamps and wood stoves, selling stiff starched collars and long woollen underwear, whalebone corsets and high-button shoes, to such old-fashioned customers as still survived in Ontario and New Brunswick. Though, to be sure, it did every now and then put up a freshly painted sign in front announcing that it had adopted a new name and was under entirely new management.

Meanwhile the Liberal department store, under the astute direction of its young manager, Mr. Mackenzie King, equipped itself with all the modern merchandizing techniques of the twentieth century. It added new departments to deal with such new commodities as old-age pensions and baby bonuses. It introduced a gaudily packaged new specialty of national citizenship for new Canadians. Its sales have therefore gone on booming from year to year; since 1935 it has blanketed the country and pretty nearly driven its rivals out of business.

In short, for the last twenty years we have had one genuinely national party, which is able to make an effective appeal in all parts of the country; and over against it a variety of special sectional, ideological or racial groups, none of which seems able to grow into the second national party that is necessary for a two-party system.

It seems to me that this has inhibited in Canada one healthy development that has been taking place all over the western world: the rise of a genuine conservatism with a conservative philosophy and conservative policies. In the middle of the twentieth century conservatism means political leadership by big business. Britain and the United States now have conservative governments that are frankly business men's governments. And the British or American citizen today knows what his politics is about. The Englishman is watching to see whether a conservative government depending upon private enterprise can put the British economy upon its feet, as a socialist government failed to do. The American is making up his mind whether it really is true that what is good for General Motors is good for the United States. And in American politics the two old department-store parties are being gradually forced into an alignment of Left *versus* Right.

But where is the conservative revival in Canada? There is a revival, I think, but it is taking a peculiar form that is unhealthy. We are now buying conservative goods from the Liberal department store. It is the Liberals who boast their belief in private enterprise — American private enterprise, if necessary. It is the Liberals who are closely associated with big business and who are committed to a programme of economic expansion under the leadership of big-business enterprise. Under Mr. King in the 1920s and 1930s the Liberals were able to frustrate the rise of any genuine party of the Left. Under Mr. St. Laurent they frustrate the rise of any genuine national party of the Right. Their blanketing of the Centre prevents our ever getting any clear sense of the direction in which we are moving or any clear sense of the alternatives between which we might choose.

All this had led to another peculiarly Canadian phenomenon. Since we seem unable to produce an effective second party, and so to produce an effective opposition on Parliament Hill, we are turning by some instinctive subconscious process in another direction. Her Majesty's Canadian Opposition is emerging in the provincial capitals. The federal government treats the little opposition parties in Ottawa with contempt, but it negotiates warily with the provincial governments. It well knows where the countervailing power is located which is really a check upon its own power. In effect, our Canadian opposition now consists of the Social Credit governments in British Columbia and Alberta, the C.C.F. government in Saskatchewan, the Conservative governments in Ontario and New Brunswick, and the Union Nationale government in Quebec.

But they constitute so effective an opposition that our politics has reached a condition of stalemate. The federal government manoeuvres skilfully so as to put the blame for inaction upon obstinate provincial governments, while they in turn try to convict the federal government of being the villain. Look at what is happening, or rather what is failing to happen, in health, in education, in road building, in housing, and so on. Moreover, far from trying to shake loose from this vicious system, we Canadian voters now elect anti-Liberal governments in the provinces to save ourselves from Ottawa, and then we turn around and elect a Liberal government to Ottawa to save ourselves from these provincial-rights wreckers.

Such conductdoes not strike me as a demonstration of political intelligence. We need some fresh stimulant in our politics that will have the same invigorating effect as the stimulant of unprecedented capital investment has had upon our economy. Being an old man myself, I haven't the slightest idea of where this stimulant will come from. But there are some four hundred thousand new babies being born every year in Canada. Surely, when the due quota of these babies eventually goes into politics, some of them will come up with some new political ideas.

6. Canada and the
North Atlantic Triangle

(This was a talk given at Michigan State University in February, 1957, in a symposium on Canadian-American relations. It was printed in the quarterly published by Michigan State University, *The Centennial Review*, Fall, 1957.)

I hold these truths to be self-evident: (1) that some effective form of North Atlantic alliance is essential for the preservation of our western civilization; (2) that it is desirable that such an alliance should develop into something more than an alliance, into a community of some kind, political, economic, cultural; (3) that this enterprise — alliance or community — can be carried out only under the leadership of the United States; (4) that it behooves the rest of us, therefore, to avoid the temptation to indulge in continuous bellyaching about American leadership; (5) that the American people are, as yet, far from being mature enough to provide the wise leadership that is needed. These being self-evident propositions, I shall not waste time in discussing them further.

I shall confine myself to a discussion of some of our particular Canadian difficulties in this North Atlantic enterprise. Because they are somewhat intangible and are mainly psychological, they are apt to be insufficiently appreciated by our American neighbours. The chief cause of trouble between Canada and the United States does not arise in differences of policy between the governments of the two countries but in lack of understanding between the two peoples. One ex-Canadian, now resident in the States, has put it in this way: Americans, he said, are benevolently ignorant about Canada, whereas Canadians are malevolently informed about the United States. Obviously he was still speaking as a Canadian. I wish to dwell upon his word "malevolently".

Americans must understand that we Canadians, like the Arabs and the Israelis, like the British and the French, are not rational creatures. The only rational creatures left in this twentieth-century world are, of course, the Americans. Let me try to explain why we Canadians are finding it difficult to respond to the challenge of the 1950s in a rational, pragmatic, utilitarian manner, with the cool adjustment of means to ends which is the temper in which international affairs should be handled. Americans are apt to see us as a calm, sensible, colourless people, because it has pleased Providence for the moment to give us a cool, calculating, pragmatic, utilitarian government. But actually, at this moment, we the people of Canada are being swept by storms of neurotic emotion.

All our Canadian existence since 1783 has depended upon our successful manipulation of our particular North Atlantic triangle — the triangle of Canada, Great Britain, and the United States. Until very recently our Canadian world has in effect consisted of this triangle. Canada could not exist for long if the relationship between the two big members of the triangle were one of war, even of cold war. She requires a state of peaceful co-existence between the British and the Americans, and has been much happier in her triangle since the Hundred Years War between Britain and the United States came to an end with the Treaty of Washington in 1871. But, given this state of peaceful co-existence, we survive as a distinct individual Canadian entity by the feat of balancing ourselves in a triangle of forces in which Britain is at one corner and the United States at the other corner of the triangle.

It is a good triangle, from our Canadian point of view, if it is an isosceles one, with both Britain and the United States pulling roughly the same weight. Such a triangle was not necessary in the nineteenth century for the British or the Americans. They could at any time have worked out a bilateral arrangement in a London-Washington axis. But an axis of this kind was of no use to us. We had to make sure that we were included, that is, that the relationship was in the nature of a triangle. Otherwise we should have remained an insignificant dependent colony of Britain or become an insignificant dependent satellite of the United States. Since it was the geographical pull of the United States which threatened our existence most directly, we balanced our historic connection with Britain against it. Our response to the challenge of the nineteenth century was to keep this triangular relationship working, and to get Englishmen and Americans acting as if they understood it and appreciated it as fully as we did. This was what Arnold Toynbee would call a creative response to challenge.

During the hundred years from Lord Durham's Report in 1839 to the outbreak of World War II in 1939 we achieved independence of Great Britain and avoided absorption into the United States. We pre-empted the northern half of the North American continent from American expansion. (This is our great historic achievement, which we expect to earn us entry into paradise when the last trump sounds.) This British century of our history was a happy century for us. We achieved independence without separation. We accepted British leadership — political, economic, cultural, and moral — and we followed Britain into two world wars. The important point to understand about us now is that since 1940 we have entered into a new era, and that we face a new challenge with the old attitudes of mind, habits of action, maxims of conduct, traditions, prejudices, slogans, clichés, and myths that we inherited from this happy British century of our experience. We made a creative response to the challenge of the nineteenth century. We are now suffering from what Toynbee would call the nemesis of creativity.

For we have gone through the revolution of 1940. In that year we passed from the British century of our history to the American century. We became dependent upon the United States for our security. We have, therefore, no choice but to follow American leadership. And our American century is going to be a much tougher experience for us than our British century was. It is the uneasy, half-acknowledged recognition of this fact that is making us neurotic today. The British, said a famous historian two generations ago, built up their empire in a fit of absence of mind. We are watching the Americans start to build up their empire now; and as their power over us expands, they seem to be even more absent-minded about it than the British were in the days of their imperial glory.

Let me refer briefly to some critical events in our Canadian history in order to illustrate how deeply the pro-British attitude became grounded in our consciousness during the period when we were using Britain to balance against American pressures in our North Atlantic triangle. In the years 1775–1783 the ancestors of the French Canadians rejected the invitation to join the American Revolution; and after 1783 there was a great influx of English-speaking "United Empire Loyalists" into the anti-revolutionary part of North America. In the War of 1812 we again rejected the American invitation. After the Rebellions of 1837 we rejected American Jacksonian democracy and adopted instead a mild British liberal Whiggism which we called Responsible Government. In 1867 we formed the Canadian Confederation in order to save the northern half of the continent from American "Manifest

Destiny" expansionism. (Manifest Destiny is what we in British countries are accustomed to call Imperialism.) In 1891 and again in 1911 we rejected propositions for close reciprocal trade relations with our southern neighbour because we feared that such economic ties might lead to political absorption. 1891: "A British subject I was born, a British subject I will die." 1911: "No truck or trade with the Yankees." In the 1930s Mr. Bennett countered the high American tariffs, which were hitting us hard, with fantastically high Canadian tariffs.

You will observe that there is a periodicity of about twenty to thirty years in these anti-American crises of our Canadian history. About once every twenty or thirty years the fever rises in our blood, we gird up our loins under the leadership of some inspiring prophet-saviour, and once again we save ourselves from the United States. Today in the 1950s the twenty-thirty years' period has come round again, and there is more anti-American speech-making and editorializing in Canada than I have ever known in my lifetime. We are waiting for the prophet-saviour to emerge.

Part of this inherited anti-American tradition of ours is to the effect that we have always been treated harshly by American diplomacy. American diplomats drive hard bargains and show a callous disregard for any particular Canadian interests that may conflict with local American interests that are well entrenched in Congress. He who sups with the American Department of State should have a long spoon. Such was the tradition on which all Canadians were reared until a few years ago. Furthermore, this anti-American bias in our thinking is the one thing that English-speaking and French-speaking Canadians have in common.

You will see what I mean when I say that we Canadians are not rational creatures. For we now live in a world in which close and intimate co-operation with the Americans is absolutely essential. However Europeans or Asiatics may delude themselves, we Canadians cannot dream of forming part of any third force or of being isolationist or neutral in the fundamental conflicts that split our world — now a much bigger and more complex world for us Canadians than the old North Atlantic triangle of the nineteenth century. The test of our maturity in facing this new twentieth-century challenge is how sensibly we adjust ourselves to the new phenomenon of American leadership. Until we have proved ourselves mature in meeting this test, we are not in a good position to indulge in sneers about the immaturity of American leadership. Mature people accept the inevitable.

What makes us more neurotic at the moment is that just when we become aware of this new challenge, we are also having it made uncomfortably clear to us that we are more dependent upon our neighbour economically than ever before in our history. We can hardly help being resentful about this fact, however profitable it may be for us for the time being. The percentage of our imports that comes from the United States and of our exports that goes to the United States has reached unprecedented figures. We operate in the dollar area, not in the sterling area of the rest of the British Commonwealth. Our spectacular boom of the 1950s derives primarily from the flow of American investment capital into Canada. Furthermore the Paley report has made it clear that the things we are specially efficient at producing are the very commodities that the American economy is going to need in ever increasing quantities — forest and mineral products. We are drifting towards an integrated North American continental economy.

Finally — and this is what causes Canadian eggheads the most worry of all, making pathetic creatures out of most of them just now — we are culturally more and more influenced by American mass-culture: Hollywood movies, Madison Avenue advertising, commercialized radio and television, mass-circulation magazines, American fashions in clothes, motor-cars, hit-parade songs, cocktail bars, and gadgets, gadgets, gadgets. Our eggheads are wont to refer to these influences as "alien" (see the Massey Report of 1951), but there is no sign that the ordinary Canadian citizen, when he welcomes them as he does, is doing anything except what comes naturally.

Against this dangerous mid-twentieth-century domination of our Canadian life by our great neighbour, what can we do? This is our modern challenge, and we cannot meet it by simply retiring to cultivate our garden.

What we can do about the economic and cultural challenge is beyond my assigned subject. In the political sphere the first thing that we need to do is to reconstruct the North Atlantic triangle. The British corner of the triangle is no longer weighty enough. We must do something to add weight in that corner. Some sentimentalists in English-speaking Canada like to think that we can do this by calling in the British Commonwealth to redress the balance. They are what Arnold Toynbee would call our Canadian Archaists.

But the Commonwealth is not a power aggregation in international politics. Sentimentalists in Great Britain have been wont to emphasize it because this is their way of affirming that Britain is still a world power; but recent hard facts have demonstrated that she has sunk to be simply a European power. The members of the British Commonwealth do not agree with each other on the fundamental questions of the twentieth century. Some of them, the Asian members, think that the essential division in the modern world is between colonial and anti-colonial powers; the North Atlantic members, along with Australia and New Zealand, think that it is between free communities and totalitarian communities. South Africa under its present government is a standing denial of all the ideals of freedom and equality and democracy in which the other members profess to believe. And in the Suez crisis Britain, the old mother country of the Commonwealth, gave the rest of us a severe moral shock which still further undermined Commonwealth unity; as the London *Economist* has put it, she was caught stealing hats in Oxford St.

The British Commonwealth is therefore not much help to us Canadians in this problem of the balance in the North Atlantic triangle. What then? It seems to me that since 1945 our Canadian policy should have been to give all possible support to projects for the closer integration of the states of western Europe. Here is where we may find our new balance against the overwhelming weight of the United States. The British, however, up to a few months ago, have always insisted on remaining aloof from schemes for western European unity. They used always to invite the rest of us to invite them to stay out of Europe for the sake of Commonwealth unity. And when Mr. Macmillan a while ago reversed this policy and announced British interest in a European free trade union, the Canadian response was disappointing. We should have been enthusiastically pushing them farther into Europe, for our sake as well as for their own. For only in a successful western Europe can Canada find that new balance which will be needed to make the North Atlantic triangle work as well for us in this new American century as it worked in the old British century. Our government, in fact, should at this moment be educating the Canadian public into an understanding of the new facts of life in the second half of the twentieth century.

There is another challenge facing you Americans as well as us Canadians. Suppose that a revived western Europe comes about, with Britain recovering some of her greatness as a partner in it, what kind of international relationship should we work for in the broader Atlantic community in which we North Americans will be co-operating with the west Europeans? Canadians have had a very different experience in international relations from that of the American people. In our British period we worked out a most satisfactory relationship with the other British countries, the so-called Commonwealth relationship. It is a loose, free-and-easy partnership of equals, who stand by each other in times of trouble as members of a happy family stand by each other, but who are not bound by any formal ties of military alliance or political federation. It is a curious, anomalous kind of partnership, for each member does what seems good to himself in carrying out his obligations to his partners and cannot be bound by any majority decisions of the others to which he is not a consenting party. It is worked, in fact, by a system of what might be called, in American language, con-current majorities. One might call it — I am referring particularly to the first Commonwealth before the Asian members came in — a team, except that it is a team without a coach, and Americans can't understand a team without a coach. All members of the Commonwealth are equal, and if the British have sometimes assumed that they are more equal than the rest of us, they are apt to be brought up sharply by the Canadian government, as they were in the Suez crisis last November or in the Chanak business — also a crisis in the Near East — in 1922.

This is the experience which has determined our Canadian out-look on international affairs. The states of western Europe have never been united even in a loose Commonwealth arrangement. So I predict that, as the North Atlantic triangle expands to include a good deal of western Europe in it, you Americans are going to make a disconcerting discovery. You are going to find time and again that the other members of the team will not go along with the big fellow — even if he has all the technological know-how, the atomic weapons, and the money — except when they see fit in accordance with their own interpretation of their own interests. You are going to acquire a lot of experience in the practical work-ing of a system of concurrent majorities. I expect that Frenchmen and Germans and Scandinavians and Belgians and Dutchmen will prove just as obstinate in insisting on their right to include them-selves out of any project of which they do not approve as will we Canadians and Britishers. I deplore most of the silly immature

anti-American declamation in Canada just now.   But I cannot hide
my conviction that we Canadians have a great deal more experience
than you Americans have in working this loose international
system of concurrent majorities.

7. The University and Politics

(At the Convocation for Arts and Science of Queen's University, 16 May, 1959, I received the degree of Doctor of Laws, *honoris causa*; and I was invited to deliver the Convocation address.)

Mr. Vice Chancellor, it is a great honour to receive this degree today; and I cannot, in any words that I can find, adequately express my thanks to Queen's University, or my pride. My feeling of pride is increased when I find myself in this distinguished company of gentlemen who have become with me this afternoon Doctors of Laws or Doctors of Divinity, *honoris causa*, of Queen's University. But now it becomes my duty to say a few words on their behalf to this audience; and I have an uneasy suspicion that a good deal of what I say may fail to meet with the approval of my fellow doctors.

As everyone knows, a Convocation address is by tradition supposed to be in the nature of an academic sermon, directed primarily at the graduating class, with some side glances at the university staff. So I propose to preach a short sermon on the topic of the university and politics, which happens to be a favourite sermon topic of mine.

My remarks are prompted by the last two federal general elections of 1957 and 1958. What was the significance of these two election campaigns? There was certainly a spectacular reversal in party fortunes. But what enlightenment did the voters receive about the real problems that confront them, about unemployment, about inflation, about our relations with the United States, about defence, about the cold war? And what can have been the nature of the mental processes of decision-making that took place in the individual voter's mind on these two occasions?

Our political scientists, sociologists and social psychologists in Canada are still too genteel to go out on doorbell-ringing expeditions to question the actual voter before and after elections, as do English psephologists and American opinion-research specialists. So we can only make guesses as to what went on in the voter's mind. My guess is that the Canadian voter had been in a deep slumber for twenty-odd years before 1957, sleeping steadily on his left side, his

Liberal side; that early in 1957 he began to stir uneasily in his sleep, to such an extent that the political doctors watching around his bedside gave out almost daily bulletins that he was waking up; but they were wrong; and on March 31, 1958, still sleeping, he turned over on to his right side, his Conservative side, and he will probably continue to sleep steadily on this side for another twenty years, dreaming happily all the time of Stanley Cup and Grey Cup finals, of nerve-wracking weekends on crowded highways, and of split-level ranch-houses.

This is our way in Canada of escaping from politics. And the fundamental urge among the mass democracies of all our western countries is to escape from the responsibilities of politics, to hand over the burden of decision-making to some charismatic leader, and to retreat into their own private lives. When they do reluctantly turn their attention to political issues, at quadrennial elections, they are submerged under such a bombardment of advertising propaganda, about complex subjects on which they have no information of their own, that rational decision becomes impossible. Between election times modern mass communications, mass entertainment agencies, provide so many distractions from politics that the ordinary citizen is no longer politically minded.

Here is one of the root problems of modern democracy. Can our universities do anything about it? I think that they can do more than they are doing. Politically, the chief function of a university is to turn out each spring a new batch of young people to become members of a political élite, young men and women with disciplined, critical, inquisitive minds, who have been immunized by their university studies against the insidious influences of modern mass communications, who are accustomed to objective, rational methods of enquiry, who have acquired the Socratic faith that the unexamined life is not worth living. If we can gradually build up an élite with minds like that, who insist on applying the Socratic technique to politics, we may eventually raise the intellectual level of our public life. I can see no other way of doing it except through the agency of this élite acting as a leaven within the inert lump of mass democracy.

I put this case to a Queen's audience because Queen's has been distinguished by the interest of its professors in current political discussion and by the high quality of the political journalism which they have produced. This is what has always made Queen's specially interesting to me. The very first Queen's professor, a professor of mathematics, is reported in the official Queen's history as having, after his last public speech, whispered to the man who was following him on the platform: "Pump it into the boys to grow up good Conservatives." That isn't quite what I mean by high-quality political discussion. The journalistic contributions of Queen's professors in the *Queen's Quarterly* for the past sixty-five years would be a better example. I need mention only such names as those of Shortt, Watson, Cappon, Skelton, from among the great Queen's men of the past.

It was Principal George Monro Grant, as far as I know, who began this kind of political writing at Queen's. In his early days, as a young Presbyterian minister in Nova Scotia, Grant had already intervened in current politics as a supporter of Confederation, and after he came to Kingston his interventions were continuous. Let me quote what his biographers have to say about this side of his academic career:

> Grant insisted on the right to be a publicist as well as a churchman; few things roused him to hotter resentment than the theory that clergymen should take no part in public affairs. He was the despair, however, of party men. No other considerable public man in Canada can have followed fixed principles with more complete indifference to their effect upon the fortunes of existing organizations. Had he been a professed independent this would have been expected. The baffling thing was that Grant, with his intense desire to effect things, instead of adopting the attitude of judicial balance usual in an independent, made himself a powerful ally on the side which he judged for the moment to be most likely to advance the interests he had at heart.

By 1896, they say, he had become "a consulting publicist". And away back earlier in his career, in 1867, they quote the remark of one of the Nova Scotia opponents of Confederation about the young men like Grant who were for it. "We shall lose in the end," said this die-hard, "because the men with ideas and ideals are against us." Well, G. M. Grant was the greatest of all Queen's men, and the greatest university head that we have had in Canada. I commend his example as a university man "with ideas and ideals" to our modern university men when they sit down to think about the relation of the university to current politics. He was the happy warrior that all Canadian intellectuals should wish to be.

The function of such a university man is to raise the intellectual level of political discussion. He will probably not make much of an impact on our mass democracy. But he will help to remedy the fundamental weakness of our Canadian politics, which is that within this unintellectual and uninterested and uncommitted mass-democracy we have not as yet built up a very effective political élite. Without this élite modern politics falls into the hands of the so-called practical politicians with their advisers from the advertising agencies. Just as war is too important to be left to the generals, so politics is too vital a matter to be left to the politicians.

What is it that makes British politics so much more attractive and stimulating to people with political interests than is our Canadian politics? Why do issues there seem to get clarified in political discussion in a way that seldom happens here? Essentially, I believe, it is because Britain throughout the past century and a half, during which she was evolving towards complete democracy, has always had this political élite to give a lead in political discussion. Originally it was an aristocratic élite, inheriting wealth and power; later it became an upper-middle-class élite. Today more and more men and women of working-class origin belong to it.

I know that the word élite is a dangerous word for a believer in democracy to use. It has been appropriated in our day by the spokesmen of anti-democratic philosophies, men who see no rôle for the masses of common people but to be bossed and manipulated by their superiors. And anyone today who begins talking about an élite in politics betrays at once that he considers himself to belong to it. But I cannot find any better term for what I mean. I mean that select minority of educated people — not necessarily all educated at a university — who are politically conscious, who are constantly subjecting politics to Socratic analysis, whose principle of action is that the unexamined life is not worth living.

This is by no means the same as a governing class based on birth or wealth or military or police power. I am speaking of an élite of intelligence, not an élite of power. Many of those whom I should class among the élite have little wealth or power. Some of them are perpetually in opposition, dissenters, non-conformists, who are always taking up the cause of unpopular minorities.

How would you distinguish the political élite in Britain? Well, they are the people who get their daily news from the London *Times*, the *Manchester Guardian*, or the *Daily Telegraph* rather than from the *Daily Mirror, Mail, Express*, or *Herald*; who read the *Observer* on Sundays rather than the *News of the World*; who read weeklies such as the *New Statesman*, the *Spectator*, the *Economist*, the *Listener, Punch,* the *Times Literary Supplement*; who read monthlies such as *Encounter,* the *Twentieth Century,* quarterlies such as the *Political Quarterly,* the *Quarterly Review*; and who have provided the audience for the Third Programme on the B.B.C. These élite journals that I have mentioned are all edited and written by university men for university men. And these people — writers and readers — are arguing about politics all the time. They are continuously educating one another. They have analyzed and clarified the main political, economic and social issues before these reach Parliament or get included in party platforms.

This British élite do not form an exclusive class. Theirs is an open society. The test of entry is a trained intelligence. In the modern affluent society the new psychological distinctions amongst brows are more significant than the old economic distinctions among classes. The élite of which I am talking consists of high-brows and upper middle-brows, with a marginal associate membership from among the middle middle-brows. As I have said, there are always new recruits being added from the working classes. Witness the excitement in Britain today over the "angry young men", who are mostly new intellectuals arriving in the élite via the red-brick universities.

Note also that this British political élite are not a social group who keep to themselves in ivory-tower isolation. Some of them, including a good many university dons, are always going out to try their hand at communicating with the mass electorate by taking part in political campaigns, running for Parliament, serving on committees that draft party programmes, etc. It is hardly necessary now to dwell on the part which Fabian Society highbrows have played in the Labour party since it was founded in the 1890s, or which the intellectuals of the Conservative Political Centre under Mr. Butler's inspiration have been playing in the contemporary Conservative party. Consider the tremendous influence in left political circles of G. D. H. Cole and A. D. Lindsay in Oxford, and of Harold Laski and R. H. Tawney in London University. Or consider the fact that what is now clearly the most intelligent statement of party policy between the two wars was the famous Liberal Yellow Book of 1928 which was produced by a committee whose most prominent members were the Cambridge economist J. M. Keynes, and the Liverpool historian Ramsay Muir.

Now the root weakness of our Canadian politics is that it is largely lacking in an élite such as this British one. We are a young country just emerging from the pioneer stage; and our high-brows and upper middle-brows, as they come out of the university, are scattered thinly across the country. One couldn't make a list of Canadian newspapers and periodicals, written by university men for university men, even remotely comparable to the English list which I have named or to the still longer American list that could be drawn up. In fact, when the more or less lonely members of our Canadian élite seek intellectual nourishment to enrich their understanding of contemporary politics, they must mostly have recourse to these English and American journals.

There has been another phenomenon in English public affairs throughout the nineteenth and twentieth centuries which seems to be necessary for the moral and spiritual health of democratic politics but which has been largely missing in Canada. I refer to the succession of prophets, seers and philosophers who have risen to ask inconvenient questions, to preach unpopular truths, to search into the moral dilemmas of politics, to make value judgments about their society. I mean persons such as Thomas Carlyle, John Ruskin, John Stuart Mill, William Morris, Charles Dickens, George Eliot, Matthew Arnold, in the nineteenth century; such as Bernard Shaw, H. G. Wells, G. K. Chesterton, John Galsworthy, in the early twentieth century; and such recent writers and broadcasters as George Orwell, Arnold Toynbee, Bertrand Russell, J. B. Priestley, Aldous Huxley, A. J. P. Taylor. These prophets differ a great deal among themselves, but they are all dedicated to the same essential activity; it is that of making value judgments which challenge and offend the prejudices of the comfortable and the complacent. Most of the earlier names I have mentioned are not those of university graduates. But today it is hard to see where such public servants can come from except from the university.

In the United States there has been a similar succession of prophets, seers and philosophers from the days of transcendentalists like Emerson and Thoreau, down through radical professors like Charles A. Beard and Thorstein Veblen, or humorists like Mr. Dooley, to modern dramatists like Eugene O'Neill and Arthur Miller, a cartoonist like Herblock, a theologian like Reinhold Niebuhr, and a mere sociologist like C. Wright Mills. I was interested recently to read two reviews of Professor Mills' latest book, *The Causes of World War III*. One, a favourable review, remarked with approbation on the Mills habit of "discussing embarrassing subjects in an embarrassing way". The other, an unfavourable review, said that this last book of Mills is like all his earlier writings, "an uneven blend of journalism, sociology and moral indignation".[1] While I don't agree with the policies proposed by Professor Mills in this volume, I wish we had a few more Canadian professors who would insist on publicly discussing embarrassing questions in an embarrassing way, and whose discussion was intense enough to mix up journalism, sociology and moral indignation. For here is one of the great weaknesses of our Canadian politics. Our Canadian society just doesn't seem to breed men like these Englishmen and Americans whom I have named. And the fact that such figures do not emerge in Canada makes our political élite, such as it is, all the less effective.

Fortunately we do have one of these prophet-philosophers in Canada today, and he is a Queen's man. I mean, of course, Professor Arthur Lower. How dull and syrupy our Canadian politics would be without his sharp and penetrating comments — even though he does discover that the whole of Canada is just the little town of Barrie writ large. If he scolds his lilliputian contemporaries too impatiently, that is because he has brooded over their ancestors with such sympathy and compassion. Incidentally, it has long puzzled me why my friend Arthur Lower, who has had the advantage of living amongst the Calvinists of Winnipeg and Kingston, should have become so pessimistic about the possibility of a Canadian elect who may yet save this nation, whereas I should remain so hopeful about this prospect, though I suffered for twenty-eight years (it seemed longer) among the Anglicans and Methodists of Toronto.

At any rate the hope of our political salvation lies in the building up of this intellectual élite within our mass democracy. It is still weak and without much internal cohesion in Canada; Canadian eggheads tend to think of themselves politically as scattered individuals rather than as members of an active social group. In Canada it is still slightly improper for professors to become too interested in current politics; and if they get into trouble for political utterances or activities, the last place in which they think of looking for support is among the organized university alumni.

---

[1] Professor Dennis Wrong, whose unfavourable review of C. Wright Mills I was quoting here, has pointed out to me that his review was of the earlier Mills book, *The Power Elite*, and that he agrees with Professor Mills in being critical of the scientism and moral neutralism of so many sociologists.

This seems to me to point to a failure in the political education given by our Canadian universities.

And here I come back to the point with which I started. The political function of our universities — they have, of course, other important functions — is to turn out each spring a batch of young recruits for the political élite within our national community. Universities, under modern conditions, are almost the only source from which such recruits can come. I have been assuming this afternoon that I was addressing a group of potential recruits. I hope that this graduating class of 1959 is going out into the world determined not to fall asleep politically for the next twenty years but to play an active part in applying to Canadian politics the Socratic principle that the unexamined life is not worth living.

Appendix

A list of some other writings by Frank H. Underhill on various topics

ON EDWARD BLAKE

Edward Blake, the Supreme Court Act, and the Appeal to the Privy Council, 1875-76 (*Canadian Historical Review*, September, 1938)

Edward Blake, the Liberal Party and Unrestricted Reciprocity (Report of Canadian Historical Association, 1939)

Edward Blake and Canadian Liberal Nationalism (in Ralph Flenley [ed.], *Essays in Canadian History*, Toronto, 1939)

Laurier and Blake 1882–1891 (*Canadian Historical Review*, December, 1939)

Laurier and Blake 1891–1892 (*Canadian Historical Review*, June, 1943)

Edward Blake (in C. T. Bissell [ed.], *Our Living Tradition*, Toronto, 1957)

ON CANADIAN POLITICAL PARTIES

Democracy and Leadership in Canada (*Canadian Forum*, April, 1934)

Some Observations upon Nationalism and Provincialism in Canada (in V. Anderson [ed.], *Problems in Canadian Unity*, Toronto, 1938. This was a talk given at the Couchiching Institute in August, 1938)

National Unity (*Canadian Forum*, January, 1945)

Political Parties (a chapter in George W. Brown [ed.], *Canada*, Toronto, 1950)

Canadian Political Parties (booklet published by the Canadian Historical Association, 1957)

The Revival of Conservatism in North America (Royal Society of Canada, *Transactions*, 1958)

The Dawson Biography of Mackenzie King (*Canadian Forum*, August, 1959)

ON CANADA AND THE BRITISH COMMONWEALTH

The Canadian Forces in the War (in Vol. II of Sir Charles Lucas, *The Empire at War*, 1923)

The Political Ideas of John S. Ewart (Report of Canadian Historical Association, 1933)

Canada in the Last War (in Chester Martin [ed.], *Canada in Peace and War*, Toronto, 1941)

Seventy-Five Years After (the 75th Anniversary of Confederation, *Canadian Forum*, July, 1942)

Reflections on the Revolution of our Time (*Canadian Forum*, March, 1944)

Dufferin-Carnarvon Correspondence 1874–1878 (edited by C. W. de Kiewiet and F. H. Underhill; Toronto, Champlain Society, 1955)

The British Commonwealth: an Experiment in Co-operation among Nations (Duke University Press, 1956)
Canadian and American Ties with Europe (*Queen's Quarterly*, Autumn, 1959)

ON CANADIAN GENERAL ELECTIONS

O Canada — Election Results of 1926 (*Canadian Forum*, May, 1930)
O Canada — Election Results of 1930 (*Canadian Forum*, December, 1930)
Our Fantastic Electoral System (*Canadian Forum*, November, 1935)
The Meaning of the Elections (*Canadian Forum*, July, 1945)
Vox Populi (*Canadian Forum*, July, 1949)
How to Vote (*Canadian Forum*, July, 1953)
The Canadian Elections (*Contemporary Review*, October, 1953)

ON SOCIALISM IN CANADA AND BRITAIN

Review of F. Borkenau, *Socialism, National and International* (*Canadian Forum*, July, 1942)
Fabians and Fabianism (*Canadian Forum*, March and April, 1946)
Review of Alexander Gray, *The Socialist Tradition* (*Canadian Forum*, November, 1946)
Review of Beatrice Webb, *Our Partnership* (*Canadian Forum*, June, 1948)
The Politics of Freedom (*Canadian Forum*, December, 1949)
Canadian Socialism and World Politics (a reply to an article by S. W. Bradford, *Canadian Forum*, October, 1950)
The Socialist International (*Canadian Forum*, September, 1951)
Review of L. Thompson, *Robert Blatchford: Portrait of an Englishman* (*Canadian Forum*, September, 1951)
Review of S. M. Lipset, *Agrarian Socialism* (*Canadian Forum*, February, 1951)
Review of Norman Thomas, *A Socialist's Faith* (*Canadian Forum*, October, 1951)
What's Left? (*Canadian Forum*, February, 1952)
Aneurin Agonistes (on Aneurin Bevan, *Canadian Forum*, November, 1952)
Review of Beatrice Webb, *Diaries 1912–1924* and R. H. S. Crossman, *New Fabian Essays* (*Canadian Forum*, February, 1953)

ON CANADIAN FOREIGN POLICY IN THE 1930s

Social Planning for Canada, Chapter 22 — Foreign Policy (a book written by members of the League for Social Reconstruction. I was one of the writers and editors. 1935)
Spiritual Enlargement (*Canadian Forum*, August, 1935)
That Clear Moral Issue; or St. George against the Dragon (*Canadian Forum*, April, 1936)

Canadian Policy in a War World (*Canadian Forum*, July, 1936)

Canada and Post-League Europe (*Canadian Forum*, October, 1936)

The Outline of a National Foreign Policy (in V. Anderson [ed.], *World Currents and Canada's Course*, Toronto, 1937)

Mr. King's Foreign Policy (*Canadian Forum*, July, 1938)

ON BRITISH THINKERS

Bentham and Benthamism (*Queen's Quarterly*, November, 1932)

Fabians and Fabianism (*Canadian Forum*, March and April, 1946)

Shaw (*Canadian Forum*, December, 1950)

Arnold Toynbee, Metahistorian (*Canadian Historical Review*, September, 1951)

The Toynbee of the 1950s (*Canadian Historical Review*, September, 1955)

John Stuart Mill (C.B.C. broadcast, printed in *Architects of Modern Thought*, Third and Fourth Series, C.B.C., Toronto, 1959)

SOME BOOK REVIEWS

The Economic Interpretation of Canadian History (H. A. Innis, *The Fur Trade in Canada* and *Select Documents of Canadian Economic History 1497–1783; Canadian Forum*, October, 1930)

Summer School Politics (Two books containing the addresses given at the Liberal and Conservative Summer Schools, 1933; *Canadian Forum*, March, 1934)

The Sirois Commission as Historians (*Canadian Forum*, November, 1940)

C. B. Sissons, *Egerton Ryerson, His Life and Letters*, Vol. I (*Canadian Forum*, May, 1937)

C. B. Sissons, *Egerton Ryerson, His Life and Letters*, Vol. II (*Canadian Forum*, January, 1948)

J. A. Corry, *Democratic Government and Politics* (*Canadian Forum*, February, 1947)

A Canadian Philosopher-Historian (A. R. M. Lower, *Colony to Nation; Canadian Forum*, July, 1947)

Harold J. Laski, *The American Democracy* (*Canadian Forum*, October, 1948)

Leslie Lipson, *The Politics of Equality* (*Canadian Forum*, October, 1948)

Julian Amery, *Life of Joseph Chamberlain*, Vol. IV, 1901–1903 (*University of Toronto Quarterly*, July, 1952)

Bruce Hutchison, *The Incredible Canadian* (*Canadian Forum*, December, 1952)

Kingsley Martin, *Harold J. Laski* (*Canadian Forum*, August, 1953)

The Hero as Engineer (Herbert Hoover, *Memoirs*, Vols. I–III; *University of Toronto Quarterly*, October, 1953)

The Historian as Prophet (E. H. Carr, *A History of Soviet Russia*, Vols. I–III, and *The New Society; University of Toronto Quarterly*, October, 1954)

Three Gullivers among the Toronto Lilliputians (J. R. Seeley, R. A.
Sims, E. W. Loosley, *Crestwood Heights* (*Canadian Historical
Review*, September, 1956)
Kenneth McNaught, *A Prophet in Politics: a Biography of J. S. Woods-
worth* (*Canadian Historical Review*, March, 1960)
J. M. S. Careless, *Brown of the Globe 1818–1859;* Vol. I — *The Voice of
Upper Canada* (*Waterloo Review*, December, 1959)

Index